Sounds

Sounds

The Ambient Humanities

JOHN MOWITT

University of California Press

University of California Press, one of the most distinguished university presses in the United States, enriches lives around the world by advancing scholarship in the humanities, social sciences, and natural sciences. Its activities are supported by the UC Press Foundation and by philanthropic contributions from individuals and institutions. For more information, visit www.ucpress.edu.

University of California Press
Oakland, California

Library of Congress Cataloging-in-Publication Data

Mowitt, John, 1952– author.
   Sounds: the ambient humanities / John Mowitt.
      p.   cm.
   Includes bibliographical references and index.
   ISBN 978-0-520-28462-3 (cloth : alk. paper)
   ISBN 978-0-520-28463-0 (pbk. : alk. paper)
   ISBN 978-0-520-96040-4 (ebook)
   1. Sound (Philosophy).   2. Sounds—Psychological aspects.
3. Sounds—Sociological aspects.   4. Sounds—Political
aspects.   I. Title.
   B105.S59M68   2015
   121'.35—dc23

                                        2014044113

24   23   22   21   20   19   18   17   16   15
10   9   8   7   6   5   4   3   2   1

To and for Bette

Contents

Acknowledgments

At some point in the early 1990s, before everything in the United States became "post-9/11," the diasporic performance practice of the "ring shout" morphed into the expression "shout-out." Turning away from a defiant acknowledgment of the ineradicable source of one's hope, the shout-out simply became an acknowledgment made, typically in the context of live performance, to "helpers" (in Propp's sense). However, from the beginning the shout-out was more than the act of calling out. It named itself in the act: "I'd like to give a shout-out to . . . my manager, my mother, my charity," who or whatever. As such, and this despite the familiar and dubious genealogy of the term, the shout-out is the deliberate forging of a sonic bond. Part of what matters about the gesture is that acknowledgment becomes attachment, an attachment that happens in the agitated void between, at a minimum, two bodies that accompany each other before others.

The shout-outs that follow, and in written form remain infelicitous (in Austin's sense), actually try to square the philological circle: they are acknowledgments both of the ineradicable source of hope and of "helpers" who, in the end, are one and the same. I hope, in this spirit, no one objects to being called out in this way and attached to the sounds that wave between us.

Sounds: The Ambient Humanities is an interspliced collection of essays, one of which, "Whistle," dates from a conference, "Warp and Woof," convened in the summer of 2003 at the University of Leeds, with which I am now affiliated. I am grateful to Barbara Engh and CentreCATH for their invitation. Adrian Rifkin, who has since left Leeds, responded to my keynote with wit, insight, and generosity. I thank them all for setting it in motion and wish to acknowledge that "Whistle" is a much extended version of "Tune Stuck in the Head," which appeared initially in *Parallax* 41

(2006): 12–25. *Parallax* is published by Taylor and Francis of Great Britain. Further details are available online at www.tandfonline.com.

One other essay, *"Tercer Sonido,"* was occasioned by a conference, and I wish to thank Silvia López for inviting me to participate on her panel for the International Congress of Americanists convened in Vienna in the summer of 2012. While there, I had hugely generative discussions with Chris Chiappari, Ricardo Roque, Fabio Durao, and Laura Novoa. Sara Saljoughi was an earlier inspired and inspiring reader of the essay. Both she and José Rodriquez Dod got me listening with *filín.* I am grateful to them all for their patience and insight.

Two other essays, "Whisper" and "Silence," were initially conceived as contributions to edited volumes. "Whisper" is a revised version of "Like a Whisper," which appeared initially in *differences* 22, nos. 2–3 (2011): 169–89 (reprinted by permission of Duke University Press). Further details are available online at www.dukepress.edu. I am extremely grateful to Rey Chow and James Steintrager (the editors of "The Sense of Sound" special issue) for both involving me in the project and pressuring my contribution in such fruitful ways. Julietta Singh deserves hearty acknowledgment for helping me hear what emerges from the horse's mouth, and Jeanine Ferguson for insisting that a dog's life is even more worth sharing than having.

"Silence" is a revised version of "Kafka's Cage," from *Freedom and Containment in Modernity: Kafka's Cages,* edited by A. Kiarina Kordela and Dimitris Vardoulakis (New York: Palgrave Macmillan, 2011), 63–86 (reprinted by permission of the publisher). Further details are available online at www.palgrave.com. Just prior to the publication of this text, Kiarina organized a panel discussion of the project at Macalester University and invited me to participate. I want to warmly thank her, her coeditor Dimitris, her colleagues at Macalester, and the friends and students who turned up to listen: Silvia López, Rembert Heuser, Verena Mund, Michelle Baroody, and Thorn Chen.

Two other professional occasions helped to shape the material gathered here. The portion of "Echo" given over to a reading of Michael Ondaatje's *Coming through Slaughter* was first presented on a panel at the annual meeting of the American Comparative Literature Association organized by Laura Zebuhr and Alexandra Morrison. I am grateful to Laura and Alexandra for their invitation but also to fellow panelist Cory Stockwell for taking us to "the end of the shit." While in attendance, I reconnected with a friend and former colleague at Minnesota, Asha Varadharajan, whose "so what are you working on?" query helped sort so much.

"Squawking" was conceived for and presented at a miniseminar here in Leeds convened during my year of transit between the United States and the United Kingdom. I want to thank my new colleagues who attended—Barbara Engh, Catherine Karkov, Eric Prenowitz, Marcel Swiboda—and the wonderful students, notably Sam Belinfante, Peter Kilroy, James Lavenier, and Lenka Vrablikova—who insisted I not get away with anything, but in the most gracious possible way. Lenka deserves considerable additional "shouting" for her brilliant work on the index to *Sounds*. I wish also to note that "Squawking" was first "picked up" in my last class at Minnesota, "Music as Discourse," and I want to thank all the fabulous students who helped me hear what I was trying to say.

Two final "shout-outs" then: first, to the brilliant colleagues, students, and friends who have allowed me to believe that what I think and write about sound matters: Maurits van Bever Donker, Alexander Cancio, Cesare Casarino, Patricia Clough, Lisa Disch, Frieda Ekotto, Carla Farrugia, Andreas Gailus, Heidi Grunebaum, Patricia Hayes, Qadri Ismail, Neelika Jayawardane, Joya John, Niki Korth, Erin Labbie, Premesh Lalu, Anne-Marie Lawless, Richard Leppert, Alice Lovejoy, Gary Minkley, Marissa Moorman, Neo Muyanga, Anaïs Nony, Laurie Ouellette, Tom Pepper, Suren Pillay, Helena Pohlandt-McCormick, Ciraj Rassool, Kevin Riordan, Simona Sawhney, Adam Sitze, Nathan Snaza, Ross Truscott, Dag Yngvesson, three of the four original members of "Ill Will and the Stale Mates"—Tony Brown, Jason McGrath, and Michelle Stewart—and, and, and Mary Francis, my unflappable editor at the University of California Press.

Finally, I just want to say again how important it has been, every day and in every way, to have my brothers and sisters and their amazing kids, but especially Jeanine, Rosalind, and Rachel, with me wherever I may wander.

"Squawking" was conceived for and presented at a miniseminar here in Leeds convened during my year of transit between the United States and the United Kingdom. I want to thank my new colleagues who attended—Barbara Engh, Catherine Karkov, Eric Prenowitz, Marcel Swiboda—and the wonderful students, notably Sam Belinfante, Peter Kilroy, James Lavenier, and Lenka Vrablikova—who insisted I not get away with anything, but in the most gracious possible way. Lenka deserves considerable additional "shouting" for her brilliant work on the index to *Sounds*. I wish also to note that "Squawking" was first "picked up" in my last class at Minnesota, "Music as Discourse," and I want to thank all the fabulous students who helped me hear what I was trying to say.

Two final "shout-outs" then: first, to the brilliant colleagues, students, and friends who have allowed me to believe that what I think and write about sound matters: Maurits van Bever Donker, Alexander Cancio, Cesare Casarino, Patricia Clough, Lisa Disch, Frieda Ekotto, Carla Farrugia, Andreas Gailus, Heidi Grunebaum, Patricia Hayes, Qadri Ismail, Neelika Jayawardane, Joya John, Niki Korth, Erin Labbie, Premesh Lalu, Anne-Marie Lawless, Richard Leppert, Alice Lovejoy, Gary Minkley, Marissa Moorman, Neo Muyanga, Anaïs Nony, Laurie Ouellette, Tom Pepper, Suren Pillay, Helena Pohlandt-McCormick, Ciraj Rassool, Kevin Riordan, Simona Sawhney, Adam Sitze, Nathan Snaza, Ross Truscott, Dag Yngvesson, three of the four original members of "Ill Will and the Stale Mates"—Tony Brown, Jason McGrath, and Michelle Stewart—and, and, and Mary Francis, my unflappable editor at the University of California Press.

Finally, I just want to say again how important it has been, every day and in every way, to have my brothers and sisters and their amazing kids, but especially Jeanine, Rosalind, and Rachel, with me wherever I may wander.

Introduction

Squawking

I

During the weeks when this text was assuming final form, a sound dominated the global news cycle. The sound was routinely referred to as a "ping," an onomatopoeic rendering of the sonic sign transmitted by the flight data recorder thought to belong to Malaysian Air Flight 370, presumed (at the time of writing) to have crashed under mysterious circumstances somewhere off the coast of western Australia in the Indian Ocean, tragically sealing the fates of all aboard. Sounds, specifically infrequently heard ones, do not typically attract this kind of global attention, and while only time will tell whether we are dealing here with what Peter Dale Scott might call a "deep event" (that is, a happening whose sociopolitical conditions of possibility are structurally repressed), what is clear enough is that this ping triggered two different but related questions: where was it coming from, and how did it get there? For many, an answer to the second question was thought to follow from an answer to the first. For others, and I count myself among them, the ping's power to trigger two searches—the one for its source, the other for its significance—was an equally intriguing, even troubling, dimension of the problem generated by the odd, and thus all the more horrible, disappearance of Malaysian Airlines Flight 370. In the studies that follow this search for significance, this work to make sense of (a) sound is precisely what provides them with a common orientation. And, at the risk of overstatement, one might consider that onomatopoeia (literally, sounds that "make names"), as exemplified in the word *ping*, registers precisely the not entirely arbitrary relation between sound and sense that my words are essaying to contour.[1]

But more than that, this text seeks to attend to the sound/sense snarl humanistically, that is, from within a problematic where the epistemological aim of "problem solving" has been displaced by the aim of what Richard Sennett has called "problem finding" (287). Perhaps because the contemporary fate of the humanities is not squarely on his radar, Sennett avoids precisions that deserve to be made. Specifically, "finding problems" is not the familiar "asking better questions" that has displaced the "search for answers" in certain quarters, and this for two reasons: first, questions, precisely to the extent that they belong to the hermeneutics of dialogue, do not in any essential way suspend the principle or practice of problem solving. Better questions are formulated so as to get better results. Second, because "finding problems" points immanently to the *problematic* within which the dialogue of question and answer is intelligible, it leads more directly into the epistemological snarl that, I argue, *is* the humanities or, to acknowledge that its now endemic crisis is shared by crucial aspects of the social sciences (frankly, on all practices of scholarly inquiry whose "outcomes" are hard to measure), humanistic inquiry. If this bears emphasis at the outset, it is because this text casts its lot with those in sound studies impatient with a certain technophilial tendency to treat sounds as mere emanations of devices, or practices and devices, or practices grasped best when placed either in some sort of chronological order of development or in a particular geographic location. Or both. Sounds, whether in the world or on the page, are Text (cf. "Echo"), that is, provocations to reading, especially readings that find problems not only in or with other readings but with the conditions and limits of reading itself.[2] Indeed, a repeated theme in what follows is the issue of whether sound is the sort of object that can be meaningfully contextualized and, if so, how the work of its contextualization must be carried out. This is a problem. It is one I find and refind even in silence, and it pricks our ears toward the very problem of the humanities as such: can the field now be justified, not in the face of the market but in the face of empire.[3] I proceed, then, prudently aware, even if incompletely, that the endeavor is fraught and that my soundings may not in the end add up. Strictly speaking, this prudence is what is required to attend and attune to the faint/feint sounds that compose this study. And, in the end, it is what I am squawking about.

Such a course prompts one to find, almost directly, another problem: that of the need to come to grips with what, following Don Ihde, I will call "visualism."[4] A clear counterweight to the "denigration of vision" set forth by Martin Jay, "visualism" and the problem it poses for this text can be detailed, its gravity measured, by retracing some of the intellectual history put in play in Jay's influential study.

The distinction between eye and gaze introduced by Jacques Lacan in *The Four Fundamental Concepts of Psychoanalysis* (Seminar XI) has had a profound and lasting impact on the analysis of visual culture within the humanities. Although this distinction, especially as it concerns the gaze *(le regard)*, had its precursors in Sartre, Merleau-Ponty, and even the diehard antiphenomenologist Foucault, it was Lacan's elaboration of it that proved decisive even when defended, as in the case of Joan Copjec's "The Orthopsychic Subject," from its devotees. Even the later innovation of distinguishing between vision and visuality (think here of Hal Foster's important anthology) can fairly be said to have its touchstone in Lacan's work. Crucial here is not the matter of who came first but the theoretical character of the distinction itself. Although it is in certain respects misleading, what is at issue in this distinction can be summoned by invoking another—that between seeing and watching. That the latter suggests a certain form of concentration is nevertheless not the decisive element, as Benjamin's well-known critique of "contemplation" in "The Work of Art in the Age of Its Technological Reproducibility" immediately suggests, for watching can also occur in a state of "distraction." Instead, what is decisive is the mediating work of sense or, to use a more Lacanian vocabulary, "signifierness," as Bruce Fink proposes to translate *significance*. Put this way, seeing is implicitly deprived of sense, and while there are ways in which this is realistic, it is not true. Seeing, as in witnessing what Freud called a "primal scene," is doubtless mediated by the work of sense but in ways that are structured by afterwardness. What is seen, to put the matter enigmatically, is always watched later and watched as if seen for the first time. The misleading complications freighted within the distinction between seeing and watching are thus here thrown into relief.

That said, if I invoke this material at the outset, it is because *Sounds* is a study that will entertain the value of floating (positing, but with the hesitation or hazard of a guess) a concept "analogous" to the gaze in the field of sound studies. Partly, this is in acknowledgment of the vexed productivity of the concept in the analysis of visual culture but not only this. As the preceding precautions make manifest, the risks of this analogical reasoning are considerable, thus inviting a careful elaboration of the reasons for taking them at all, but by way of adumbration, at issue here is the entwinement of sound and sense outside the frame of linguistics. Put differently, we need to insist on a difference between the phonic and the sonic. This difference, in order to matter methodologically, will call for a name.

To be sure, there is an available parallel distinction between hearing and listening that might well be deployed in this context, and several important theoretical examinations of it offer themselves as touchstones. I am thinking here of, for example, Adorno's "On the Fetish-Character in Music and the Regression of Listening," Barthes and Havas's "Listening," Chion's chapter dedicated to the three types of listening in *Audio-Vision*, Szendy's *Listen: A History of Our Ears*, and Nancy's two studies of listening (one of which serves as the foreword to Szendy's text). To justify the logic of the analogy itself, one might also add to this short list, Adorno and Eisler's discussion of the differences between hearing and seeing (the ear archaic, and the eye modern) in *Composing for the Films.*

These texts, in their own ways, admit of difficulties very much like those that haunt the seeing/watching distinction. To take a still resonant case: in Barthes and Havas's study the authors differentiate among three modes of listening, the first of which is named the "alert." In precisely bridging between human and nonhuman animals, the alert appears to introduce within listening itself something like a faculty unmediated by sense. The alert is simply perceived, and if it carries a sense, it is one reduced to the binary of flight or fight. One might expect this to generate a distinction like that between hearing and listening (and French has the relevant vocabulary, *ouïr* versus *écoute*), but it does not. Barthes and Havas fold this *into* what they mean by listening, as if to stress the precariousness of both the modes and the faculties.

Here again what this foregrounds is the prudence with which one is advised to approach the work to come. But let's cut to the chase. Looming before all other difficulties of the sort entertained above is the terminological and, in the long run, conceptual one. In English we have no convenient analogue to *gaze* in the auditory or sonic domain. In *Audio-Vision* Chion runs into a version of this problem when he tries to think the sonic equivalent to "point of view," and he quite reasonably proposes "point of audition," only to immediately complicate its implied isomorphism with "point of view." This, while instructive, does not help. *Audition* cannot substitute for *gaze* any more than it can substitute for *view*. Or, at least this substitution is not entirely satisfying, and not simply because, as Chion worries, *point* means little in the sonic register. Let me then propose *audit* as, if not an entirely satisfying substitution, at least a coherent one, and let me further suggest that its awkwardness as a name bounces back from the discourse of "visualism" in relation to which we hear it.

Audit? In contemporary English usage *audit* can refer to the review of financial records, as well as to an attenuated form of enrollment in a college or university course. As such, a student listens but does not, at least in principle, speak or write. The former, an audit, is a noun, the latter, to audit, a verb. Etymologically, *audit* bears the semantic profile that allows us to recognize its presence in *audition, auditorium,* and *audience*. It is a "hearing."

Beyond that, and the following chapter on "the gasp" will elaborate the matter in detail, this hearing, as a mode of perception, has a primordial tie with aesthetics, with what Rancière has called "the distribution of the sensible" (Rancière, *Politics* 12). Pulling these threads together, one arrives not so much at a perception or sensible event but at a fold where perception turns back or over on itself, traversing the faculty of hearing with the angle, the posture of listening. It is here that the audit serves as a coherent analogue to the gaze.

To bring out necessary conceptual detail regarding this analogy, it is useful to revisit the debate between Merleau-Ponty and Lacan on the question of vision, or the visible. No less redoubtable a figure than Sartre urges this on us when in his "eulogy" (published in *Les temps modernes* as "The Living Merleau-Ponty") he draws attention to the precise point of contact between the two writers in adducing the Lacanian formula, "the unconscious is structured like a language." This encounter is a vexed one because when the formula is deployed in the posthumous *The Visible and the Invisible*, it is qualified if not repudiated altogether, whereas in Sartre's eulogy it is proposed as a tenet with which Merleau-Ponty is in accord. The theoretical contours of this discrepancy are teased out in Lacan's own enigmatic eulogy for Merleau-Ponty aptly titled "Merleau-Ponty: In Memoriam" (Hoeller 73–81).

Published in the issue of *Les temps modernes* immediately following the one in which Sartre's statement appeared, Lacan's essay—as if vying for attention—takes up the same text characterized by Sartre as the crystallization of Merleau-Ponty's philosophy, the late (indeed last) "Eye and Mind." Ostensibly a phenomenological account of painting, Merleau-Ponty's text, in establishing the ontological character of painting, is keen to elaborate what about vision exceeds mere seeing. Lacan, while compelled by this strategy, works hard to stress that, at the end of the day, Merleau-Ponty folds this excess back into a body present at the fleshy seam between itself and the world. In effect, Merleau-Ponty draws on a phenomenological account of sense, the embodied proprioceptive ground of intentional consciousness, to get at what about vision cannot be squared with seeing, now understood as the recognition and appropriation of things seen. What he means by the invisible has precisely to do with what exceeds and conditions seeing.

Lacan and Merleau-Ponty disagree about the theoretical status of the invisible—not in the sense of disagreeing about whether something exceeds the limits of seeing but in the account of sense required to think this limit. Whereas for Merleau-Ponty this always comes back to the matrix of perception and conception, for Lacan—following a post-Saussurean Freud—sense always derives from the slither of the signifier, or "signifierness."

Crucial here is the equation Lacan draws between the spatiotemporal coordinates of the signifier and what he means by the unconscious. Put differently, and this was something of a mantra in the 1960s, phenomenology had no real account of the unconscious, Sartre famously equating it with censorship only to then show that the censor must recognize what it seeks to censor, meaning that even what is unconscious is part of consciousness. Even more recent exertions, such as those in Jean-Luc Nancy or Michel Henry, take their cues from this snarl of theoretical problems.

For Lacan this means that the concept of the gaze must be produced, and this is precisely what he undertakes in *The Four Fundamental Concepts*. In effect, the gaze (and he uses the same term, *le regard*, found in Sartre's *Being and Nothingness*) comes to designate that which limits seeing, or organizes the field of the visible, at the level of the encounter not between "eye and mind" but between "eye and the signifier."[5] Thus, if the audit might be said to serve as a coherent analogue to the gaze, it is because it bears the same, if not identical, relation to "signifierness." The theoretical parallel might then be not ear and mind but ear and signifier.

Interestingly, one finds comparatively little in the Lacanian corpus that deals in equivalent detail with the ear. Eye and voice, yes, but not the ear. The recent publication in *Lacanian Ink* of two interviews with Lacan about the topic of music suggests that this might be a good thing. Just the same, it gives one pause. Specifically, it invites prudence about the conceptual tie between the audit and the theoretical framework of psychoanalysis. In the chapters that follow, I give expression to this prudence by exploiting the resonance between *le regard* as deployed by Lacan and *le regard* as deployed by Foucault, not as subsumed within the motif of "panopticism" but from the latter's discussion of "the medical gaze" in *The Birth of the Clinic*, a text in which no scorn for the "mindless phenomenologies of understanding" (xiv) is withheld. In the Sheridan translation, where the titular gaze is rendered as perception, the phenomenology in question would appear to be that of Merleau-Ponty. This is confirmed when only pages into the portentous introduction Foucault urges us to concentrate our attention on the unsteady division between "the visible and the invisible insofar as it is linked to the division between what is stated and what remains unsaid" (xi). While this might imply that Foucault harbored ill will toward Merleau-Ponty, he did not. Their disagreement was largely a principled philosophical one (although their views of Stalinism differed); in fact, one of Foucault's first editorial projects upon joining *Tel Quel* in the early 1960s was to assemble a special issue of the journal dedicated to *The Visible and the Invisible*. The point is this: he knew this material backward and forward and was thinking about it while finishing *The Birth of the Clinic,* perhaps even while writing the introduction from which I have been quoting.

Five years after the publication of *The Birth of the Clinic,* Foucault— responding to a series of questions put to him about his work by the editors of *L'Esprit*—used the very tension between the said and what remains unsaid to explain what he meant by discourse (see "History, Discourse and Discontinuity"), and it is this term that now calls for attention. In ways that one does not find in the later Foucault, he engages a frankly Lacanian vocabulary in the introduction to *The Birth of the Clinic,* gesturing, in his then customary critique of commentary, to the "superabundance proper to the signifier" (xvi), in effect, "signifierness." That said, Foucault is careful to separate his project from a "'psychoanalysis' of medical knowledge" (x) by giving priority to the concept of discourse over and above that of the signifier. Indeed, although the entirety of *The Birth of the Clinic* might be seen as a response to Merleau-Ponty (see especially the chapter "Seeing and Knowing"), it in fact must be seen as part of a dispersed but precise triptych whose opposing panel is *The Four Fundamental Concepts.*

But what hangs on the commitment to discourse? To the extent that it traverses and cuts through the divisions between the said and the unsaid, and the visible and invisible, it accomplishes the same conceptual work as the Lacanian unconscious. It thinks where one does not think to think (to use Lacan's account of the Cartesian *cogito*) the limits of seeing and saying. But it does so in the theoretical vocabulary of what Foucault was later to call historical ontology. Against a presumed universalism of the signifier, discourse is deployed to bring out the regional and provisional character of the work of the signifier, not to suspend the gravity of being but to situate that gravity within a paradigm of thinking the articulation of language and matter. Many thorny problems thus follow from Foucault's commitment to discourse—many of them implicitly aired in the recorded disagreements between Žižek, Butler, and Laclau—but sorting them is not my aim. I want only to invoke them so as to state what it might mean to formulate the concept of the audit in their wake.

Again, prudence. My point here is not to demonstrate that the audit belongs to a certain discourse but rather to prompt consideration of whether the conceptual construct of the audit helps us think about the degree to which sound and the very distinction between hearing and listening belong to a materialization of discourse with which academic intellectuals are inti- mate, namely, discipline. Or, more specifically, I approach the discipline of sound studies to trace how it thinks the relation between its ways of know- ing and the sounds it purports to know.

But what of the problem of visualism? In essence, as I have been suggesting, it is precisely its disciplinary sway that compels one, especially a partisan of sound studies, to entertain methodologically what I have here called the audit. Again, this is not in order to ridicule or abandon the powerful insights produced by adherence to the concept of the gaze (little could be more absurd), nor is it merely to mimic a certain style of analysis. Rather, I wish precisely to draw attention to a systemic foreclosure that conditioned those insights, a foreclosure legitimated by a set of theoretical habits grounded in the paradigm of visualism. And frankly this—the *problem* posed by the concept and disciplinary deployment of the gaze—more than the legitimacy of the dissonant term *audit* is what all the squawking is about.[6]

II

In 2005 Michelle Hilmes reviewed Jonathan Sterne's *The Audible Past* and Emily Thompson's *The Soundscape of Modernity* in the pages of *American Quarterly*. Her title: "Is There a Field Called Sound Culture Studies? And Does It Matter?" In the opening paragraph of the lengthy review that followed, Hilmes referred back to her title:

> I pose the two questions above in the face of mounting evidence that the study of sound, hailed as an "emerging field" for the last hundred years [1905–2005] exhibits a strong tendency to remain that way, always emerging, never emerged. This may suggest an answer to the second question: perhaps it doesn't matter to enough people in enough disciplines that the study of sound consolidate and declare itself. Perhaps sound study is doomed to a position on the margins of various fields of scholarship, whispering unobtrusively in the background while the main action occurs elsewhere. This would echo the position that most writers on the topic attribute to sound itself—constantly subjugated to the primacy of the visual, associated with emotion and subjectivity as against the objectivity and rationality of vision . . . in essence, fundamentally secondary to our relationship to the world and to the dominant ways of understanding it. (Hilmes 249)

Hilmes then segues to consideration of the texts under review, noting—based on the strength of a decade's worth of important scholarly work—that things may be on the verge of changing. Significantly, she associates this possibility with the fact that the potential disciplinary object of sound study has shifted from "the study of sound itself" to "*sound culture*" (ibid.; emphasis in original); indeed, it is the fact that Sterne and Thompson share a tenacious interest in the latter that recommends them for scholarly attention and in doing so signals the arrival rather than the endless emergence of sound studies.

Although I share Hilmes's enthusiasm for these two texts (if not her *sotto voce* preference for *The Soundscapes of Modernity*), the topic of the emergent, derived one assumes from the work of Raymond Williams, warrants more attention than can be given it in a review that has other concerns. Brought to bear on the field of academic disciplines, the emergent—expressly divided by Williams between the "oppositional" and the "alternative"—invites one to consider whether the "arrival" of a field is all it is cracked up to be. In what follows, I will attempt to animate this problem, assigning very special import to the term *echo*, evoked almost in passing in Hilmes's review as a way to designate the relation between the subjects and objects of sound studies. Put differently, to borrow from another assessment of the importance of the work of Sterne and Thompson: "The overarching goal of this new aurally based work is not to create an alternate world of sound studies. Rather, it is to demonstrate the unique possibilities that thinking about sound can open up" (Suisman and Strasser 5). As is still said of the devil and the details, the interesting even crucial problems posed by sounds are found precisely in these unique possibilities.

Like many vital things, resisting the impulse to create an alternate world is easier said than done. With the recent appearance of *The Sound Studies Reader* and *The Oxford Handbook to Sound Studies* (both 2013) it might indeed appear that what Hilmes heralded as the Zeno-like progression of sound studies has concluded and that, as the young Charles Sanders Peirce predicted, Achilles has overtaken the tortoise. If not deceiving, appearances can always be misleading, and if earlier I stressed the importance of the concept of "emergence," it was to underscore that what rarely appears in the formation of a field are the political and theoretical stakes *of* that formation. To trace these, one might consider that they fall within what Suisman and Strasser call "unique possibilities" of "thinking," possibilities that in tracing the limits of the sayable expose a field—in its grammar, its logic, and its rhetoric—to the floating concept of the audit. In effect, the emergence of a field is yet another context in which the audit might be put to the test.

Consider, for example, the case made for the development of sound studies in a 2004 special issue of *Social Studies of Science*. Edited by Trevor Pinch and Karin Bijsterveld, "Sound Studies: New Technologies and Music" (also the editors of *The Oxford Handbook*), the papers collected there derive from a conference that took place in the Netherlands in 2002, that is, two years before Hilmes was speculating about the emergence of sound studies. As if sharing her caution, the editors chime in on the status of their object when situating the concerns of the conference: "This territory can be thought of as part of a wider field of what we shall call 'Sound Studies.' Sound Studies is an emerging interdisciplinary area that studies the material production and consumption of music, noise, silence and how these have changed throughout history and within different societies, but does so from a much wider perspective than standard disciplines such as ethnomusicology, history of music and the sociology of music" (Pinch and Bijsterveld 636). The territory referred to here is the one defined by the encounter between music and technology, and it is presumably what motivated the conference title: "Sound Matters." This pun is deliberate, and it gives rhetorical expression both to the conviction that technology "materializes" music and to the vexed disciplinary matter of concern.[7] Who is concerned with sound and from within which "area" is this concern expressed? Without wishing to make a mountain out of a molehill, what Suisman and Strasser call "unique possibilities" for thinking are here given a rather limited remit. They are expressed in the form of a disciplinary affiliation that appeals to the concept of matter without bringing this affiliation to bear on this concept. The dilation effected by the series "music, noise, silence" is reversed at the same rate of speed that the concern about disciplinarity converges on the object of music. Here, the still-emerging field of sound studies has a name—"we shall call it 'Sound Studies'"—and, somehow, through a precipitous superimposition of music and sound, it constitutes an alternative to more traditional fields. But does it oppose them, and, if so, what might such opposition mean? Does matter matter differently from within or as part of an oppositional practice of sound studies?

In certain respects these are unfair questions. The text at hand is merely an introduction to the special issue of a journal, so precisions of the sort I am calling for are not to be expected there. Nevertheless, what is in evidence in any gesture to inaugurate a conversation in the not merely academic public sphere are what earlier I called the grammar, logic, and rhetoric of a field—in effect, the terms of debate. The role such terms might play in stimulating the possibilities of thinking opened up by sound studies is worth pondering, especially if we value Foucault's construal of discourse: the difference between the virtual and the actual in the expanse of statements.

Both Pinch and Bijsterveld are researchers in the fields of science and technology studies, but lest one think that the matters raised here do not resonate in the humanistic disciplines, it is worth consulting yet another introduction to a special journal issue dedicated to sound studies, Gustavus Stadler's "Breaking Sound Barriers." This piece appears in *Social Text* 102

("The Politics of Recorded Sound") from 2010. The punning title, with its play on "barriers," is followed by a punning epigraph that is in turn followed by an opening paragraph that reads in part:

> This special issue of *Social Text* emerges from the current excitement, audible across a number of disciplines, about new ways of studying sound and sound reproduction from cultural and historical perspectives. It offers a range of such work—produced by scholars in history, African American studies, English, history of science and performance studies— positioning the production and consumption of recordings as social and cultural practices; from this perspective, the essays herein illuminate both the political contexts surrounding such practices and the way these practices mediate understandings of such contexts. A number of the articles are also concerned with historiographic questions and seek to complicate simplified, apolitical narratives of the "evolution" of sound recordings. (Stadler 1)

As with Pinch and Bijsterveld's introduction, Stadler (an English professor at Haverford) moves deftly to tie sound to technology, specifically the technology of sound recording. He also retrieves the insistent theme of emergence, although now applied to the journal rather than the area of sound studies. What is different is his somewhat more polemical tone, the fields covered by his contributors, and the explicit way he situates the journal as a historiographic intervention. Of the several contributors only one of them (David Suisman, in fact) is affiliated with the history of science; the rest hail from various fields within the humanities, including, of course, history. Indeed, it is around the theme of history that Stadler's "polemical" tone becomes audible. Note the "air commas" that draw attention to the dubious authority of evolution when deployed as an explanatory concept in the frame of a historiographic practice concerned to think the interplay between practices and contexts.

Crucial here is Stadler's sense that historical narratives become apolitical (by which he, like so many, means either conservative or reactionary politics, not the absence of politics) when they submit historical change to the implacable vagaries of something resembling natural selection. I do not disagree. In fact, polemics aside, this dimension of Stadler's statement, his insistence that the study of recorded sound ought to involve us in a theoretical and political consideration of the very terms of this study, is precisely what *Sounds* seeks to amplify and extend. Where Stadler and I differ is on the level of theoretical abstraction: he is concerned with historical contextualization; I am concerned with contextualization as such, although my approach will proceed in somewhat closer proximity to the problematic of the "sociology of culture." We are both, in this sense, seeking to find the problems that provoke and to proliferate unique possibilities for thinking, and it is because of this baseline solidarity that I want to quibble with his easy recourse to the figure of illumination when characterizing the impact of his special issue on the dialectic of practices and contexts. Why this recourse to the rhetoric of "visualism" precisely when he has so carefully, so attentively, stressed the need to hear in sound the challenge to the categories of our thinking about it? As has already been suggested, I will turn to echo to retrieve and reweave this particular theoretical thread.

Would it be fair to say that in all that has been gained in "Breaking Sound Barriers," the problem of materiality has effectively dropped out? That this is the price of putting into question the very terms of debate? I think not but for perhaps odd reasons, reasons having to do with the insistent figure of the pun, of paronomasia as it ricochets through sound studies in our present. Technically, paronomasia refers to words that, while sharing a sonic signifier, proliferate signifieds, and I have been drawing attention to their prevalence in the discourse of sound studies. Of course, one might always chalk this up to cleverness, but this explanation preempts a more profound puzzle: why the distinctive receptivity to paronomasia in the emerging field of sound studies? Could it have something to do with the distinctive way that phonic sounds (what Saussure famously called "acoustic images"), even homonyms, materialize meanings and that they do so precisely by dispersing meaning along a syntagmatic chain where a certain irreversible spacing of the signifier actually constitutes the possible meanings of a particular word? The spirit does not call for the letter; instead, it is called up *by* the letter, and it is this effect that Lacan sought to designate with the term *signifierness*. Even if, as the object-oriented ontologists warn, objects—such as sounds—withdraw into their own strangeness, it is the signifier that gives us what access we have to this flight.

Moreover, above and beyond the material productivity of the signifier, what the paronomastic dimension of discourse underscores is the way sound studies registers, in the very choreography of its endless emergence, the ubiquity of sounds not simply as phenomenal events in the field of human perception but as sonic fossils embedded in the medium of thought. The now commonplace therapeutic formulation "I hear you" is only the most banal instance of the ubiquity invoked here. Indeed, Derrida's well-known picking apart of Husserl's theory of signs might be said to rest, at the end of the day, on what in other contexts we might call a *double entendre*, where hearing itself doubles over, thickens. All of this is to say that the way materiality reasserts itself in the very discourse of sound studies, in its rhetorical turns, points to a crucial way in which materiality is questioned differently by being approached through sound or through a problematic in which the sonic and the phonic are allowed to sound without drowning each other out. Attuning to this is essential to stimulating the unique possibilities of thought inscribed within sound studies, possibilities that may well call for an audit to attend to. So let us then pose for ourselves the following problem: how might sound studies refresh the way we think about what it means to, as Stadler put it, articulate cultural practices and their sociohistorical contexts—not how we situate sounds but how sounds situate situating? How do sounds stir us to recognize situating as a problem?

III

Not long before Roland Barthes shifted from "work to text," he shifted from "institution to work"—a prepositional prototype. That we have remembered only the former is a disciplinary symptom that will receive comment in what follows. At issue here is the question of context or, more precisely, the question of how we are to think about the work of situating a text in its context in the wake of the advent of what Barthes, among others, called textuality, that is, the methodological field that displaced the object of scholarly attention known, almost retronymically, as "the work."[8]

Barthes made the shift from "institution to work" during the 1960s, as he was struggling to come to terms with work of his colleague Lucien Goldmann. As Julia Kristeva herself has testified, it was Goldmann that directed her to Barthes's seminar after her arrival in Paris on Christmas Eve, 1966. In December of 1963, on the pages of the weekly *France-Observateur*, Barthes published a review of Goldmann's work titled "Les deux sociologies de roman" (The two sociologies of the novel). Although brief, the review makes crystal clear (a) that Barthes regards Goldmann's sociology of literature as the leading edge of a field that reaches back to Lukács if not to Marx himself; (b) that Barthes recognizes the challenge posed to this field by the advent of structural anthropology; and (c) that, for him, the urgent task of "the new criticism" (to sound the battle cry that arose in his quarrel with Raymond Picard) was to develop the theoretical and practical implications of that challenge. Barthes does this, as the title of his review suggests, by splitting the sociology of the novel (and literature more generally) in two.

In his review Barthes states the point as follows: "One is thus led today to conceive of two complementary critiques (or two sociologies): an ideological critique that, for my part, I will call *semantic* because it concerns itself with content (what Goldmann calls 'form') and a *semiological* critique that concerns itself with 'forms.' One could call this sociology of forms a *socio-logic* to the extent that it attempts to take account of the eminently significant manner in which novelists *classify* their words" (250; my translation). His formulation here of a "socio-logic" is recycled from an earlier review of the work of Lévi-Strauss titled "Sociology and Socio-logic: With Regard to Two Recent Works by Lévi-Strauss," where socio-logic is contrasted with sociology precisely *not* to ignore or evade sociology but to subject it to what Adorno and Benjamin might call immanent considerations or critique. Hence the importance of *complementarity*, a term deployed in physics to think the dual nature of light as both wave and particle. If I stress this, it is because I want to complicate a now rather prevalent tendency to treat Barthes and all of his "poststructuralist" sympathizers as formalists, as intellectuals dedicated to resisting the very notion of contextualization so as to better obscure the petite bourgeois and thus reactionary character of their own thought.

So what issues from this "immanent critique" of sociology? Put differently, what does socio-logic do that sociology, especially the sociology of literature or culture more generally, does not or cannot? To approach this, I urge that we trace more carefully the shift from "institution to work" before returning to the discussion of Lévi-Strauss.

Beginning in the early 1960s, Goldmann was convening seminars/ workshops and publishing their proceedings under the general title of *Études de sociologie et de la littérature*. In 1967 the topical seminar was convened in Brussels, and Barthes was invited to participate—presumably *not* because he was perceived as an unrepentant formalist (and doubtless Goldmann had read "Two Sociologies of the Novel"). Barthes's text was titled, "Rhetorical Analysis." He writes:

> Literature presents itself to us as an *institution* and as a *work*. As an institution it gathers all the uses and all the practices that regulate the circuit of the thing-written in a given society: the social and ideological status of the writer, the means of distribution, the conditions of consumption, the strictures of criticism. As a work, literature is essentially constituted as a verbal message of a certain type. It is to the work-object that I wish to attend, so as to suggest that we pay attention to a still unexplored field (aware that the word is very old), that of *rhetoric*. (83; translation modified)

On the face of it this sounds like the formalist gesture par excellence, but if read in the wake of the earlier review, where sociology is split in two, one might readily sense that what is at issue here is not an opposition between rhetoric and society but the evocation of a sociology specific to rhetoric, that is, to literature conceived as a work.

For the sake of brevity let us consider that such a sociology, a sociology of the work, is what Barthes was attempting to formulate by confecting the term *socio-logic*. What justifies such a claim is the characterization of *socio-logic* that appears in the review of Lévi-Strauss, where Barthes counterpoises a sociology of the symbol to a structural sociology that attends to the sign as a signifying element in a spatial distribution of functions. Moving beyond methodology—the analysis of forms rather than analogically grounded contents—Barthes draws attention to the phenomenological proposition that mind mediates matter and that, as a result, cultural analysts must attend to the "trace of mind, the collective work which has been performed by mind in order to subject reality to a logical system of forms" (Barthes 1162). His later appeal to "rhetoric" would appear to rhyme with this call for attention to "the logical system of forms," and it certainly echoes his anxiously voiced concern about the "verbal surface" that Goldmann seems, at least from the vantage point of the review in *France-Observateur*, to be prepared to sacrifice to his "macro-criticism" of the novel, to use Barthes's characterization.

To summarize: what is legible in Barthes's encounter with Goldmann is a desire to formulate a sociology of literature attentive to signs rather than symbols, that is, to the proposition that mind is structured by language (related obviously to the Lacanian formula discussed in section 1 above), *not*, as one often hears, to abandon society for textuality. In fact, what emerges clearly in Barthes's writing of the early to mid-1960s is a critique of sociology that establishes an important theoretical solidarity between semiology and the critique of positivism one finds in many figures we now affiliate with the Frankfurt School.

This is all well and good. But as everyone knows, Barthes shifted from the "work," which he had contrasted with the "institution" in 1966, to the "text." My question is this: what were the consequences of this shift for the critique of sociology and, by extension, for the analytical practice of the sociology of literature and its attendant concept of context? Precisely to the extent that academic literary theory has only remembered—doubtless for largely polemical if not mythomorphic purposes—the shift from work to text, the question of the text's relation to the critique of sociology calls for elaboration if the problem of con-textualization is to be brought within range.

Famously, Goldmann developed his approach to the sociology of literature—and Barthes acknowledges this—by inventing the concept of what he called a worldview or vision. Supporting this vision was, to invoke another Goldmannian *mot d'art*, a "trans-individual subject." In effect, what allowed him to link Pascal and Racine—the prime suspects of his study *The Hidden God*—was the fact that their works gave expression to the doctrinal conflicts of the social actors, that is, readers who took these writers seriously. Aware of the vulgarity of a literary sociology concerned to establish how literary content reflects certain class interests, Goldmann stressed that literary *form* is the true object of sociological attention, adding that to grasp its relation to a world vision, the concept of homology is required. For him, the form of Racine's plays and the architectonics of Pascal's thoughts stood in a homological relation to the consciousness of the transindividual subject of eighteenth-century France.

Two points are worth emphasizing here. First, it seems clear that Barthes finds this compelling because of the way "world vision" insists on the mind's mediation of matter. If sociology can resist its tendency toward vulgarity, this will be because it can grapple adequately with the form and content of expression or, put differently, because it can take seriously the "consciousness" side of "collective consciousness." Second, and Barthes draws attention to this by emphasizing the limits of Goldmann's concept of form in his review, the shift to homology, though meant to overcome the constraints of "reflection aesthetics," repeats those constraints by not truly complicating the "visualism," organizing the concept of homology. While it is true that Barthes does not frame the matter in these terms, I think there is much to be gained in doing so precisely because, as I have indicated, his elaboration of a "socio-logic of textuality" remains unfinished. Perhaps sounds, as the very principle of wanton radiation, can lead us on.

To pursue the socio-logic of textuality, I want to explore the theoretical and practical potential of the concept of "echo" as a way to tease out of the endlessly emerging field of sound studies not just another phenomenon of scholarly or aesthetic attention—*the* echo—but a supplemental concept for thinking the work of contextualization in the humanities. This does not mean that I am unattuned to the sound of an echo—what one really sounds like, for example, in nature—but rather that I take this sound to be resonant with problems. In the chapter that follows, "Echo," I listen to Michael Ondaatje's stunning little text on the birth of jazz, *Coming through Slaughter*, especially to the squawking that riddles it, for riffs on the theoretical practice of contextualization. Ostensibly a "bio-text" on the jazz trumpeter Buddy Bolden, this study is also a sustained, high-pitched meditation on what it means to situate a musical sound in a sociohistorical context. As proposed above, what pricks one's ears to this is a certain alertness to the problem of the audit, that is, the methodological effect that enables a text to sound along the unraveling seam where sound and sense traverse one another.

"Echo" is followed by "Whistle," the first of three chapters that concentrate on sounds designated as nonvocalized vocalizations (sounds that occur in or on speech but that lack phonemic value). In this chapter the whistle—like wind over a fissured wall, perhaps a rendition of the slippage between the discourse of sound studies and its objects—is tracked in relation to the phenomenon of the "tune stuck in the head," or what Theodor Reik called the "haunting melody." While the mnemonic character of this phenomenon is pronounced, what is equally striking—especially when brought into contact with Benjamin's meditation on Proust's concept of the *mémoire involontaire*—is the motif of haunting as a name for an unconscious memory. An unknown known. To tease out the political valence of this feature, the chapter lingers over the "criminalization" of haunted whistling in Fritz Lang's first sound film, *M*, where the oft-noted mirroring in the image between the police and the gang has its startling echo in the "whistling" that blows through the film. Bringing the problem of psychopathology and whistling closer to us, I tease out what is repeated differently in the whistle as it figures in Roy Boulting's film from the mid-1960s, *Twisted Nerve.*

The third chapter, "Whisper," develops further the problematic linguistic status of the whistle as a nonvocalized element of speech. By bringing the sound of the whisper into proximity with Foucault's use of the term *murmur* in *History of Madness*—especially as it is used there to limn the mad line between the said and the unsaid (or even, the unsayable)—I tease out the problem posed by the whisper: not what, but how does it mean? I do so by reading it in relation to two textual articulations of whispering: Robert Redford's *The Horse Whisperer* and the long-running but now defunct television series *The Ghost Whisperer*, specifically the crossover episode in which Cesar Milán, the dog whisperer, makes a guest appearance. By theorizing the drone note that links the mad, the unsayable, the animal, and ghosts, this chapter identifies a political valence of whispering that falls between the more typical politicizations of whispering as either anonymous denunciation or persecuted speech. Here, the audit imposes itself as a way to think a certain political foreclosure in our reflection on sonic (as opposed to phonic) practice.

"Whisper" is followed by "Gasp," the last of the three chapters devoted to the liminal phenomenon of nonvocalized speech or what I have also called "faint/feint sounds." This chapter stumbles upon the problem of whether the aesthetic, as such, can be theorized within a distinctly sonic problematic. It pursues this question by puzzling over the classical motif of the *thymos*, typically rendered in English translation as "spiritedness." Following Francis Fukuyama's once influential translation of *thymos* as "the desire for recognition," and Derrida's reading of the impasses that follow from this translation in *The Specters of Marx*, I return via Richard Onians's work to the classical and distinctly prephilosophical sources of the *thymos*. This allows us to hear its decisive relation with breath, especially breath as sucked in and heated by the blood. In effect, what Derrida and Fukuyama miss about the *thymos* is that it pertains to a subject centered not in the brain (consciousness) but in the lungs. The root, *ais*, an onomatopoeic rendering of the gasp, is to be found lodged in the lung of *aisthesis*, the Greek term used to designate individuated perception and later elaborated by Edmund Burke and others to refer to the perception of art as a whole. Elaborating this through readings of *Last Gasps*, by Terrence McNally, and *The Moor's Last Sigh*, by Salman Rushdie, I trace how the sonic root of this development puts a different spin on the persistent association of the beautiful, wonder, and last things. Here, too, the hypothesis of the audit helps us think through why this has been difficult to see.

Chapter 5 turns its attention to the putative absence or complete suppression of sound, "Silence." Opening with a different pass over the motif of context, and especially the problem of "influence" (how, for example, one subject or a body of works can be said to influence another), "Silence" moves on to a sustained reading of the encounter between four intellectual figures and traditions: John Cage and his various engagements with silence (*4′33″* but also his several lectures and comments on silence); Franz Kafka and his stunning parable "The Silence of the Sirens"; Adorno and Horkheimer's allegorization of the Sirens episode in Homer's *Odyssey;* and Lyotard's clever deployment of Cage against Adorno's championing of Schönberg in the former's short statement "Several Silences." Precisely in multiplying silences, Lyotard brings out the cacophony that attends silence as a discursive or disciplinary object, whether musicological or philosophical. Are all these nonsilences the same, and if not, what do they sound like? Or, just as important, how do these differences bear on what sound sounds like as a provocation to thinking?

Echo, whistle, whisper, gasp, and silence are common enough instances of sonic signals (by the way, an English rendering of the French expression for *ping*). The sixth and final chapter of *Sounds* attends to the odd sound, or sound oddity, of "thirdness," or as it is pronounced in the chapter title, *tercer sonido* (third sound). A term that finds its current philosophical footing in the work of Charles Sanders Peirce, *thirdness* (one of his "new categories") designates the substance of mediation. But, less abstractly, thirdness also figures decisively in the discursive field of cinema studies. There it resonates as a form of filmmaking, often tied to Latin America in the 1960s, that designates what falls between the global cinema of Hollywood and the various national cinemas that have risen to challenge its cultural and economic hegemony. Noting that despite the enormous theoretical attention given to the phenomenon of "third cinema," the soundtracks of *tercer cine* films have largely lapsed into silence; the chapter explores the deployment of "the third" in the work of Roberto Esposito *(The Third Person)* and Hélène Cixous *(The Third Body)* as a way to track the work of the audit in our "deafness" to mediation in the works of cultural revolution. The political problems posed by sound are manifest here as a set of practical assumptions that silence without silencing an adjective, *third*, whose founding abstraction (what does *3*, whether ordinal, cardinal, or nominal, stand for?) is further and relentlessly modified by the morphological supplement of -*ness*.

Plainly enough, the "sounds" attended to in the chapters introduced above are not precisely those to be found in Nabokov's short story from 1923, whose title, "Sounds" *(Svuki)*, is otherwise identical to my own.[9] It is true that we share an interest in noises both cultural (piano playing) and natural (rain), and various iterations of silence, but whereas in Nabokov's text the titular sounds are narrativized, that is, embedded in the feeling tone of "the end of an affair," in *Sounds* they are treated more paratactically, that is, set near without precisely following on or from one another. For me, this bears on crucial methodological problems that thus invite elaboration as a way to orient readers to the way this text is written. Style? Yes, but not as stylus so much as *punctum*, as prick, that is, the attunement or pointing of the ears.

Succumbing to Barthes's warning about the lure of the adjectival when prose confronts the ekphrastic challenge of music, Nabokov devotes considerable energy resisting the temptation to leave his sounds in their acousmatic state. They are rendered as they melismatically glide from what Barthes and Havas called "the alert" to the "sign" (245) and put to work to capture, or simply evoke, the consonance of mind and world. Losing the resonance of the correlation between silence and "habitually untalkative women" (Nabokov 15), the story culminates in a final word, "silence" (24), that cashes out the narrative tension, the formal arc, in an easy correlation of silence and the end of narration. The skillfully deployed "I," "you," "she," "he" knotted around a certain Pal Palych, converges around a narrating *I* who, for that reason alone, gets the last word. The last word is silence. The ekphrastic teetering is brought to a standstill.

The sounds that will be attended to here are inscribed so as to end up differently. This is not a question of genre (that Nabokov was working in literature, writing a story) but of method. Even if we grant the fragility of such a distinction, the matter of emphasis is important. I am trying to say something about sounds by working on and with them in a certain way. I have come upon them as problems, provocations for thinking, and wish to leave them there—not undisturbed, but in some sense unmoved, resonating on what we might call their own frequencies if we had some reliable way of knowing what those might be. That, after all, is the lesson of silence: not only may we not know what it is, but we certainly remain unsure about how to write about it without reducing it to an academic topic of dubious professional value.

Some of these studies—even exercises in listening—were written for particular occasions and bear those rather local signs. Some were written expressly for this project, but all are presented here as occasions for attending to faint yet obvious events in ways meant to amplify how sound studies can be involved with and committed to the distinctly humanistic effort to open up unique possibilities for thinking. I do not mean thinking as opposed to feeling (no one believes in this binary any more) but thinking in the sense of being swept into what Marvin Gaye astutely called "what's goin' on." As it will be one of my aims to establish: there is much to hear here.

1. Echo

> So it happened that a nightingale sang in the garden of a country home. Her voice could be heard clearly in the house. A radio company that discovered the nightingale decided to place a microphone next to the tree where the bird had its nest. The tenant of the house, listening to the broadcast and the live voice of the nightingale at the same time observed that the broadcast nightingale was heard earlier than the live one,—the difference being due to the different velocities of electrical and acoustical waves. The real nightingale sounded like her own echo.
>
> —ADORNO, *Current of Music*

The accent I have placed on the problem of how sound challenges our thinking about context calls for elaboration and development. Although concerned here to trace the catachrestic loop between the contextualization of sound and the pressure of sound on the work of contextualization, my attention to echo is meant to tease out of the emergent field of sound studies not just another phenomenon of scholarly or aesthetic attention—the echo—but a supplemental concept for thinking the work of contextualization in the humanities as a whole. The value of the audit will be put to the test, quietly (that is, on the expository periphery), in helping fix (on) the constraints brought to this problem by the gaze and the logic of specular reflection.

I open this line of inquiry by reading an early "novel" of Michael Ondaatje's, *Coming through Slaughter*. What strongly recommends this text for consideration is the fact that, in exceedingly intricate ways, it addresses the problem of thinking the origin of jazz by connecting it to the figure of Charles "Buddy" Bolden and, in turn, connecting Bolden to New Orleans at the beginning of the twentieth century. The text, in short, is a snarl of contextualization and sound, and what attracts attention is the place of echo in this snarl. Or, stated in terms put in play in my epigraph, the text sings and acts like a nightingale.

For those unfamiliar with Ondaatje's text, a sketch of some of its defining contours will prove useful. Generically, and according to Barthes, this is what Goldmann means by form; the text exhibits qualities of a police procedural or detective novel. Not far into the text we are introduced to a character named Webb, who is a cop looking for Buddy Bolden, a friend who has gone missing under somewhat mysterious circumstances. Ondaatje works the discrepant relation between story and plot to give us insight into Bolden as a person but also to deepen the enigma around his disappearance. The reader is coaxed into caring about the question: why would a guy like this just up and disappear?

The text is divided into three sections, and in the first we are introduced to Bolden, who is depicted as a caring father (he walks his kids to school); passionate husband (he is a dexterous and attentive ravisher of his bride); talented, if inebriated, barber (his shop, "N. Joseph's Shaving Parlor," buzzes with activity); and a daring, even dangerously talented, cornet player. In large part this section is focalized through an omniscient narrator but one whose omniscience is constantly interrupted by "testimony" from friends of Bolden who narrate from within the narration, hovering between first and third person. Webb appears in this section setting the dynamics of the narrative in motion around a double enigma: where is Bolden, and why is he there? In a deft metafictional gesture Ondaatje has the reader following the steps of Webb's investigation. In strict conformity with Hitchcock's dictum, "never give away the beginning," the text—apparently narrated after the fact of the resolution of the enigma—solves the mystery by insinuating that, despite all appearances, Bolden is mad. It is not that he has gone away; it is that he is put away. Significantly, this positions the reader ahead of Webb, but it does so before one knows quite what to do with this information and, in effect, after the fact.

Sections 2 and 3 of Ondaatje's narrative trace out the pertinent plot details. We learn that Bolden's wife, Nora, is a former prostitute; that he has a friend, Bellocq, who photographed prostitutes and other denizens of Storyville and who, after being visited by Webb, immolates himself in his shop; that a friend of Bolden's, Tom Pickett, sleeps with his wife and that Bolden retaliates by taking a straight razor to Pickett's face and body; that during a gig in Shell Beach—not far from New Orleans—Bolden abandons his band and moves in with the Brewitts, a married couple; that Bolden is seduced by Robin Brewitt and reconstructs the fateful triad of his own home (Bolden-Nora-Pickett cum Bolden-Robin-Jaelin); that Webb finds Bolden and convinces him to return to New Orleans and to his family; and finally, that while struggling to reestablish himself, Bolden, as he is blowing his horn in a street parade, succumbs to his demons and is institutionalized at the East Louisiana State Hospital, where he dies. Unlike section 1, sections 2 and 3 are focalized through multiple narrators, including Bolden himself. Although there is considerable reported speech, none of it—with the exception of recorded testimony—is marked as such through punctuation. This touch draws direct attention to the problem of punctuation in the "novel," a problem to which I will be compelled to return.

What makes this text vital for my purposes is the fact that it quite explicitly seeks to contextualize the origin of a sonic practice, of jazz. Charles "Buddy" Bolden is largely recognized—most recently in Ken Burns's monumental *Jazz* from 2001—as the horn player who synthesized the decisive musical components—ragtime, the hymnals of the black church, the Afro-Caribbean rhythmic patterns (the so-called Big Four), and the call and response structures of field hollers—that modulated the blues up into jazz. In Bolden, Ondaatje is attempting to inscribe the relation between a music and a place into a text. Indeed, Bolden is depicted as someone whose "mind became the street" (Ondaatje 42). But Ondaatje is also and above all trying to write a text that meditates in a distinctly metafictional register on its *own* relation to the work of contextualizing jazz. It is here that *Coming through Slaughter* engages most directly the structure and logic of the echo.

While one might certainly want to draw attention to the turn-taking among multiple narrators that organizes the text so as to capture the peculiar way in which the text "solos," more important I would argue is the shape, the syntax of the text when considered from the point of view of its source material. Here is what I mean. The text opens with two mechanically reproduced images: a photograph of Bolden's band (the very photograph Webb goes to Bellocq to secure) and three sonographs of a dolphin's "voice" taken from John Lilly's *Mind in the Water*. It closes with reels from a film and a list of credits, sources, and acknowledgments. The mechanically reproduced images are indices, that is, signs formed by having entered into what Peirce called actual physical contact with their objects. As such they underscore the text's ambition to render the causal connection linking Bolden, jazz, and New Orleans.

Even as the text puts these indices to work, however, it interferes with their functioning. The photo, the only really existing image of Bolden, appears in the plot as the object of Webb's quest: he wants an image of Bolden so that as he approaches people along the path of his search, he can ask, "Have you seen *this* man?" Significantly, the photo fills the space of a disappearance. Bolden, thus, both is and is not where jazz begins. In fact, after Bellocq prints a copy of the negative for Webb, he destroys the negative saying of Webb, "Hope he don't find you" (Ondaatje 53). But a further detail of this exchange bears emphasis.

Once Bellocq decides to accommodate Webb, they develop a print. The narrator describes the process thus: "Watching their friend float into the page smiling at them, the friend who in reality had reversed the process and gone back into white, who in this bad film seemed to have already half-receded with that smile that may not have been a smile at all, which may have been his mad dignity" (Ondaatje 52–53). Here the development process is compared directly to Bolden's absence, but just as importantly, it has Bolden "floating" into view, coming not so much through Slaughter (a nearby town) but through water. I stress this because it helps us think about the syntactic function of the sonographs of the dolphin's voice, the other mechanically reproduced images with which the text begins.

The text that accompanies, even captions, the sonographs reads:

> Three sonographs—pictures of dolphin sounds made by a machine that is more sensitive than a human ear. The top left sonograph shows a "squawk." Squawks are common emotional expressions that have many frequencies or pitches, which are vocalized simultaneously. The top right sonograph is a whistle. Note that the number of frequencies is small and this gives a "pure" sound—not a squawk. Whistles are like personal signatures for dolphins and identify each dolphin as well as its location. The middle sonograph shows a dolphin making two kinds of signals simultaneously. The vertical stripes are echolocation clicks (sharp, multi-frequency sounds) and the dark, mountain-like humps are the signature whistles. No one knows how a dolphin makes both whistles and echolocation clicks simultaneously. (Ondaatje, no pagination)

While these too are indices, they are indices of sounds, sounds humans can hardly hear. Like Bolden they are present, but as absences *for us*. If this were all they were, little more comment would be warranted, but one of the intriguing features of Ondaatje's text is that it seeds itself insistently with material from this unpaginated page, the zero degree of the text.

One senses this first perhaps in a passage like the following, where Bolden is narrating an interaction with Webb and the Brewitts: "and me rambling on as they were about to leave, leaning against the driver's window apologizing explaining what I wanted to do. About the empty room when I get up and put metal into my mouth and hit the squawk at just the right note to equal the tone of the room and that's all you do" (Ondaatje 101). This is the first of four "human" squawks that punctuate the text. The last, in fact designated as the "last long squawk" (Ondaatje 131), marks the moment of Bolden's collapse in the parade, his last performance. Not only is this squawk tied to Bolden's instrument, the "impure" sound of his cornet, but it is also depicted as "emotional," just as the sonograph commentary specified. Bolden's squawk is at once a signal in a lonely room and a death rattle.

A similar point can also be made about echolocation or, more particularly, the echo. In a passage narrated by Frank Lewis, the clarinet player in Bolden's band, Lewis muses about Bolden's music: "We thought it was formless, but I think now he was tormented by order, what was outside it. He tore apart the plot—see his music was immediately on top of his own life. Echoing. As if, when he was playing he was lost and hunting for the right accidental notes.... He would be describing something in 27 ways. There was pain and gentleness everything jammed into each number" (Ondaatje 37). The stress here on "pain and gentleness" restates the theme of the squawk, its emotional character, but the sound's lack of purity is given important detail. Specifically, Bolden's notes, earlier described by Lewis as calling out to be "cleaned," are here characterized as oxymoronic. This particular quality gestures back to a different sonogram, the one that prompts the narrator to observe: "No one knows how dolphins make both whistles and echolocation clicks simultaneously." Indeed, this double character of Bolden's sound—his signature (the whistle) and his situation (the echolocation click)—is expressly developed in the text as a way to describe jazz. The relevant passage, narrated by the trombone player in his band, reads as follows:

> Thought I knew his blues before, and the hymns at funerals but what he is playing now is real strange, and I listen real careful for he's playing something that sounds like both. I cannot make out the tune and then catch on. He's mixing them up. He's playing the blues and the hymn sadder than the blues and then the blues sadder than the hymn. That is the first time I ever heard hymns and blues cooked up together.... It sounded like a battle between the Good Lord and the Devil. (Ondaatje 81)

This "first time" is presented as a birth, the beginning or upsurge of jazz as the unholy fusion between the blues and hymn music. From a musicological perspective this may ring false, but in the text it is clear that Bolden's capacity to blow two sounds at once explicitly "echoes" the dolphin's capacity to whistle and click simultaneously, and both are connected to the emergence of jazz in New Orleans at the threshold of the twentieth century.

But other details in Frank Lewis's observations bear comment as well. Recall that he also drew attention to the dual character of Bolden's notes—at once gentle and filled with pain—and added that they sounded as if Bolden was lost, hunting for the right notes. The fact that he also invokes "echoing" as a way to describe the relation between Bolden's life and his music strongly suggests that Lewis understands Bolden's music, jazz, as a form of echolocation. The "right accidental notes" are not necessarily ones that work musically but ones that articulate, even if accidentally, signature and situation, whistle and click. In this, Ondaatje's text offers up the echo as a figure for the work of contextualization. As Lewis says, Bolden's music and life were on top of each other, "echoing." Or, put differently, *Coming through Slaughter* urges us to think of the echo as a way to designate how jazz belongs to without reflecting the African American experience in the southern United States.

The figure of the echo echoes repeatedly in Ondaatje's text; in fact, at times it organizes the very logic of its sentences, as when, for example, Bolden bids farewell to one of his bandmates in Shell Beach: "They were shouting back and forth in musical terms. Crawley knew he was saying goodbye to his friend. He was saying goodbye to his friend" (Ondaatje 33). Although the Ovidian allusion is certainly interesting—the two subjects, the water, the incompletion and distortion of echo's utterance—I want to stress something else about the material narrated by Lewis—namely, the fact that this narrator appears in the text as one of its sources. He is not merely another narrating soloist; he is a "real person" who "really appears" in the only really existing photograph of Bolden and is a person whose contribution to the text is acknowledged, albeit implicitly, in the acknowledgments.

This bounces us back to what I referred to earlier as the syntactic structure of the text, the photos with which it opens and the acknowledgments with which it closes. If, as I have proposed, the text floats "echoing" as a way to think the relation between signature and situation, text and context, then the syntactic structure of the text—including, of course, the relay between story and plot, the past and present of narration—could be said to be structured like an echo. This means not only that the text's beginning and end echo one another but that Ondaatje's text, at a metafictional level, understands itself as the echo of its source material, some of which is charged with the authority of oral history. It is not, however, uninteresting that *Coming through Slaughter* places the echo in the beginning, and while it is certainly worth thinking about the specific way in which Ondaatje invites us to ponder the relation connecting cetaceans, language, and music, it is likewise important to recognize that Ondaatje's ontology insists that this relation is echoes "all the way down."[1] In other words, if the source material echoes the text matter, then the latter can hardly be said to "reflect" the context secured by such materials. Nor, I should add, does it make sense to simply reverse the problem and propose that the source material, the context, reflects the text, for the problem is with the specular character of reflection itself.

Certainly one of the more powerful theoretical treatments of reflection is found in Macherey's "The Problem of Reflection" from the mid-1970s. This is an intricately argued text, one that seeks to formulate an aesthetics consistent with the tenets of "structural Marxism," where, among other things, it is conceded that the lonely moment of the last instance may never come. Perhaps this is because it is echoing. Regardless, what bears emphasis here is the motif of a foundational distortion or disorientation. At bottom, reflection—modeled as it is on the logic of specular repetition—gives expression to an epistemological axiom consistent with "visualism." Mind mirrors world, and the putative task of human endeavor is to perfect this mirroring. This does not mean simply bringing mind and world into an alignment that is free of distortion but one that it is immediate. Reflection is, in effect, what Paul de Man meant by the symbol when he contrasted it with allegory in "The Rhetoric of Temporality," and it is on this epistemological basis that one sustains political evaluations of "correct ideas" or, for that matter, "realism."

The echo would appear to operate in accord with a different epistemological axiom, one that interferes with mirroring by insisting on a foundational (thus antifoundational) distortion. Although the point can always be dragged in the direction of positivism, where the difference between the transmission of light and sound becomes paramount, the fact is that echo is structured by delay, by time. Moreover, the delay always marks a decay. Something is missing from the sound source, and as a consequence the "mirroring" is more than simply reversed; it is systemically imperfect. This imperfectness might then be construed as the derivative or passive character of the echo, but as is clear in Ovid's remarkable poem, decay can also assume an ironic function, where delay displaces the authority of its source material.[2] In effect, echo, while not giving up on source, refuses to enshrine a simple principle of derivation at its core, thereby obliging literary or cultural sociologists of all stripes to respond to the theoretical gauntlet it throws down. Gilles Deleuze, puzzling over the problem of Destiny, puts it beautifully: "it [Destiny] implies between successive presents *non-localizable connections*, actions at a distance, systems of replay, resonance and echoes, objective chances, signs, signals and roles which transcend spatial locations and temporal successions" (Deleuze 83; my emphasis).

Before turning to consider how echo might then bear on what in the introduction I called Barthes's split sociology, I wish to acknowledge that my own musings on echo are echoing those of Joan Wallach Scott, who in "Fantasy Echo: History and the Construction of Identity" has proposed echo as a way to refresh feminist historiography. At the risk of casting Scott in the role of Narcissus, my commentary will seek to deploy the decay between us as an opening, an opportunity to further clarify what echo is doing here.

Scott's piece begins with an anecdote. She explains her title by reporting that she stumbled upon it while working as a teaching assistant for George Mosse, whose multiply accented pronunciation of the French expression *fin de siècle* was transcribed in a student paper as "fantasy echo." Scott astutely comments that this transcription is itself an echo, thereby generating the need to define what about an echo could be said to describe the conceptual difference between fantasy echo and *fin de siècle*. After deftly summarizing how Western feminism has tended to articulate history and identity (the latter typically located in history but not itself historical), she turns to a theoretical discussion of both fantasy and echo. Fantasy is developed through a reading of its deployment in psychoanalysis from Freud to Žižek, and Scott presents it as a way to give tight, even theatrical, form to material premised on the foreclosure of difference. It is both defensive and enabling. Echo, however, Scott teases out of Ovid and important subsequent interpretations of the poem. She underscores many of the same points I have made above: delay, decay, founding repetition, and so on. Indeed, it is precisely the quality of decay that explains her interpretation of Mosse's student. Taken together, the two theoretical discussions justify a founding antimetabole: "The echo is a fantasy, the fantasy an echo; the two are inextricably intertwined" (Scott 287).

In her conclusion Scott moves to extend her observations beyond the field of contemporary historiography and Western feminism, proposing, "Fantasy echo is a tool for analysts of political and social movements as they read historical materials in their specificity and particularity" (304). Here, one might say, our interests echo one another most intently, and for this reason I am called to give some account of my relative lack of interest in fantasy.

Put succinctly, the matter comes down to "visualism." Although Scott, spurred by Laplanche and Pontalis, returns to Freud's discussion of fantasy in the essay "A Child Is Being Beaten," she pursues her elaboration of the concept by turning to Žižek's Lacanian-inspired treatment. This brings fantasy largely under the auspices of the imaginary, where it works to secure a precariously unified, because specular, identity. It incorporates what doesn't fit, in fact, what will never fit. Echo is then the foreclosed delay *within* this identity. I agree with this. But what happens if one retrieves the discussion of fantasy from Freud's correspondence with Fliess? There, fantasy is expressly counterpoised to dreams. As Freud puts it in a draft on the architecture of hysteria: "They [phantasies] are built up out of things that have been heard about and then *subsequently* turned to account; thus they combine things that have been experienced and things that have been heard about past events (from the history of parents and ancestors) and things heard about the subject himself. They are related to things heard in the same way as dreams are related to things seen" (Freud 197–98). A formulation such as this would suggest that fantasy is better grasped by situating it not within the imaginary but within the sonic field of echoing (the subject's past echoing in its present). Indeed, the imaginary itself might be similarly resituated, a maneuver that would transgress the very logic of "visualism."

Of course, once thought within the sonic field of echoing, fantasy loses its status as the counterweight to echo, reducing the antimetabolic loop to nil. In Scott's text one senses something like her resistance to such a proposition but less in the text's explicit formulations than in the syntax of key sentences. For example, Scott has repeated recourse to sentences like "Yet there is no denying the persistent fact of identification, for echoing through the twists and turns of history is the fantasy scenario: if woman has the right to mount the scaffold, she has the right to mount the rostrum" (Scott 297). Here, the antimetabolic with its defining delay loop appears to be flattened out so that fantasy is a thing conveyed *by or through* the process of echoing. Thing is followed by process. True, this protects the loop from closing, but it also risks a different problem: phantasmatic capture. If one recalls that in her unpacking of the concept of fantasy, Scott has recourse to Žižek's characterization of the narrative of fantasy as that which resolves "some fundamental antagonism by rearranging its terms into a temporal succession" (Scott 289), then one might well wonder whether a version of this formula animates a locution like the one cited above, where the loop between fantasy and echo is, as I said, flattened. In short, is the fantasy echo more fantasy than echo?

If this is the case, and my question, while perhaps rhetorical, is not merely so, one needs to proceed cautiously in wielding the tool Scott has placed in our hands, especially when shifting from the terrain of identity construction, whether feminist or not, to the problematic of contextualization as such. Doubtless, certain aspects of the fantasy echo might be usefully deployed in thinking about *Coming through Slaughter*—a Sri Lankan author in Canada might well "enjoy" (in the strong psychoanalytical sense) identifying with an African American musician and troublemaker in New Orleans—but as concerns the methodological question of how to situate a text in its context, other aspects of the tool, notably its missing aspects, might prove even more useful.

Here, reengaging Barthes's discussion of the two sociologies acquires fresh urgency. To reiterate, we are not dealing with the familiar differentiation between qualitative/hermeneutic and quantitative/positivist sociology. Instead, Barthes is differentiating between two sociologies of literature, one that attends to the literary institution and the other to the literary work. Nor, despite certain affinities, is this a restatement of the distinction between dialectical and so-called vulgar sociologies of literature to be found in Lukács and Mikhail Lifshitz. As I have noted, Barthes invokes the term *socio-logic* to designate the sociology of Goldmann's theory of the novel. While the distinction is sharp, Barthes insists that they are complementary, although in the last line of his review he hints that because a socio-logic thinks the activity of classification as such, it can assign sociology its value. But what precisely is a socio-logic?

Barthes introduces this term in another review (this generic repetition merits attention in its own right), one dedicated to two texts by Claude Lévi-Strauss, *Totemism* and *The Savage Mind*. It predates the review of Goldmann by a year and, as with the later review, was written while Barthes was offering a seminar on the "system of objects" at the *École pratique des hautes études*. Yes, Jean Baudrillard wrote his dissertation under Barthes's supervision. As if predicting my interest in it, the review begins at the water's edge by discussing the formal logic of a beachside tent village. What is meant by *socio-logic* can be gleaned from a set of important formulas that mark out the geography of the text. I will simply list them: first, a socio-logic gives expression to a responsibility of forms. This implies a sociology attentive to form and function but also an analyst responsible for the system of objects thought to be comprehended through such attention. Second, a socio-logic proceeds on the assumption that because all societies (whether "primitive" or "modern") structure reality, all aspects of the social formation can and should attract "socio-logical" analysis. Third, whereas a sociology of contents places a premium on statistical averages and norms (especially when studying deviance), a "structural sociology" (a synonym for "socio-logic") is attentive to variation, aberration, in effect, the exceptional. And fourth, sociology is concerned with normality, typicality, while a socio-logic is a sociology "of totality" (Barthes, "Sociology and Socio-logic" 163). Taken together, these might all appear to be an elaboration of the gnomic formulation in *Mythologies*: "I shall say that a little formalism turns one away from History, but that a lot brings one back to it" (Barthes, *Mythologies* 112), where "History" serves as a metonym for *context*.

Of these formulas the ones that attract more than heuristic attention are those in which appear the words *responsibility* and *totality*, words often understood to be anathema to devout "poststructuralists," at least from the vantage point of those who regard the latter as a late (yet oddly pre-Nietzschean) variant of nihilism. But even from the perspective of a more immanent engagement with Barthes's texts these terms are ones that also seem difficult to square with the tenets of "textuality." Does Barthes not rather directly confront totality with plurality and responsibility with pleasure in the programmatic statement "From Work to Text"? He certainly appears to, but he also begins this piece (he insists on calling it a "text") by indicating that the development whose tentative propositions he is attempting to distill is "linked" (his word) "to the present development of (among other things) linguistics, anthropology, Marxism, and psychoanalysis" (56). Moreover, in concluding the text, he also insists on the fact that Text (sans definite article and capitalized) constitutes a properly social space that leaves no language safely outside. In short, even as Barthes moves to leave aside what he had earlier counterpoised to the institution, namely the work, he retains a vocabulary utterly consistent with his earlier theoretical reflection on the two sociologies. Again, the problem is *not* the antisocial character of textual analysis but the problem of formulating a sociology of literature cut to the measure of textuality.

It is interesting that Barthes no sooner invokes the "link" between the text and the developments of linguistics, anthropology, and so forth than he draws attention to its function: "(the word *link* [in French, *liaison*, a term with significant linguistic and sexual resonance] is used here in a deliberately neutral manner: no determination is being invoked, however multiple and dialectical)" ("From Work to Text" 56). Thus, Barthes grasps Text as precisely the methodological field within which one needs to think carefully, not about whether text has a context but *how* it has a context and what might be the *responsible* way to establish this without appealing to the epistemology of determination, whether Freudian (the plurality of "overdetermination") or Marxian (dialectical). "Neutral" here, as we know from his late study on the topic, does not mean "agnostic." It means "confounding" when applied to the procedures of binary classification (i.e., neither marked nor unmarked), and in that sense Barthes is deliberately exposing himself to the task of refining what a "link" links. Again, the point is *not* indecision or denial but assuming theoretical and political responsibility for thinking the articulation of literature and society in a manner that eschews or delays appeal to the binary formulas of determination.

My immodest proposal is that echo might be a productive way to think about what Barthes calls "link." Given that I have hinted at this by proposing that "echo" functions in the metafictional register of Ondaatje's text as the concept through which it thinks its own link to its material, it is crucial to note that both in "Sociology and Socio-logic" and in "From Work to Text" literature might be said to repeat, or echo, its function.

In the review of Lévi-Strauss, Barthes invokes literature as a way to concretize the distinction drawn between a sociology of normality and a "socio-logic" of totality. Drawing first on Foucault's *History of Madness* and the importance attached there to the social logic of exclusion, Barthes argues that even though literature is consumed by a small demographic, the social distinction between literature and popular fiction is, as Durkheim might say, a *total* social fact. In the end literature is "unintelligible" without such a distinction. His deft evocation of Goldmann (also an enthusiastic partisan of "totality") is designed to keep the debate over the sociology of literature in the wings of his argument, and what is achieved here is, among other things, the principle of the constitutive exclusion. Anticipating Deleuze and Guattari's concept of minority literature, Barthes here insists that a sociology driven to normalize the abnormal is a sociology doomed to misunderstand the relation between literary art and society, modern or not.

A decade later, in "From Work to Text," Barthes ties textuality and literature together in a remarkably similar way. This occurs in his second proposition regarding textuality, the one referred to under the heading of "genre" in his opening summary. With a symmetry that seems calculated, the evocation of Foucault in the earlier piece gives way to an evocation of Bataille, whose collected works were being edited by Foucault at the time. Why Bataille? As Barthes explains, his writing is difficult if not impossible to classify. More specifically, it is not clear that Bataille belongs to literature at all. In effect, the evocation of literature functions to again put in play the social logic of exclusion. What is different here is the metacritical twist by which Text is made more than the principle of a constitutive outside. As Barthes puts it: "If the Text raises problems of classification (moreover, this is one of its 'social' functions), it is because it always implies a certain experience of limits" (58). In other words if the logic of exclusion operates to manage a social formation by legitimating the demarcation of what is asocial, then Text is precisely what interferes with this by restlessly agitating the forming of any and all limits. Even this one. Crucial here is not *what* is excluded—the mad, literature, or the sacred—but the necessary social work of exclusion. Doubtless, this is precisely the kind of formulation that makes Text appear allergic to "totality," but it is crucial here to note that Barthes is not, thereby, prepared to abandon the social. In fact, in the parenthetical phrase cited above, Barthes specifies that the problematization of classification is *one of the "social"* functions of Text, suggesting not only that Text's capacity to confront us with an experience of limits (one of Bataille's formulas) makes it social but that this is only *one* of the ways in which Text is social.

Or "social." Key here is that in and around Barthes's sustained engagement with something he persists in calling literature, he maintains contact with the Goldmannian legacy, even as he teases apart its conceptual tapestry. This is what it means to put *social* in quotation marks: he does not so much wish to put it under erasure as to attach "the social" to a different sociological paradigm, one closer to what we have seen that he earlier called a "socio-logic." Now, if this, too, is what warrants his knowing appeal to "link" as a way to attach Text and context, then what does echo help us grasp about this predicament?

Coming through Slaughter provides us with vital clues. As my reading of the text has established, it is not simply metafictional. It is concerned to think as part of its relation to itself (both its phatic and metalinguistic registers) its relation to a life, a place, a time, and a sound. It is all that jazz. At the core of this relation is a disappearance, an index that traces and then corrodes its object. The challenge for a sociology of literature is how to think the specificity of *this* relation. How to think the way jazz's relation to slavery, to New Orleans, to Congo Square, to Bolden repeats in Ondaatje's relation to the text woven of these sources?

It seems crucial to recall that when Marx took up the problem of the epic at the end of his introduction to the *Grundrisse* he quite deliberately complicated the question of context and in ways that have not always mattered to the dialecticians among us. He first urged that we recognize how the epic belonged to a specific moment in the history of myth (I am thinking here of his telling query about the impact of gunpowder on Achilles), but he then urged that we recognize how the tradition of the epic, something like the Western cultural tradition "itself," had other contexts. Indeed, the fragment concludes by pivoting on a distinction between *childish* and *childlike*, a distinction that matters only when we understand in what way epic does not and cannot "belong" to the society that determined its production. If we moderns (and Marx invests solidly in the primitive/modern distinction) still value the epic, it is because it resonates within our present in much the same way that Freud thought our childhoods remain active in our adult life. For reasons that might have "something" to do with the fact that, by 1857, Marx had lost four of his own children (one in July of that year), his discussion is more elegiac than it might otherwise be. That is, he links the enduring value of the epic to its capacity to index a historical past that has been absolutely sacrificed to modernity, the very point later made by the pre-Marxian

Lukács in *The Theory of the Novel*. In this sense the present's attachment to the epic is childlike, not childish.

What this brings out is the fact that the epic, as a form of literature, relates, one might say, repeatedly, not to its social context but to its social contexts. The point is not the trivial one about the need to pluralize concepts. Instead, what bears emphasis is the notion that in a certain sense literature and society are never *not* linked to one another. What the demand for determination achieves, whether in the first instance or the last, is the unwitting production of the very problem it then seeks to solve, namely, how to fix something that is not broken. At the very least, what the example from the *Grundrisse* makes clear is that Marx was aware of the intricate ways in which historical (the present's valuation of the epic) and social (the past's mythological discourse) contexts proliferate instances of determination, a proliferation that has only intensified as the cultural tradition of the epic (largely the Eurocentric cultural tradition) has been dispersed across the places and times of what Gayatri Spivak has called "planetarity" (Spivak 2003, 71). So much so, that the conceptual tool of determination and all the analytical devices supported by its causal logic—correspondence, reflection, homology, and so on—seem quite feeble, quite inadequate to the task of thinking how literature and society link with one another. Walter Benjamin, deeply caught up in the warring of the worlds that was to find its echo in the concept of "planetarity," seems concerned about the same problem when, in the last of his theses "On the Concept of History," he insisted—as if commenting on the relation between their insights and his own life— that "historicism contents itself with establishing a causal nexus among moments in history. But no state of affairs having causal significance is for that very reason historical. It became historical posthumously, as it were, through events that may be separated by thousands of years" (397).

To give credit where credit is due, Benjamin was also among the first to float the idea that *echo* might be a keyword in the fight against historicism, a position he explicitly associates with Ranke's demand that we recognize the past "the way it really was." In his second thesis he writes: "The past carries with it a secret index by which it is referred to redemption. Doesn't a breath of the air that pervaded earlier days caress us as well? In the voices we hear, isn't there an echo of now silent ones? . . . If so, then there is a secret agreement between past generations and the present one" (4: 390). In concluding this aphorism by insisting that the historical materialist knows this, Benjamin positions echo in a quarrel that bears more than a passing resemblance to the one Barthes is engaged in with Goldmann. Benjamin wants to split history; Barthes wants to split sociology. If we split, as it were, the difference, we come rather abruptly to context and the problem of whether echo helps us think about literature or culture more broadly and society as articulations of delay, displacement, and decay. This is testimony, I should think, of how sound studies opens "unique possibilities of thinking."

Having already drawn attention to the important ways that Ondaatje's text points us forward on such questions, I believe a concluding series of observations about it are in order. In stressing the syntactic structure of the text—the placement of echo before its sources—I meant to emphasize that Ondaatje appears willing to entertain the Deleuzean proposition that echo is but another name for the "nonlocalizable." I hope it is now clear that by this I do not mean to breathe fresh life into the stale notion that since all that is human transpires within the immanence of representation, there is no point in making any literary critical appeals to society, or history, or politics. The issue is what invocation of such things one is willing to assume responsibility for in producing and disseminating a reading. I take this to be Barthes's "the responsibility of forms," where, lest it pass unnoticed, one is obliged to take responsibility for the *form* of one's responsibility. With this in mind, and here I retrieve an earlier thread, it seems unwarranted to overlook a conspicuous peculiarity of the punctuation of *Coming through Slaughter*, namely, that many of the text segments are set off by asterisks. Indeed, the text contains no fewer than sixty-nine such marks in its mere 157 pages. As the word suggests, the asterisk is the sign of the star, and, as this might in turn lead one to assume, the figure of the star assumes thematic contours in the text.

Two important invocations of the star occur in part 2 of the text, and both involve Buddy's relation to the Brewitts. In the first, stars are listed as a topic of conversation among Robin, Jaelin, and Buddy. As the narrator goes on to report, Jaelin, at a certain point, revisits this topic by announcing that there is a new star called the Wolf-Ryat [*sic*] star, named after the two people who discovered it. Buddy responds by saying that "Wolf Star" would be a better name for it. In the concluding sentence of this section the narrator observes that they were talking about Robin.

In the second invocation Buddy is swimming with Robin, and they are discussing the impact of his presence on the Brewitt marriage. The passage opens with an echo: "As long as I don't hurt you or Jaelin. As long as I don't hurt you or Jaelin, she mimics" (Ondaatje 69). It then moves through the surrounding darkness to "the dull star of white water under each of us. Swimming toward the sound of madness" (69). Here, too, the star appears attached to Robin, or attached to Buddy's attachment to Robin, but in the second passage this attachment assumes the form of a sonic link to madness,

Buddy's madness. One might reasonably propose that this is what motivates the echo that sets the passage in motion.

What ties the passages together around the figure of the star becomes clearer once the Wolf-Rayet star acquires some specificity. First discovered in 1867 by Charles Wolf and Georges Rayet, Wolf-Rayet type stars are massive stars in the process of falling apart. Under certain conditions Wolf-Rayet stars can become black holes. They can be recognized by the spectacular and erratic emission bands that gather around and extend outward from them. In effect, these stars, the new star mentioned by Jaelin and the dull star beneath the white water, point either through madness or implosion to a text limit where Buddy stands as that which will go missing—the dead, mad star of jazz.

What brings these thematic treatments into association with the asterisk—aside from the fact that asterisks punctuate the sections in which these passages appear—is made evident in an earlier passage in the text. This is a passage in which the narrator reports an outburst of anger between Buddy and the other woman in his life, his wife, Nora: "Furious at something he drew his right hand across his body and lashed out. Half way there at full speed he realized it was a window he would be hitting and braked. For a fraction of a second his open palm touched the glass, beginning simultaneously to draw back. The window starred and crumpled slowly two floors down. His hand miraculously uncut. It had acted exactly like a whip, violating the target and still free, retreating from the outline of a star" (Ondaatje 16). Here, at a window, on the very surface that articulates the inside and outside of the structure in which it is set, two stars meet: the star of the cracked glass and the imprint of a hand, both teetering between the literal and the figural. The "outline of a star" draws attention to the specific graphic features of the splayed hand and thus the five points/digits that form the asterisks that appear in *Coming through Slaughter* (font selection is relevant here), linking the shattered glass, Bolden's madness, and the imploding massive star. While this thematic series might well urge one to think about the asterisk as a sign of disaster (literally, *dis* + *astro/star*), it seems even more pertinent to note the star's relation to the limit, the surface on which it is insistently outlined. From this perspective the asterisk, the figure of the star, marks the limits of the text within the text, both syntactically and philologically.

Philologically?

One of the more unusual pieces that appears in Adorno's *Notes to Literature*, from 1958, is the one titled "Punctuation Marks." It is unusual because, as his English translator, Shierry Weber Nicholson, points out, it is an exercise in metacriticism. In it Adorno, who otherwise scrupulously follows the German scholarly protocol of referring to himself in the third person, appears here to be engaging with his own practice, and doing so under the general heading of "physiognomy." As in his radio studies from the late 1930s he is thinking about punctuation marks as faces behind which deeper text layers are discernible as sites or even sources of expression. If Nicholson is right, then these marks—exclamation marks, colons, dashes, and parentheses (to name ones he discusses)—are bits of his "own" face behind which, Hegel's hostility toward physiognomy notwithstanding, lie not only his thoughts but the matrix of thought and sound. As he says at one point: "There is no element of language that more resembles music than in the punctuation marks" (92).

It is interesting that although many marks are both mentioned and used (the typesetter at Columbia University Press has introduced elaborate text separators between each paragraph/fragment/aphorism that composes the text), Adorno does not discuss the mark of the asterisk. Of course, one might always conclude that this mark is physiognomically irrelevant—and I have not combed the corpus to determine whether the asterisk is entirely absent—but one might argue that Daniel Heller-Roazen's philological, as opposed to physiognomical, account of the asterisk in *Echolalias* offers a more theoretically satisfying explanation of Adorno's reticence.

Heller-Roazen's discussion occurs in the chapter "Little Stars," which begins: "It is always possible to perceive in one form of speech the echo of another" (99), an intertextual appeal to Benjamin that might suggest that he, too, wishes to comment on the problem of historiography. But he does not. Instead, his interest lies in the philological, even linguistic, problem of explaining *why* one language echoes in another. He observes, "No necessary logical link ties the consideration of the echoes between languages to that of their cause" (100), a problem that only compounded itself when, at the end of the eighteenth century, the project of thinking the continuities between Sanskrit and, say, Greek or Hebrew, situated, at least in principle, all languages on a plane of immanence. The political theology of this development has been well studied in Jean Oleander's *The Language of Paradise*.

But what does the chapter title "Little Stars" have to do with this? "Stars" here refers to asterisks, and as Heller-Roazen details, asterisks (in German *der Stern*) emerged as a typographical expression "that designates forms that have been deduced" (107). In effect, asterisks came to function in philological compendia, even dictionaries and lexicons, as the way to mark that a relation—typically etymological—between one language and another is, strictly speaking, unattested—that is, deduced. In my edition of

The American Heritage Dictionary of the English Language this function is realized by the mark of the dagger, a sign typically followed by the gloss: "origin obscure." Heller-Roazen is careful to differentiate the two signs (the asterisk and the dagger), but in both cases what matters is that the asterisk signals a problem: is there a cause outside of language for the echo of one language in another, and what might constitute decisive evidence for this? In the absence of such evidence one marks the surface on which it may or may not have been inscribed with a star.

For his part Adorno echoes this appeal to the echo by proposing that punctuation should be handled the way musicians handle "forbidden chord progressions" (Adorno, *Notes to Literature* 97). What is revealed through such handling is whether one is skilled or sloppy. "To put it more subtly, one can sense the difference between a subjective will that brutally demolishes the rules and a tactful sensitivity that allows the rules to echo in the background even where it suspends them" (97). Although he goes on to foreground the use of commas, his point clearly applies to the entirety of punctuation. All punctuation effects the choreography of sensitivity and will, and as such, effects the asterisk-function, the marking on the text surface of the text's relation to the causes that echo there. Perhaps it is because this function cannot assume the profile of a face, an identity that gives itself *to be seen;* and thus seen through, it eludes the attentions of physiognomy and therefore does not figure in Adorno's discussion.[3]

My point then is this: if the asterisk figures so prominently in *Coming through Slaughter*—both syntactically and thematically—this is because it is required by the metafictional protocols of the text. Not only is the text's narrative and hermeneutic development transferred by the device of the "small star" (where is Bolden, and why is he there?), but through the motif and practice of the echo it attaches itself both to itself and to a context that insists on being deduced, unattested. The point is not that there is no origin, no encounter with anything but language. Instead, whatever limit is ascribed is one that readers—whether close or distant—are responsible to and for. Ondaatje wrote under the pressure of this insight. If this is one way to think the "responsibility of forms," then it is also a way to think the socio-logic of textuality, one that took the emergence of sound studies to echo back—but is it back?—in our direction.

A closing thought: in ways that will require further attention (see chapter 6), throughout *Roland Barthes* Barthes refers to himself (the *lui-même* of the French title) in the third person: *he.* This linguistic and rhetorical rigor (in an opening aphorism he stresses its novelesque character) assumes an especially rich articulation in the aphorism/entry called "The Echo

Chamber," a formulation that in French *(la chambre d'échos)* evokes almost immediately the title of his last book, *La chambre claire* ("camera lucida" in Latin). Setting aside this enormously suggestive architecture of the adjoining rooms of clarity and echoes (Barthes's reproach to "visualism"?), I turn to the theme of this aphorism. It is stated in the opening line: "In relation to the systems which surround him: what is he?" (*Roland Barthes* 74). "He" responds by characterizing himself as an echo chamber. While it is clear that Barthes deploys the figure as a way to explain how and why he is such a fickle adherent to any of the grand causes of his day, one ought not ignore the fact that he is here repeating his concern about "the link" at a "personal" level. In presenting "himself" as an echo chamber, Barthes authorizes one to belong to any context, even to one's "own" context, in the medium of sound—not in the sense of noises or tunes that haunt one from Combray-like places but in the sense of a discursively mediated perception of what it is like to belong anywhere. Why deploy the concept of the gaze to think this predicament? I am not seeing it.

2. Whistle

> Is not the involuntary recollection, Proust's *mémoire involontaire*,
> much closer to forgetting than what is usually called memory? And
> is not this work of spontaneous recollection, in which remembrance
> is the woof and forgetting the warp, a counterpart to Penelope's work
> rather than its likeness? For here the day unravels what the night
> has woven.
>
> —BENJAMIN, "On Some Motifs in Baudelaire"

> Such a perfect democracy constructs its perfect foe, terrorism. Its
> wish is to be judged by its enemies not by its results.
>
> —DEBORD, *Comments on the Society of the Spectacle*

SOUND POLITICS

I

The whistling that will concern me in this chapter occurs in the medium of
the cinema. It derives what sense it has from the films within which it takes
place, and responding to the problems posed by this instance of a nonvocalized vocalization pressures the concept of the audit I am here inventing in
a rather overdetermined way. Specifically, when dealing with the textual
analysis of films, it is difficult to avoid the analytical legacy of the gaze. This
is because it was in relation to the cinema that this concept first fatefully
passed from the encounter between philosophy and psychoanalysis
sketched earlier to the field of visual studies. Thus, if the audit can be treated
as a coherent analogue for the gaze, then it is in the work of film analysis
that the details and merits of this analogy confront most directly the discourse of "visualism."

In the spirit of Steve Martin's witty observation that the French have a
different word for everything, I note that the French word for *visualism* is
to be found in the work of Jean-Pierre Oudart and Serge Daney, in whose
hands it is rendered as *ocularcentrism* or, even more comprehensively, *pho-
tology* (both here translated back into English). If I emphasize this here, it is
because *ocularcentrism,* first articulated in the pages of *Cahiers du cinéma,*
has the dual advantage of amplifying the political dimension of the critique
of "visualism" while keeping the problem of the cinema in the foreground,
thus pressuring the concept of the audit from just the right angle.

The relevant political dimension of *ocularcentrism* can be teased out by contrasting two critiques of what was once called mass culture: a critique centered on the motif of deception (consider here Adorno and Horkheimer's well-known chapter in *Dialectic of Enlightenment*, "The Culture Industry: Enlightenment as Deception") and a critique centered on the motif of positioning (consider here Althusser's account of "interpellation" in "Ideology and Ideological State Apparatuses"). In a nutshell what is at stake is that whereas deception is assumed to befall a preexisting subject whose capacity to make rational political choices is thereby diminished, positioning is understood to produce and sustain the illusion (quintessentially visual) that there is a subject of deception whose choices, whether rational or not, are his or hers to make. This complicates in a rather fundamental way not so much political behavior but our sense of the agent of such behavior. It also thus complicates the task of any cultural analysis that purports to have political implications.

Although the point is not often stressed, positioning, as an effect of the operation of the basic cinematographic apparatus, did not immediately express itself as a theory of the gaze. This required the intervention of feminist scholars such a Laura Mulvey, who shifted attention to film narrative, where the gaze could be attributed to characters as opposed to the apparatus as such. In effect, Mulvey engendered the position of what Oudart, Daney, Comolli, and others had called "the Absent One" (the empty vantage point providing the visual field with its perspectival coherence). What was gained at the level of political precision, notably the heuristic device of the "male gaze," was, if not lost, certainly obscured, at the level of the critique of mass culture. If visual pleasure was the problem, it was everywhere. It had no particular relation to mass culture generally or the cinema in particular, a situation that called for a modulation of the kind of political analysis brought to bear on what Adorno and Horkheimer had called "the culture industry." An instructive response to this call pertinent to the tension between the concepts of gaze and audit is to be found in Walter Benjamin's theoretical and political account of memory.

II

"When Marx undertook his analysis of the capitalist mode of production, this mode was in its infancy." This, the opening sentence of Benjamin's "The Work of Art in the Age of Its Technological Reproducibility," at once preempts all subsequent discussion of so-called postindustrial society and underscores his ambivalent relation to Marxism, an ambivalence that culminated in the years immediately prior to his suicide in a theory of history where the dwarf of dialectical materialism was borne on the shoulders of the Jewish Messiah. Benjamin's sentence, underscoring as it does the break before and after language *(Anfang* from *infans)*, not only explicitly foreshadows the necessity of a historical supplementation of Marxism; it confronts us with the task of tracking what happens to Marxism in the course of its properly messianic supplementation. It asks, in particular, what happens to the production of critical consciousness once the mode of production passes from, as it were, the silent era?

It is not difficult to show that much of Benjamin's writing during the 1930s traces the impact of commodification on the cultural field. In the "Work of Art" essay this takes the form of showing how, in a certain sense, the structural logic of proletarianization has spread from the field of production to the field of consumption, indeed, to the consumption of culture. How else are we to understand the confidence with which Benjamin, in his notes for the essay, aligns the shock experience of spectatorship with the worker's shakedown at the assembly line? (Benjamin, "Formula" 94). As odd as it may seem, when, at the essay's close Benjamin calls for the politicization of art, he is doing so on the basis of his belief in the broadly cultural politicization of the masses. The point is not, as the obtuse have uncharitably asserted, that watching a film either politicizes one or triggers revolt. Rather, Benjamin is insisting that as the capitalist mode of production came of age (after it became possible not to imagine but to hear commodities speaking, as Marx does in *Capital* I), it began to redistribute the structural occasions for the production of critical consciousness. As one might assume, this did not leave the redistributed elements untouched. Indeed, Benjamin proposes a new dyad of proletarianization. In the place of a palpable encounter with the expropriation of surplus value and collectivized association, he stresses the masses' desire to get closer to things and to overcome their uniqueness—both critical rearticulations of commodity fetishism. But here's the problem one stumbles upon: how precisely is this displaced structure of proletarianization secured at the level of the subject positions constituting the masses?

Although the "Work of Art" essay appeals to the concept of the optical unconscious and its structurally critical character (one sees the limits of one's seeing), better resources for responding to such a question appear in contemporaneous essays, indeed ones often regarded as at odds with the "utopian" aspirations of the "Work of Art" essay. Perhaps the most pertinent of these is the equally well-known "On Some Motifs in Baudelaire," where through a formulation cited from *Beyond the Pleasure Principle*—to wit "emerging consciousness takes the place of a memory trace" (Benjamin,

"Some Motifs" 317)—Benjamin not only thematizes the crucial link between memory and the production of consciousness, but he forever complicates all political deployments of memory. He achieves this by retrieving and developing Proust's distinction between voluntary and involuntary memory. As my epigraphic evocation of "On Some Motifs" makes clear, this distinction had mattered to Benjamin for some time, certainly for more than a decade. And, interestingly, it is one whose provenance Benjamin and Julia Kristeva disagree about, the former proposing that it derives from Bergson's *Matter and Memory*, the latter tracing it to Schopenhauer as mediated through the teachings of Gabriel Séailles, an aesthetician whose seminar "Studies in Sensibility" Proust followed in 1894–95 (Kristeva 262). Although the matter of its derivation is interesting, clearly more important is the way Benjamin interprets Proust's distinction.

As with so many of Benjamin's conceptual touchstones the distinction between voluntary and involuntary memory resists summary. This is due, in large part, to the fact that so many of Benjamin's touchstones are piled, as it were, on top of each other like the rubble left in the wake of progress. So, to exhaust the memory problem, one would have to take up the related distinction between the novel and the story, and the two modalities of experience, *Erlebnis* (or immediate, lived experience) and *Erfahrung* (or experience mediated by meaning). This is not the place to attempt such an exhaustive survey. Thus, let us make the best of a difficult situation and settle for a consideration of the *fundamental* difference between the two Proustian memories. If Benjamin appeals here to psychoanalysis, it is because Freud provides him with the concept of the unconscious, and, as it turns out, what is distinctive about involuntary memory is that it is, properly speaking, unconscious. Not only is it a memory one does not know she or he has, but it is a memory one cannot set out to preserve. By contrast, voluntary memory—and it is crucial here that Benjamin associates it with the explosion of mnemotechnics (steam printing, photography, phonography, cinematography, etc.) in the nineteenth century—is deliberative, conscious as a matter of principle, but for precisely that reason voluntary memory is memory that contains no trace of the past whatsoever. In effect, voluntary memory is the process whereby the mind is simply cluttered with souvenirs of what Gayatri Spivak has called the vanishing present.

The political importance of this distinction becomes clear when to it are added the modalities of experience. For, what matters, if consciousness (whether critical or not) does indeed form on the site of a memory trace, is memory. On Benjamin's account what constitutes the content of memory, not its mechanism (voluntary or involuntary) but its content, is meaningful experience, that is, *Erfahrung*, precisely what Proust retapped through the medium of the tea-soaked *madeleine*. Now, there are two political aspects to Proustian memory. The easiest to discern is the one that deals with the moment of recognition, that is, the moment when Proust's narrator discovers not only that he has been trying too hard but that everything around him—all social institutions and practices—everything has been conspiring to keep this from him. This is the moment, albeit clichéd, of ideological unmasking. More difficult to discern is the second aspect. This is the one where what stands out behind the isolation defining every souvenir that clutters voluntary memory is the collectivity latent within all experience whose meaning endures. Here it is important to resist the impulse, succumbed to too readily by Jennings et al. (the editors of Harvard University Press's "selected writings") to temporalize experience—to, in effect, overlook Benjamin's insistence on the *social* forces registered in the discourse and practice of involuntary memory. Otherwise, when in "On the Concept of History" Benjamin reanimates the figure of the chronicler, a figure aligned in 1936 with the storyteller into whom has been dipped all transmissible, hence meaningful, experience, the light cast on the politics of messianic Marxism is too faint to be picked up. Memory has become, and a certain hyperbole is important here, the locus of what is politicizable in the late capitalist, and now globalized, mode of production. Indeed, memory is structured by the factions warring over not just its contents but the form of its contents.

UNSOUND FILM

Let us say, for the sake of argument, that a certain link has now been forged between politics and memory—not a sufficient link but a necessary one—whereby any account of the production of critical consciousness will at some point have to confront the problem of memory. Specifically, such accounts will have to struggle, like Penelope, with the warp of recollection and the woof of forgetting, in effect, with what Spivak has called the "textility" of experience (*Critique* 337). Now while Benjamin, for reasons not hard to discern, concentrates on the memory that is forgetting (voluntary memory), one is not thereby entitled to ignore the forgetting that is recollection, or at the very least, repetition. Of the many instances of such forgetting—and it is important here to insist, against Nietzsche, who counseled learned forgetting, upon the involuntary character of the forgetting—one that cries out for attention is that of the so-called haunting melody or, put more mundanely, the tune stuck in one's head. Benjamin himself points us in this direction, not by discussing the phenomenon per se but by unpacking his discussion of the two memories through reference to a little known work of Theodor Reik's, *Surprise and the Psychoanalyst* from 1929.[1]

In this text Reik, too, resists discussing the haunting melody directly. Instead, he lays out the fundamental concepts—surprise, memory, reminiscence, attention—drawn on in his later study *The Haunting Melody*. Indeed, Reik's discussion of the voluntary/involuntary distinction revolves round the concept of attention, thus revealing that a chief concern of his study is the choreography of the transference in the clinical setting. How, in other words, is the analyst to get in tune with the analysand's process of free association? What form of attention must be paid to what the analysand says? Key here is the theme of surprise (in German, *Uberraschung*), denoting as it does the feeling that arises when, through the distinctly open receptivity of involuntary attention (also called "hovering attention"), an affect or thought abruptly enters consciousness. In striking a chord with Benjamin's discussion of Proust, but also in defining the concept crucial to Reik's analysis of the haunting melody, surprise springs the trapdoor that fashions communicating vessels of Benjamin's "On Some Motifs in Baudelaire" and *The Haunting Melody*. Through this surprising portal a problem concerning the politics of memory can be brought to bear on a specific form of forgetting that is, just the same, recollection.

Reik's study of music has been largely ignored. In this it repeats what Reik himself characterizes as the status of music in Freud's corpus. A notable, indeed *the* notable, exception here is Philippe Lacoue-Labarthe's remarkable chapter "The Echo of the Subject," from *Typography*. Concerned with the relation between autobiography and music, Lacoue-Labarthe deftly teases out the relation between Reik and Gustav Mahler, showing the depths to which autobiography is in fact propped up on the reiterated failures of others. Because Reik does not do much of anything with the politics of memory, it would appear that this otherwise ignored text may yet contain surprising insights.

For those unfamiliar with it a brief summary of its concerns is warranted. Although it is presented as a general study of psychoanalysis and music, the text orbits tightly around Reik's own struggle with a haunting melody. Here is the scene: On Christmas Day of 1925 Reik, while on vacation, was informed by a colleague that Karl Abraham, Reik's own analyst, had died the day before and that Freud wanted Reik to give a eulogy for Abraham at the next meeting of the Vienna Psychoanalytic Society. To process the shock of this news, Reik promptly left his hotel and went for a walk. Predictably, as he walked, he thought back to the various moments spent with his analyst and friend. In the midst of this somber reverie, to Reik's surprise, he found himself humming a tune fragment. It was the first bars of the ethereal chorale (emerging, as it does, from an almost interminable silence) from the last movement of Mahler's Second Symphony. Thinking little of it, Reik returned to his hotel, and over the ensuing days he began to work on the requested eulogy. Again to his surprise, every time he sat down to work on the eulogy, indeed every time he even so much as thought about the task, the melody would return. Reik describes it as "following" him, even "casting a spell on him," both characterizations that call out, do they not, for the more comprehensive term *haunting*, on which he ultimately settled? (Reik, *Haunting Melody* 222). To make sense of this "tune stuck in his head," this "ear worm," Reik turned to the project of theorizing the relation between music and psychoanalysis. Why the haunting melody as such calls for this act of theorization is not a question posed, much less examined, by Reik. It is a question I, too, will be obliged to set aside in passing.

Reik's basic approach lends itself well to the treatment given it by Lacoue-Labarthe; that is, by sleuthing out the Oedipal rivalry between Mahler and Hans von Bülow (Mahler's teacher and later sponsor) expressed in the chorale, Reik is able to recognize a similar thought concerning his relation to Abraham as the "involuntary," in fact unconscious, trigger of the melody. Indeed, Reik's study reads as though all haunting melodies are triggered by unconscious anxieties about professional fathers who must be killed off in order for their otherwise terminally insecure children to thrive, a proposition whose unquestioned investment in Oedipalization now leaves us all a little flat. But this is why it is important to sound the theoretical depths of the text and draw out its surprising links to Benjamin's musings on the politics of memory.

What emerges clearly from Reik's discussion is the notion that the haunting melody haunts precisely because it is involuntary. It results apparently from having heard a melody, perhaps even in a state of distraction, but certainly without committing it to memory, and then, in effect, forgetting that one has heard it. When later it is recollected, when it returns, it appears to come from nowhere, further consolidating its uncanniness by exhibiting a certain obsessive, even uncontrollable, rhythm of repetition. Less typically, although this is prominent in Reik's example, the rhythm of haunting interrupts to distract one's attention, rendering a certain kind of deliberative concentration impossible. While this quality aids in its interpretation—one can assume that what gets interrupted is relevant to the significance of what interrupts (an assumption crucial to Reik's self-analysis)—it is also what exposes the distraction produced by the haunting melody to the work of "criminalization."[2] Indeed, this perhaps is the hallmark of a forgetting that is a recollection. From the perspective of a certain deliberative or calculative rationalism, such forgetting is decidedly *not* regarded as the surprising condition of possibility for a significant cultural event, say the writing of a novel. Instead, the forgetting that returns to distract is simply criminal. It is regarded as nothing more or less than the menacing encroachment of banality, perversely diverting the flow of isolated lived moments, especially moments of concentration. Perhaps predictably, this is what makes it at once fascinating and important.

To establish the political importance of the haunting melody as an involuntary memory, it is necessary to appeal to the work of Michel Chion, an appeal justifying the assertion that, prior to the advent of "the new musicology," much of the most interesting thinking about music was taking place outside academic musicology. In *The Voice in Cinema* Chion reintroduces a concept developed by Pierre Shaeffer (although classically linked to Pythagoras, who is said to have lectured from behind a curtain or drape), the "*acousmêtre*," a neologism derived from the French *être acousmatique* used by Chion to designate a voice without a visible source (17). Elaborated as the adjective *acousmatic*, the term is used to designate all sounds (not only cinematic ones) lacking attribution in the visual field. For reasons that will soon become clear, it is important that Chion identifies the radio as a quintessentially acousmatic medium. What makes this relevant to the problem of the haunting melody is that the tune stuck in one's head is significantly acousmatic, even more so than the superego's voice, which in its tone, diction, and word selection is identifiable and to that extent visualizable. As is often said: I can just hear what my mother would say about that! The haunting melody is obviously identifiable, but who precisely is the source of its high-fidelity playback? Drawn more by the pre-Oedipal than the Oedipal, Chion proposes to link the acousmatic with the mother's voice, a voice that in necessarily passing from acousmatic to visualized (assuming the sighted infant), falls short of the profound uncanniness of the haunting melody. So here's the problem: how do we, in getting at this uncanniness, amplify the importantly involuntary character of the haunting melody?

Benjamin gave us an important clue when he framed matters in terms of a tension between isolation (the experience recorded in voluntary memory) and tradition (the experience inscribed in involuntary memory). If voluntary memory contains no trace of the past, this is not because it has liberated us from it. On the contrary, it has surrendered us to a past that appears to us simply as the implacable unfolding of the present, a present in which we are isolated from the social work involved in producing and sustaining it. By contrast, what was triggered by the *madeleine* (or the paving stone) was Combray, not just a location but an intricate social configuration where the labor and desire that conditioned Proust's literary act disclosed itself to him. The aspersions cast on "tradition" in the "Work of Art" essay, should not deafen us to the important way it metonymizes the social bond in the Baudelaire essay, for although Benjamin appears to have had no knowledge of Saussure, his analysis confirms the latter's insight that "because the sign is arbitrary it follows no law other than that of tradition, and because it is based on tradition it is arbitrary" (Saussure 74). In thereby drawing the conventional, the social, nearer and depriving it of its uniqueness (two features of the politics of reception), without however converting it into an analogue for the collective unconscious, Benjamin makes the involuntary character of memory take on a distinctly political value. It indexes the experiences that, precisely to the extent that they defy calculation and elude deliberation, become politicizable beyond the memorable context of the prevailing consensus. The reluctantly cultivated forms of "never forgetting," in fact, crowd such experiences out but only to intensify their aleatory power. In this sense Proust is only one of many who carry with them the points of reference for a serious problematization of the largely corporatized mass culture now seeking to imagine itself as a wholly global phenomenon. Under such circumstances it is worth insisting that the reifying or utopian character of mass culture may not be as important as the status of memory, whether highbrow or low.

Let me return, then, to the problem of criminalization. Complicating our relation to involuntary memory is its status, perhaps even its cultural value, within Western modernity. Quite apart from the link between reason and action forged within political philosophy and covetously sheltered within certain strains of political science, involuntary memory, specifically as incarnated in the haunting melody, has maintained an assiduously cultivated association with both madness and fascism. It has been officially criminalized and thus depoliticized. While it would be presumptuous to claim that this precise association begins with Fritz Lang's *M* (1931), it is certainly given a full hearing there, one that would confirm that the encounter between sound and the cinema was just as fateful for the medium as that between the cinema and fiction (to repeat Metz's famous observation). Granted, given the sort of persistent scholarly attention the film has received, it may seem like an exercise in futility to invoke it here, but this is no argument against the possibility that this film may still be capable of surprising us. Screen it and check.

Consider the following lines from the concluding scene, where the trapped Hans Beckert is pleading for mercy before what has been described as a kangaroo court.

> But I . . . I can't help myself. I have no control over this, this evil thing inside me. The fire, the voices, the torment! . . . It's there all the time, driving me out to wander the streets, following me, silently, but I can feel it there. It's me, pursuing myself. I want to escape, to escape from myself! But it is impossible. I can't escape. I have to obey it. I have to run . . . endless streets. And I am pursued by ghosts. Ghosts of mothers. And those children . . . they never leave me. They are there, always there . . . except when I do it. When I . . . (Lang)

These remarks are preceded by a distinction drawn by Beckert between himself and criminals, that is, people who, unlike him, have chosen evil. This is the significance of the "But I, I can't help myself" (or, as the German has it, "you can, but I must!") with which the cited passage begins. In a film, one of whose oft-cited formal characteristics is the systematic collapse it effects between crime and law, such a gesture shifts immediately into the realm of metacommentary. Beckert is thus giving voice to the logic of criminalization in general and for that very reason provoking the charge. Moreover, in the course of the cited passage both the subject and the object of crime undergo a tortuous mutation, effected largely through the subtle inflections of the "it" (or as Freud put it, and the neuter gender—as Blanchot was ceaselessly to remind us—is crucial: *das Es*). Initially associated with "this evil thing inside," the "it" effects a Moebian transformation becoming the outside that pursues, indeed that—like a ghost—haunts Beckert, culminating in the "when I do it," the unspeakable act subject here to the figure of aposiopesis. Thus, both the fact and the cause of criminality are fatefully suspended.

Of course, *das Es*, as Lacan later insisted, is also the letter—indeed, the letter *S* that in his rewriting of Saussure's algorithm assumes the position of the signifier. No doubt this powers its Moebian maneuvers. But the *S* is also a sibilant (from Latin, *sibilare*, to whistle), that is, an onomatopoeic phoneme that, in this film especially, attaches all the *it*s, all the *(E)s*'s, to Beckert's whistling, to that obsessively repeated melodic fragment from Grieg's setting of Ibsen's *Peer Gynt*. For the spectators/auditors this, too, is the *it*, the *Es/S*, that pursues, follows, haunts. In effect, "it is" the haunting melody of Lang's *M*. Reik, of course, would urge us to explore which involuntary memory is indexed by this melody, and, truth be told, it would be interesting to think about why Grieg, why this fragment—one whose rhythmic design (at least in the score) lends itself to the acceleration of tempo that bespeaks the frenzied violence of the trolls it is scripted to convey, etc.—but surely one would have to pursue this not in relation to Beckert but in relation to Lang, who, let us recall, only the year before writing and directing *M*, scoffed loudly and publicly at the very concept of the sound film.

A full accounting of the status of whistling in the film is impractical, but in addition to the fact that it appears in many incarnations, indeed as the very trace that finally, through the agency of a blind man, attaches the *S* to the *M*, whistling turns out to be something Beckert, Lohmann, and Schränker share. True, Lohmann and Schränker are haunted by different melodies, but it is perfectly clear that whistling is part of the intricate aural and visual interweaving deployed by the film to collapse the distinction between crime and law, an effect perfectly rendered in the persistent use of whistling to relay signals from one group to another. To that extent, it too situates every scene in which it occurs immediately at the provocative level of metacommentary. Moreover, when we consider that because Peter Lorre could not whistle—alas, he met Lauren Bacall, the consummate whistling coach, only after he left Germany—Lang himself had to overdub the whistling parts, then the full complexity of the film's texture comes into focus. In effect, Beckert's haunting melody hooks what Raymond Bellour in his study of Hitchcock's signature cameo roles called "the enunciator," onto the chain linking law and crime. As a result the film situates the collective apparatus of enunciation that is the cinema within the frame of its metacommentary on the *it*, *das Es*, that whistles through the crack between a law that is no longer simply law and a crime that is no longer simply crime. Chion, whose comments on *M* are otherwise quite penetrating, decides not to draw attention to the provocatively acousmatic character of a whistle that even when visualized only points more insistently at the unattributable source of the apparatus itself.[3]

No doubt the decisive link between the cinematic apparatus and its sound was given its conclusive formulation by Adorno and Eisler when they wrote, "Motion picture music corresponds to the whistling or singing child in the dark" (75). Like Freud, who associated this precise situation with *Angst*, or anxiety, they stressed that the child's fear was not directed outward toward the screen but inward toward what they call its "muteness," the traumatic folding of its own voice. This predicament is figured with an arresting richness in a brief but crucial scene. Here, precisely in protesting the silence imposed on him by the police, Beckert turns to the press. He does so while whistling the Grieg melody, thereby consolidating its status as a haunting melody and not simply a motif employed as a stalking device.[4] Moreover, he presses his case while writing a message that ends with the enigmatic signifier *En* (the first syllable of *Ende*) but here broken off by shadow to leave what . . . "Es"? As the graphologist consulted later explains, "The broken letters reveal the personality of an actor," Lorre, of course, but also anyone whose speech is prompted or otherwise displaced by the words of others. And remember, Lorre could not whistle. Thus, the haunting whistle in *M*, Lang's first sound film after all, might be said to bespeak a rather particular involuntary memory, that is, the onset of a general muting wrought, paradoxically, by the coming of sound. If Heinz Pohle (in *Der Rundfunk als Instrument der Politik*) is right about the role of radio in Germany during the 1920s and 1930s—he argues that with the establishment of *Deutsche Rundfunk* radio broadcasts quite literally saturated every aspect of urban space throughout the country (the *Ur*-boom box?)— then, the coming of sound happened both inside and outside the cinema; indeed, the coming of sound to the German cinema was preceded by a deafening din. *M* confronts us with this vividly when for much screen time it is precisely this din that has been uncannily silenced. Think here of the many urban scenes where traffic, largely manifested in car horns, only intermittently breaks through the dead air of the soundtrack.

Is this inversion—the big city reduced to an anechoic chamber where precisely what is missing is the hustle and bustle of the socius—is this inversion the content, what Benjamin would call the *Erfahrung*, of the involuntary memory inscribed in Beckert's serial whistle? Is the haunting melody the inscription of experience that endures, not simply because it is part of tradition but because where it comes from has arbitrarily been cast as that which tradition must now drown out? If so, is Lang not then pricking our ears, leaving us with the sounds of what fades when attentive listening, especially to not the political but politics, becomes the order of the day? And, as a final rhetorical salvo, is *M*—and the heteronymic ambiguity is deliberate (the murderer/the film)—in a strict sense a criminal of the political?

The effects achieved by Lang's film have been given more recent expression in Roy Boulting's 1968 film *Twisted Nerve*, a film recently, if obliquely, resuscitated by Tarantino in the *Kill Bill* microseries. While Boulting and Tarantino both indulge in the criminalization of haunted melodies—and this despite the anxious disclaimer that heads *Twisted Nerve*—the details separating them are telling.

In the late nineteenth century, when John Langdon Down isolated the defining features of the syndrome that now bears his name (Down's Syndrome), he first designated it by appealing to racial categories introduced by Johann Friedrich Blumenbach. In Down's estimation those afflicted with the syndrome exhibited phenotypic features consistent with what Blumenbach described as the yellow or Mongoloid race; thus emerged the term *mongolism,* as the name for the condition, a designation that survived well into the 1970s. It is this term that appears in the disclaimer to *Twisted Nerve.* Before audiences have encountered so much as the credit sequence, the film is telling us that it will not be about what it is about: the tie between crime and genetic defects. As with all such utterances, it infects all that follows with a form of attention attuned to precisely the link being disclaimed. The disclaimer, perhaps all disclaimers, is a form of what Freud called "negation" *(Verneinung).* As such, it implants the twist that gives shape and consequence to the "twisted nerve," cited from George Sylvester Viereck's poem "Slaves," by a clinician lecturing in a teaching hospital as Martin (the "Mongoloid" murderer of the film) claims his second victim.

Of course, what invites comparison with *M,* aside from the sustained meditation on the politics of criminality, is the use of whistling to convey the haunting melody.[5] As if driving the point home, in an early scene Martin/Georgie is depicted following/stalking Susan as she hurries down the pavement with what Martin later calls a "black man," Shashie, a South Asian medical student boarding in her mother's home. Boulting's camera pans to follow Martin (and the initial *M* is not insignificant, especially once we later learn that he has been practicing writing it cursively), as he follows his prey. On the soundtrack we hear the melodic theme of his whistle. This theme, in fact the exact recording of it (note the reverberating space of the sound), was presented in the title sequence, but here it is strictly marked as diegetic. Indeed, as if calling up Lang's film *ex negativo,* Martin is framed in a medium shot walking and whistling directly into the camera. Unlike Peter Lorre, Hywell Bennett can pucker up and blow. He is coming for us, and the whistling is coming from him. It seems to empty from him precisely as a haunted melody triggered by a prior experience, perhaps even an involuntary memory, we as yet know nothing about. As in a tense scene from *M,* this stalking episode is interrupted as Susan, leaving Shashie at his bus stop, turns into the public library where she works. Adumbrating the crucial role of Shashie in the sequence, Martin later leaves the library with a copy of Kipling's *The Jungle Book.*

That said, many sonic details separate the two films, and while some might be chalked up to technological advances in filmmaking, such "advances" themselves call for interpretation. Certainly a crucial difference between the two films is that the whistled melody in *Twisted Nerve* is not derived from previously recorded musical material. It is written by the incomparable Bernard Hermann for the film; indeed, it bears resemblance to some of the melodic themes heard in Hitchcock's *Marnie* from four years earlier. In fact, despite Hermann's assertion that once a film is scored, the music then belongs to the director, the credit sequence in *Twisted Nerve* reserves a title card on which Hermann's "ownership" of Georgie's theme is established. Although the motivation for my emphasis awaits elaboration, it is important here that the problem of who or what whistles is unleashed by the titular *by*.

A second differentiating detail between the two films follows. What helps to produce the oddly silent feel of *M* is the fact that the distinction between diegetic and extradiegetic sound is largely mapped onto a distinction between onscreen and offscreen sound. Car horns that sound on the street radiate from cars that are outside the frame, but their vehicular presence in the world of the plot is established. Moreover, there is no musical score, no "unheard melodies." As I have observed, *Twisted Nerve* has a fully developed musical score, and Boulting deploys it to work carefully both the onscreen/offscreen and the diegetic/extradiegetic distinction. Perhaps the most extravagant articulation of this approach occurs during a sequence set at Susan's home, where she is hosting the quintessential 1960s dance party. Present are Martin (shot glowering over a comic featuring, who else, "The Avengers"); Susan; her boyfriend, Philip; and two friends. The music to which everyone is dancing is provided by a "record player" brought by Philip. Although the music is unmistakably British pop of the period (in fact, it harks back to an earlier scene in which Martin listens to a "hi-fi" in his own room), the melodic line of Martin's whistle, with its tense little intervallic oscillations between E, D, C, and B—music that we have heard both as his whistle and as part of the thematic organization of the musical score—floods into the room from the portable loudspeaker. As if to underscore the peculiarity of this iteration of the whistling, the record player's status as an object brought from outside the room by Philip (he takes it with him when Susan asks him to leave) is coupled with the technological detail that although it is in the room, the sounds it reproduces were made and remain elsewhere. Here the whistle cuts through or across the very distinction between the inside and the outside of the diegetic world.

One could go on, but let a final distinguishing detail suffice. Unlike *M*, where the whistling of the haunted melody precedes murder (and while we know of several, we only bear "witness" to one murder), the two murders we witness in *Twisted Nerve*—the death of Martin's stepfather and the death of Joan, Susan's mother—take place in the absence of whistling. In the first stealth is essential, and in the second Martin is cast as the "cougar" bait that simply snaps in response to Joan's advances. This would appear to break the tie between the haunting melody/memory and criminal violence, but I think not. To appreciate why, it is important to consider how the respective films attempt to ground the haunted melody in human pathology.

As we have seen, in *M* the whistling of Hans Beckert is presented under the broad heading of compulsion, a compulsion fueled by a whistling fissure in his psyche (the *S, das Es*). The odd coda that concludes the film, however cruelly it blames the mothers of the dead children for their demise, nevertheless tries to maintain a broadly psychoanalytical framework within which to comprehend the tragedy we have witnessed. It's all in the family. By contrast, *Twisted Nerve* moves directly and decisively onto the territory of genetic inheritance and the structure of chromosomes. Indeed, a decisive parallel syntagma late in the film has the plot shifting between a lecture about "mongolism"—a lecture that echoes an earlier exchange between Martin and his brother Pete's doctor in which the event of "entitlement" (where the film assumes its name) occurs, an event that in citing the Viereck poem calls up through the figure of the puppet master's pulling strings a vital image and theme from Lang's film—and Martin's murder of Joan Harper. A match on action cut between an ax blow and the wave of a pointer cements the two halves of the segment, tying together both "mongolism" and criminal violence while exposing the film's disclaimer for what it is: negation. Complicating this is the pivot therein established between lecturing and murdering, but because lecturing and murdering are shown to be the cause of each other, the pivot spins without traction.

In characterizing the relation between lecturing and murdering in this way, I mean to suggest that unlike *M*, where the gang and the police are formally and thematically equated, in *Twisted Nerve* science and pathological violence are equated but in order, finally, to exonerate or empower the police. Crucial to the dénouement of the plot is a collaboration—put in motion earlier—between Susan and Shashie (referred to by his medical colleagues as "Maharaji"). She comes to him during the lecture, set in parallel to Martin's murder of Joan, and explains her suspicions about Martin. Earlier, around the breakfast table at the Harpers, Shashie has invoked medical science to complicate Jerry's (Joan's then current love interest, who is also a boarder) racist attack on the killer of Martin's father, a wealthy white entrepreneur. In effect, Shashie repeats the arguments of Hans Beckert, claiming that people suffering from mental illness are every bit as "disabled" as people who lack capacities or competencies. This bit of dialogue rhymes semantically with a terse exchange at Mr. Durnsey's (Martin's stepfather) crime scene, where the lead detective and his expert criminologist square off about the knowledge crucial to good policing. The lead detective, Superintendent Dakin, prevails then and although called to the final showdown by Shashie (himself an "expert"-in-training), he and his police force prevail in the end. They overtake, as Dakin says, "the nutter" and save Susan. In both cases what is at stake is the shaving of a point about who or what is truly capable of protecting society from crime rooted in madness, a madness sonically encoded as a haunting melody. And, whereas in *M* Inspector Lohmann and the police arrive merely in the nick of time, the police in *Twisted Nerve* arrive in, to invoke the cliché, white hats. The stain is on medical science (whence the disclaimer), not policing.

These plot details find their thematic resonance in the two pathologies: one rooted in genetics, the other in family romance. The whistling in *Twisted Nerve* is apparently fueled by a chromosomal translocation. In fact, precisely through its intricate replotting of the family romance—Martin's older brother, Pete, is institutionalized so that his mother, a character lifted from the pages of Dolto's *The Backwards Child and His Mother,* can (re) marry Martin's patrician stepfather, who attempts to skip the "step" by imposing on him an austere form of Oedipal rivalry that predictably ends in patricide—*Twisted Nerve* chimes in with the now prevalent repudiation of psychoanalysis, proposing that everything psychoanalysis thought it could illuminate can now be more scientifically illuminated by genetics. Martin's whistling thus does not emerge from the *It (das Es),* but neither does it emerge precisely from the gene. If anything, it emerges from the displacement of the *It* by the gene. Its timbre is tempered by knowledge. Hence the importance not only of the police—it must prop up, or supplement, a science indistinguishable from violence (think here of eugenics)— but the importance of the distribution of the whistle across the soundtrack.

As has been noted, the whistle in *Twisted Nerve* ricochets through the entire film. There are times, such as in the title sequence, where it might as well have been performed by an expert whistler like Wittgenstein, who, in apparent defiance of Adorno's ban on humming, accompanied his friend David Pinset in performances of Schubert's *Lieder* (and I leave aside here the urgent and intriguing problem of how Wittgenstein's thought might be said to echo his whistle).[6] It then emerges from the pursed lips of a "mongoloid"/psychopathic son who, in addition to *The Jungle Book,* is reading Krafft-Ebing's *Psychopathia Sexualis,* only to later emerge as part of a prerecorded pop tune played when Susan is propositioned by her beau, Philip, and all the while maintaining a perplexing, even disturbing, relation to the meditation on traumatically induced female frigidity in Hitchcock's

Marnie. As I asked before: who or what is whistling here and with what implications for the haunted melody?

The matter might be put thus: between the early 1930s and the late 1960s the war fought to defeat fascism and secure democracy in Europe had both been won and lost: won because the Allies had prevailed on the battlefield; lost because the cost of doing so—colonialism, anti-Semitism, racism, sexism, anti-Communism, positivism (especially in its pharmacological approach to the human mind), consumerism, Eurocentrism, and so on—had gutted democracy. As a pure form compromised by the particulars of any content, democracy had little but its own enemies to sustain it. This is Debord's point. Under such circumstances the political articulation of democracy, as Jacques Rancière has more recently proposed, contends constantly with policing, with, in effect, the regulation and neutralization of politics. As with democracy itself, policing is sustained by the fear that it will always be outmaneuvered. Whatever his faults—and they are legion—Hoover understood that policing needed to become scientific, bureaucratic, and professional precisely to respond to the threats it implanted, threats only policing could manage. This is the logic of cultural politics and the new social movements: everything everywhere becomes a place where democracy might break out, so why not see whether it can?

Twisted Nerve is sociographically ensnarled here, and as a sign of this, the melody that haunts, the whistling, howls from everywhere. It ricochets inside and outside the film, especially as this border is presented to our ears in the soundtrack's distribution of the haunting melody. Even the gesture of the disclaimer, which says that the melody does not emanate from a chromosomal translocation, nevertheless derives its authority by appealing to the very "evidence" that genetics has set the new standard for. This is not a matter of collapsing the moral distinction between the police and criminals; it is a matter of inviting policing into sexual reproduction and doing so in a way that makes Martin's Hamlet-like whining about his mother's remarriage ring deliberately false—just as false as does his lighting of a cigar in his first confrontation with his stepfather. The *It* is nothing compared to the chromosome, and policing, whether benign (treatment) or malignant (sterilization), must increase and extend its readiness to protect democracy from itself.

So, to return to an earlier moment in the problem that consumes this chapter: is *Twisted Nerve*, like *M*, a criminal of the political? Does this uneven parallel establish that the cinema has a necessary role to play in the criminalization of involuntary memory? Is this precisely what attention to the audit can bring to the critique of mass culture? As tempting as it may be to say "yes" immediately to such questions, prudence is again warranted.

Precisely because it leaves the terms of penal discourse intact, the romance of decriminalization is its own ruse, and, after all, articulating the politicizable leaves the work of the political undone. Thus, a cautionary tale may be the fitting way to end. In "The Name of a Dog, or Natural Rights" Emmanuel Levinas tells us the story of Bobby. Bobby was a stray dog that befriended Levinas and others when they were held at a forced labor camp shortly after the onset of World War II. As Jews the prisoners were, from the point of view of their captors and the local townspeople, not human beings. They lived this inhumanity in the most intimate way. What made Bobby—a name given to the dog by Levinas—matter is that he barked. He woofed. In doing so, he rehumanized the prisoners, delivering them from what had so completely othered them. Levinas's gratitude to Bobby (the definitive Fido) causes the page on which it is expressed to tremble. So another problem presents itself: what did Bobby make of the whistle that hailed him? Or, to end on a less warped note, what precisely are we to make of the whistling that strikes out everywhere toward that dark forgetting from which we imagine Bobby to be approaching us? Who or what are we calling to come?

3. Whisper

I have given a name to my pain and call it "dog."
—NIETZSCHE, *On the Genealogy of Morality*

In 1964 the US Air Force conducted Operation Bongo II over Oklahoma City, Oklahoma. As the name might suggest—I am thinking of the onomatopoeic *bongo* (in Spanish, *bongó*, where the tones of the differently tuned heads are rendered)—this operation centered on sound, specifically, the deafening din of a sonic boom. During the six months of aerial "bongo playing," more than one thousand booms were dropped on the residents of Oklahoma City. The purpose: to gauge whether residents could grow to tolerate the effects of supersonic flight. Thirty years later a different boom, more horrifying than annoying, was imposed on the residents of Oklahoma City in the form of Timothy McVeigh's devastating assault on the Alfred P. Murrah Federal Building. Citing John Locke on liberty, McVeigh compared his boom to those visited on Hiroshima and Nagasaki. His boom was "the bomb."

Like *bongo, boom* is onomatopoeic. It is also semantically resonant, having primary meanings as both a verb and a noun. Crucial about the sonic boom, however, is the way it channels this resonance and concentrates it on breaking what is called the sound barrier. *Boom* thus appears to designate the sound that arises when something delimiting sound gives way. It is an onomatopoeia that also names the collision between names and their making. From this angle, an angle that an audit may help to isolate, the boom is both a limit and the trace of the transgression of that limit. *Deafening*, to use a now discredited word. As such, while it might be thought to stand opposite those sounds so faint as to defy both hearing and listening, does it really? In what follows I take up this gambit by attempting to write on the faint sound of whispering. Why whispering? Most fundamentally, whispering recommends itself in this context because it, like the boom, is a sound problem. A limit sound. As I will propose, whispering is not only a problem for linguistics—where one might expect it to be grasped—but for philosophy and politics as well. As a problem it calls to us not so much for a solution as to answer its problematic status—that is, to render in theoretical terms the source or condition of its "problematization" and to do so aware that the sonic boom currently swelling, if not rattling, the frames of intelligibility at the barrier between the humanities and the social sciences is as blatant as it is undertheorized. Today, many scholars are making noise about sound but often in ways that feel resolutely empirical. Obviously, sound is insistently emerging, booming (as was once said of writers in Latin America), as a new object of academic attention but in ways that have made it difficult, if not impossible, to think about why those of us monitoring this barrier had not heard it before. Maybe the profession offered (up) theory prematurely? Maybe sounds, like trees in forests, demand an audit.

To make headway here will require that we approach the whisper from the side (it being, often, an aside). We will need, in effect, to start not by trying to say what the whisper *is* (perhaps "problem" is the only name it can bear) but by tracking what whispering seems to be *doing* in some of the insistent discursive practices active in and around us. We will need to think patiently about what such practices show it is *like* to whisper in the Global North. As this geopolitical specification makes clear, this reflection is far from the whole story, even about those narrative practices it purports to address. Nevertheless, because it leads to various facets of the problem that is whispering—the nonvoiced in vocalization, the "absence of work" in the labor of the concept, not to mention the traumatic snarling of the nonhuman animal and the human—it touches on matters that have global reach if only in ways as yet unrecognizable from here. Reading under such circumstances—neither closely nor distantly, but carefully—is where theory comes and goes. This is more important than we think.

Doubtless because in Saussure's characterization of the object of linguistics—the double articulation of the sign—he insists that it is "unrelated to the phonic character of the linguistic sign" (Saussure 7), he says little about vocalization of any sort. Indeed, the struggle to specify this object virtually consumes the *Course* and nowhere more openly than when Saussure addresses the question of the relation between linguistics and semiology. It is not, then, altogether surprising that when the British linguist John Laver takes up the matter of the "whispery voice," he does so by insisting on the need to supplement the linguistic account of speech with a semiological one that expressly engages what he calls the "paralinguistic" (Laver 171) dimensions of speech activity. Although Laver does not declare himself on the matter of epistemic subordination, his appeal to the Peircean concept of the index as a way to grasp how signs referring to the speaker appear in his or her speech represents a challenge to Saussurean phonocentric orthodoxy. In fact, one of Laver's important insights is that the whisper is a nonvoiced vocalization, in effect, a part of the voice that is not the voice and thus not used phonemically in any known language. The whisper is in that sense a signifier that although capable of bearing a signified fails to. This complicates the whisper's very indexicality. As Laver writes in "Language and Non-verbal Communication": "Consider the case of a participant in a conversation speaking in a *whispery voice*. The listener has to decide whether the speaker is using whispery voice as a paralinguistic feature, signaling secretive confidentiality, or whether whispery voice is part of the speaker's voice quality (either habitually or because of temporary laryngitis). Listeners often draw the wrong conclusion, and sufferers from laryngitis have often had the experience of people whispering back at them, mistaking the physical medical side of laryngitis for a psychological, attitudinal index of conspiracy" (Laver 143). In other words, precisely because the whisper lacks even a reliable indexical signified, it frustrates interpretation and complicates speech activity from within.

Laver, having repeated the well-known Saussurean distinction between physiology and psychology, turns much of his analytical energy to describing carefully the physiology of whispering. This is a sensible strategy, but his doggedness only underscores the malingering confrontation with psychology, drawing attention to what strikes me as the fundamental issue, namely, how precisely is one to grasp the meaning of whispering as the nonvocal part of the voice, or, in disciplinary terms, the nonlinguistic part of linguistics, or even the nonsemiological part of semiology? For just this reason whispering leads without delay to a disciplinary reflection on the limits of knowledge in its encounter with sound. In effect, it solicits the audit.

To flesh out the general problem of the disciplinary frame, consider the status of "the murmur" *(le murmur)* in Michel Foucault's *History of Madness*. I cite from the preface:

> History is only possible against the backdrop of the absence of history, in the midst of a great space of murmurings, that silence watches like its vocation and its truth: "I will call desert this castle that you were, night this voice, absence your face." . . .
> . . . The plenitude of history is only possible in the space, both empty and peopled at the same time, of all the words without language that appear to anyone who lends an ear, as a dull sound from beneath history, the obstinate murmur of a language talking *to itself*—without any speaking subject and without an interlocutor, wrapped up in itself, with

a lump in its throat, collapsing before it ever reaches any formulation and returning without a fuss to the silence it never shook off. The charred root of meaning. (xxxi–ii)

The "absence of history" invoked here is an allusion to Blanchot's "absence of an *oeuvre*," and it designates Foucault's argument that both history and historiography, grounded as they are in the principle of reason, are actually founded on the exclusion of madness. Put differently, history has as its condition of possibility an absence produced by its unfolding, which means that Foucault's text is as much about madness as the tremulous politico-epistemological boundary that reduces its unintelligibility to a murmur. In short, *History* poses as a critique of the history of philosophy from the standpoint of what it can neither think nor work out.

It is telling that Foucault—who frames his discussion around language, speech, words, etc.—appeals repeatedly to the motif of murmuring to designate where philosophy cannot think. This prompts us to recognize that *murmur* is deployed here in a self-consciously disciplinary way, presumably to get at what is unreason in reason, the unthought. Significantly, Foucault does not appeal here to the unconscious, a gesture indicating that his focus is not on the ontology of the psychical apparatus but on the historical ontology of knowledge. Although one could argue that some such distinction lay at the core of the heated exchange with Derrida, more immediately pertinent is the theoretical status of the murmur, particularly as it exemplifies the disciplinary provocation of whispering.

Laver is not alone in differentiating murmuring and whispering (the former is "voiced," whereas the latter is not), but compared to what is at stake in Foucault's analysis, this seems like a quibble whose explanatory power falls flat when faced with a methodological formulation like the following, also from Foucault's 1961 preface: "This [adopting a 'structural study'] will allow the lightning flash decision [*for* reason, *against* madness] to appear once more, heterogeneous with the time of history, but ungraspable outside it, which separates the murmur of dark insects from the language of reason and the promises of time" (xxxiii). The murmur of dark insects? Contextually, this formulation appears to reiterate the reason/unreason distinction but in a way that associates the mad and "dark insects," a gesture one would not expect from someone otherwise concerned to destigmatize those deemed mad. Although the more interesting and pressing matter is the way Foucault uses the distinction between language and murmuring to reiterate that between reason and unreason, the figure of the insect swells.

At a minimum it reminds us that French prompts one to distinguish murmuring *(murmurer)* from whispering *(chuchoter)* and to do so along the human/nonhuman animal frontier. In general usage, whispering applies to people, the wind, or leaves, but one characterizes birds as murmuring, that is, twittering. Although the distinction is certainly not policed by "the immortals," it seems important to Foucault that *insects* would murmur, for, among other things this lexical association of animal and sound evokes the so-called *langage des oiseaux*, that is, the archaic secret language thought to allow initiates to predict or otherwise control events. A conceptual cognate of "Adamic language," the "language of birds" installs the language-like sounds produced by nonhuman animals (whether birds or insects) in the space of the encounter between humanity and creation. As such, "the language of birds," like murmur, is a way to think the limits of reason if clairvoyance and the episteme that supports its authority are recognized as correlates. That "language" is consistently attached here to murmur is likewise important, for it means that murmur is a way, however compromised, to sound the "name" of what incessantly breaks contact between reason and unreason, philosophy and its others. This is the problem it stirs, and here this problem expressly involves animals other than humans.

Doubtless, one of the more probing recent challenges mounted within and against philosophical reason has been the emergence of "animal studies." In the hands of some this challenge has restricted itself to the ethical strand of philosophy, but for Cary Wolfe (and Derrida before him) "animal studies" has reached so intimately into the concept of the subject that its preoccupations have been made to resonate, as madness did half a century ago, in every corner of Western thought. In his 2003 anthology, *Zoontologies: The Question of the Animal*, Wolfe had the foresight to include among its contents a treatment of the animal, specifically the horse, that in putting linguistic knowledge back on the table points us in a useful direction. Paul Patton's "Language, Power and the Training of Horses" discusses the horse trainer Monty Roberts and reminds us of the puzzling but altogether enigmatic place of "whispering" in the face-off between humans and horses. Patton's piece sets the stage for Wolfe's own later remarkable study of Temple Grandin, "Animal Studies and Disability Studies, or Learning from Temple Grandin," a study that also appeals to the figure of Roberts. Doubtless because they have other fish to fry, neither Patton nor Wolfe do little more than mention whispering, thereby soliciting my effort to attend and attune to what I have called the sound problem of whispering, especially as we are given discursive access to what it is *like* to whisper in fiction, film, and television.

"Horse whispering" is a technique for training horses that may date back to Kikkuli in Asia and Xenophon in the Mediterranean but that consolidates historically in the nineteenth century first in Ireland with Daniel

Sullivan (literally called a "horse whisperer") and later in Britain and the United States with Willis Powell, John Solomon Rorey, Monty Roberts, the Dorrance brothers, Ray Hunt, and Buck Buchannan, the man who served as "adviser" to Robert Redford when Redford adapted Nicholas Evans's novel *The Horse Whisperer* for the screen.[1] Surely it is not without interest in this context that when this film was released in France, it was titled *L'homme qui murmurait à l'oreille des chevaux*, literally, the man who murmured at the ear of horses, where the idiomatic link between murmuring and nonhuman animals redirects such that it is the man who murmurs, not the horse. Either way, whispering and murmuring assume a proximity that prompts one to hear in whispering echoes of the problems heralded in Foucault's agitation of the murmur.

In Evans's novel the sense of what "whispering" does is developed in deeply suggestive ways. This occurs in the opening chapter of part 2 as Annie Graves (the mother of the traumatized daughter) spends an afternoon researching horse care and rehabilitation in the New York Public Library. After establishing the prehistoric presence of horses in North America and the deep fear lodged in their "souls" as a result of being driven off cliffs by early humans, Evans writes:

> Since that neolithic moment when first a horse was haltered, there were men who understood this. They could see into the creature's soul and soothe the wounds they found there. Often they were seen as witches and perhaps they were. Some wrought their magic with the bleached bones of toads, plucked from moonlit streams. Others, it was said, could with but a glance root the hooves of a working team to the earth they plowed. There were gypsies and showmen, shamans and charlatans. And those who truly had the gift were wont to guard it wisely, for it was said that he who drove the devil out, might also drive him in. The owner of a horse you calmed might shake your hand and then dance around the flames while they burned you in the village square. For secrets uttered softly into pricked and troubled ears, these men were know as Whisperers. (Evans 94)

The narrator follows this by noting Annie's surprise at the fact that most whisperers were men and then reports descriptions—found presumably in texts consulted by Annie—of famous male horse whisperers, Sullivan, Rorey, and the like. While it is true that the accent here falls less on whispering than on whisperers, the problem of whispering manifests in the question: so why are people who talk to, or otherwise treat, horses *called* whisperers?

Surely it is significant that in the passage, whispering is plotted along the decisive biohistorical transition of domestication. First is the moment when horses exist prior to human beings, then the moment when they are herded/hunted by humans, followed by the moment when they are "haltered," and concluding with the moment in which domesticated animals exhibit "wounds" that postdate domestication itself. A link is forged here between training and healing, and while whispering seems to apply more directly to the latter—it is a channel through which secrets pass from humans to horses through pricked and troubled ears—it is clear that the link joins the capacity to heal with the capacity to train. Indeed, the whisperers described by Evans are all characterized as individuals who know how to *retrain* horses that, for whatever reason, have forgotten their training. This relation is given acute shape in the scene where Tom Booker (the name of the whisperer in *Horse*) meets Pilgrim (Annie's daughter Grace's horse) and encounters two kids attempting to manipulate two colts using a whip. In a fit of disgust Tom takes the whip and throws it in a ditch as he departs. Whipping is thus marked as whispering's other.

But the passage from the novel is also filled with the figures and rhetoric of what Freud famously called "demonic possession." Precisely to the extent that the whisperer is not a gypsy, showman, shaman, or charlatan, he—if truly gifted—may be a witch or even the devil. He may for that very reason be subject to the hysterical persecution inflicted on witches both in Europe and North America prior to and during the Enlightenment. This, at first, strikes one as odd. Why would the domestication of animals— especially a working animal—be linked to possession? Here what seems urgent is precisely the divide between training and healing, where the latter is set off from the former in order to protect domestication, let us say, the benevolent violence of training, from critical scrutiny. *This* encounter between the human and the nonhuman animal carries biblical sanction (Genesis 1:26), whereas the encounter between a human and an animal that has become dangerous to humans is conducted under the sign of Satan. The passage suggests a reason for this. It begins by linking the whisperer to those who recognize in horses their archaic fear of human violence, stressing the importance of relating to horses responsibly. In effect, the whisperer recognizes the horse's inability and thus refusal to separate herding from haltering. As such, the whisperer bears witness to the violence of domestication and acts as if in consort with the devil. That the *Compendium maleficarum* would figure the devil as a goat god with whom "possessed" women copulate should come then as hardly a surprise.

Although it might otherwise pass unnoticed, it seems important to stress that in his evocation of the persecution of witches, Evans is linking domestication with enclosure and the epistemic violence perpetrated typically against women healers by the forces of the Enlightenment. In this he is channeling a rich vein of feminist scholarship that extends from Ehrenreich and English in the early 1970s to Silvia Federici, who, in *Caliban and the Witch*, both links the persecution of witches to the enclosure of the commons and aligns the rise of science with the decline of folk culture and knowledge. Even as she criticizes Foucault for his lack of attention to the place of witches in the history of sexuality, she insists that his account of the development of "modern" power/knowledge is crucial to a political understanding of the disciplining of witches. This is significant because it again points to the decisive way that whispering touches directly on a fraught disciplinary matrix. Even Annie's expectation that whisperers might actually include more women than men appears, however faintly, to mark the text's acknowledgment of precisely this fraught history.

But how, precisely, are we to think the *sound* of this disciplinary problem, of the "secrets uttered softly into pricked and troubled ears"?

For reasons that may seem obvious to readers who do not listen to texts, the novel is not as forthcoming on this front as is the film, which, paradoxically, contains no clear depiction of secrets or anything else uttered softly by Tom Booker to Pilgrim. At best, late in the film, we witness (and overhear) a scene where Tom walks up to Pilgrim in his stall and says, stroking his blaze, "There is something you gotta do tomorrow." The camera has tracked Tom's approach, and when the preceding line is uttered—in a "normal" speaking voice—he and Pilgrim are shot in profile. We are close to their closeness. But there is nothing secret about the "something" Tom is asking Pilgrim to do. At this point in the film every spectator knows that the broken relation between Grace and Pilgrim needs to be mended. She must ride her horse again. Here whispering just sounds like "dialogue," its sole complexity residing in the by no means insignificant matter of to whom Pilgrim is being asked to submit: Tom or Grace.

A far more resonant scene occurs earlier in the film. It is divided into two major sequences, with segments lending interior structure to both. It is composed of more than a hundred shots, some barely a second long. The novel dispatches with it in a few lines from chapter 5. The scene opens with a medium long shot of Pilgrim chest deep in water. Voices and splashing dominate the diegetic sound, guitar picking the extradiegetic sound. By the fourth shot the extradiegetic sound has faded, and everything is focused on the horse and those watching him, principally Tom, Annie, and Grace. In the fifth shot Annie, wearing sunglasses and clutching a sheaf of papers, asks, "What's he doing?" No reply. Three shots later she adds: "Is this some sort of physical therapy?" No reply. In a brief cutaway Grace glares at her mother in silence. Then, in shot ten, Annie's cell phone rings cutting across all other diegetic sound, notably Pilgrim's breathing and snorting, producing an answering sonic binary—ringing/snorting—to the visual binary of people/ horse. Instantly, Pilgrim lets out a vigorous, panicked neigh, rearing up in the water and thrashing out with his front legs. Tom is seen glaring back at Annie, who in the subsequent shot turns away to take the call, saying in shot 17, "No, you're breaking up," emphasizing that she is attending to the wrong "break." This sequence ends with Pilgrim, whom Tom has managed with considerable exertion to calm, all of a sudden bolting and knocking Tom down into the water. As others seek to restrain or chase Pilgrim, Tom says, "Let him go, let him go." In the penultimate shot of the sequence the camera pans right to follow Tom as he sets out walking after the fleeing horse.

The second sequence opens with an extreme wide shot. Montana. On the far left and in the distance stands Pilgrim. As the shot unfolds, a match on action cut allows Tom's head and then body to enter the landscape of the frame from the lower right. There is still no extradiegetic sound; indeed, the soundtrack is dominated by the hum of insects and the rustle of wind in the brush. In the following shot Grace is shown sitting with Tom's nephew, Joey, on the slope of a hill, where the two observe Tom and Pilgrim. A stilted conversation ensues, and insects and wind are joined by Thomas Newman's score on the soundtrack. As the two kids talk, Tom sets up his own observation point opposite the meadow from Pilgrim. Eventually he sits and begins to wait in the "silence" that constitutes the mysterious frontier between the score and the wind as registered in the flora of the meadow. The conversation between Joey and Grace breaks off when Joey asks, "How was he to ride?" Grace turns abruptly away, linking the traumatic question to the mysterious silence defining Tom's relation to Pilgrim. If one were to infer, at this point, what whispering *sounds* like, it would appear to be the sound(s) of this painful waiting.

With obvious emphasis as Joey turns to leave and Grace looks away and down, Annie enters the extreme wide shot in which Pilgrim stands in the left background and Tom sits in the right foreground. Newman's score bridges the two segments. She clears her throat softly and then says, "Are we in the way?" As before, Tom says nothing, turning only to acknowledge her presence. Annie persists: "Should we leave?" No reply. Tom's nonreaction is framed in direct address to the spectator, a position—the object of Tom's stare—consistently marked as Pilgrim's point of view. With audible frustration Annie adds, "I guess we'll go then." No reply. She leaves the frame, walking away from behind Tom, and this segment ends with the first of three overlap dissolves all meant to enunciate "waiting." Then as night falls,

Pilgrim begins slowly to approach Tom from across the meadow. Added now to the wind and score are the blows, grunts, and snorts of the horse. If secrets are being softly uttered, Pilgrim is doing the uttering. Again with obvious emphasis, as the horse begins its wary approach to Tom, Annie and Grace drive up on their way out. The music on the soundtrack fades, giving way to Tom's waiting and Pilgrim's snorting and blowing, sounds soon accompanied by the slow thud of hooves and the hum of insects. Annie gets out of the car and looks on in disbelief. Now *she* says nothing. As the scene concludes, Pilgrim makes his way over to where Tom is waiting. He lowers his head and Tom strokes his cheek and blaze. No "words" are exchanged. As Tom leads Pilgrim out of the meadow, passing Annie, the horse's tread, the wind, and insects are accompanied on the soundtrack by the final line of dialogue. Tom says to Annie: "From now on leave your phone somewhere else."

None of the dialogue spoken in this scene is "actually" whispered, yet surely whispering takes place. Tom has "bewitched" Pilgrim; indeed, it is the scene that establishes clearly Annie's belief that she has found a true whisperer. The effect, therefore, is to complicate what we might be listening for when listening for whispering. It is neither what nor where we expect. Sonically, the scene puts this puzzle in motion by organizing it around a ringtone. That is, whispering is the sound that opposes without answering the cell phone. It is the muted backdrop against which the "ring" becomes audible. In one sense, of course, the sound of the cell phone might be heard as a metonym for "modernity." Given the scene's studied repetition of heterosexual coupling (Grace and Joey, Tom and Annie), the cell phone "sounds like" Annie's professional identity pulling her out of the moment and away from what matters: the relations developing around and through the horse. In the novel the issue here is put with telling concision: "The whole had become clear. All three—mother, daughter, horse—were inextricably connected in pain" (Evans 175). The cell phone is thus the sonic signifier of Annie's attachment to this pain, her guilty relation to a daughter she "neglected" for her career and to whom she gifted a horse in futile compensation. It traumatizes the horse precisely because the ringtone bespeaks the "neglect" that occasioned the freak accident Pilgrim should not have survived. As both novel and film make clear, Grace *sneaks* out to ride with her girlfriend Judith on the snowy morning of the accident.

Opposite this is the whispering, the secrets delivered into Pilgrim's pricked ears by Tom, secrets apparently conveyed in the sonic weave—buzzing, rustling, and finally snorting—of waiting. It seems crucial, then, that every time Annie actually tries to speak to someone in the moment, her words are met with silence. She is not there. In this sense she, too, is waiting, which suggests that, as if in analysis, what waiting achieves is the space within which one's ears open to secrets. Remarkably, one such secret is that Pilgrim is telling these secrets to himself or picking them up from the insects, the wind, the thud of his own hooves. Here, the whisper begins to approximate "the voice that keeps silent," which may well explain why none of the dialogue is presented as "actual" whispering.

As the film winds down, we learn that Annie is most guilty about her loveless marriage and the sacrifice of desire for duty it has gently extorted from her. This crystallizes as she enters into an affair with Tom, who remains haunted by the failure of his own previous marriage. He thus attaches himself to the chain of pain linking the mother, the daughter, and the horse, and despite his strong messianic power (the novel is rife with the rhetoric of Christian apologetics) he, too, needs a whisperer. His link to the chain of pain produces an equation between the traumatic hobbling of both Grace and Pilgrim and the lived failure of heterosexual monogamy. It is in this sense that Tom's line to Pilgrim, "There is something you gotta do tomorrow," refers to him.

This reading raises two important issues. On the one hand it suggests that the unspeakable character of traumatic experience serves in this discourse as an incarnation of the nonvoiced vocalization of whispering—not simply that trauma is addressed through whispering but that trauma, because words fail it, bears within this unspeakable relation to language the nonvoiced character of whispering. On the other hand whispering also seems to take on an allegorical function. The disjuncture that binds whispering to and separates it from speaking functions as a realization of the analytically charged notion that trauma, regardless of its precipitating cause, repeats the becoming human of the animal. Freud, in *Civilization and Its Discontents*—where guilt is installed as the drive of civilization—puts this in terms of the triumph of the eye over the nose when hominids achieved erect posture, but much of what Nietzsche earlier called "asceticism" is clearly caught up with the torturous fight against the animal in the human.

One might argue, then, that human susceptibility to trauma is conditioned by the phylogenetic significance of the triumph of sight and that this is perhaps the deepest articulation of the film's obsessive allegorical impulse: Grace, Pilgrim (Judith's horse is named Gulliver), Annie and Robert Graves (in the film they are the MacLeans), not to mention the novel's repeated intertextual engagement with John Bunyan's *The Pilgrim's Progress*. As with Bunyan himself, who insisted on the decisive role of grace in salvation, both novel and film pivot on the figure of Grace, whose "recovery" provides the narrative with its arc. Indeed, the very name of the

Booker ranch, "The Double Divide," would appear to draw attention to the allegorical structure of a textual enunciation split by another scene. By proposing that whispering assumes an allegorical function, and does so by touching on the traumatic confrontation in the human with the nonhuman animal, I mean to argue that "whisper" is a sonic signifier divided by its oblique address to the side. It speaks about speaking, but it does so inaudibly.[2] In that sense it is not just taking place within an allegorically charged context, but it is structured by allegory, that is, a speaking that is phatic in the metalinguistic sense, where *meta* is beyond linguistics in such a way that invites the philosophically charged question: where must language come from such that animals do not have access to it? It must come from what passes between what is neither human nor animal.

The link proposed here between allegory and whispering is not fortuitous. Two other examples will suffice to drive home the point. In 2004 the National Geographic channel began broadcasting a dog-training program hosted by César Milán. Clearly trading on the figure of the whisperer, the program was titled *The Dog Whisperer,* and its success has both spawned imitators and provided Milán with a lucrative career as an author and speaker. A year later, in 2005, CBS aired a series starring Jennifer Love Hewitt titled *The Ghost Whisperer* that ran successfully for five seasons. While both shows appealed directly to the figure of the whisperer, both also introduced nuances in this figure that bear on the allegorical structure of whispering, perhaps most dramatically with Melinda Gordon (Love Hewitt's character), who, under the influence of the "spirit communicator" James Van Praagh, uses whispering to open a channel with dead humans, in other words, ghosts.

In the second season of *The Ghost Whisperer,* in an episode entitled "Children of Ghosts," the two shows, as is said in the industry, "crossed over" (an expression with strong Bunyanesque resonance also used in *Ghost* to connote passing into "the light"). The scene in which this "crossover" is effected warrants sustained attention.

As is typical of broadcast-television narrative, "Children of Ghosts" twists together two story lines. The more substantial line narrates Julie's story. She is the abandoned daughter of a woman she believes is her mother but who turns out to have kidnapped Julie in the wake of a traumatic miscarriage. Melinda comes to be involved first as a foster parent but then as the whisperer who discovers that Julie's kidnapper died before she could "take her back" to her biological mother, who lives in Grandview (Melinda's hometown). The second story line is Bob's. Bob is the golden retriever that belongs to Melinda's coworker, Delia Banks. For reasons unknown, Bob has been disturbing Delia's sleep by barking uncontrollably. As the episode unwinds, we discover that Bob is haunted by the ghost dog Homer, an animal visible only to Melinda. The "crossover" is set in motion early when Delia, who has lost patience with Bob, tells Melinda that a "superstar dog therapist" is visiting Grandview. They agree to seek his counsel.

Needless to say the "superstar dog therapist" is César Milán, identified as the Dog Whisperer both on posters displayed around the book signing and by Melinda when she gets face-time with César. The whole scene unfolds in fewer than fifty shots and divides roughly between two sessions: one with Delia and Bob, the other with Melinda and Homer. Both are short. Both make persistent use of the shot–reverse shot enunciative pattern, here recrafted as the very rhythm of transference. In Bob's session Delia begins by explaining that he has been behaving strangely. César asks whether anything has changed in his world. Delia responds, "You know, I am dating someone new, but Bob seems to really love him." César listens and nods. Delia adds, "He gets very excited every time he's around." During this exchange Delia strains to control Bob, who pulls at his leash and barks. César then offers his "diagnosis." "He is exhibiting something more territorial-like, as if there is another dog around us here. But there is no dog in here." Throughout this scene the camera cuts, often briefly, to shots of Homer as seen by Melinda, underscoring the limits of César's powers. In fact, there *is* another dog there but one that César senses only through Bob's behavior, a set-up complicated by Delia's line, "He gets very excited every time *he's* (Delia's new beau? Homer?) around."

The second session, in some sense already under way, begins in earnest when Bob, as if in pursuit of Homer, yanks Delia after him out into the street. Important dialogue ensues:

MELINDA. Can I ask you a question about my dog, since you are the Dog Whisperer?

CÉSAR. Sure. Is he here?

MELINDA. In a manner of speaking. I need for him to go somewhere.

CÉSAR. Um hum.

MELINDA. Let's just call it a room.

CÉSAR. Okay.

MELINDA. It's not a living room, but a . . .

CÉSAR. Um hum.

MELINDA. Anyway [aware that her aposiopesis has failed], he doesn't want to do it.

CÉSAR. All right, what you need to do is you need to embrace a pack leader mentality. Become calm and assertive. And then he will go. He will follow you.

MELINDA. [As Delia and Bob storm back into the bookstore behind her.] Okay, problem. I don't really want to go into that particular room. Not yet anyway [anxious laugh].

CÉSAR. Well, it's actually very simple. Your dog is feeding on your energy. He's not hearing what you're saying. So, until you change your feelings about the room . . . Then he will go into that room.

MELINDA. Thank you.

DELIA. [To Bob.] Sit!

CÉSAR. You're welcome.

The scene and session conclude with Melinda leaving the bookstore (signed copy of *Cesar's Way* in hand) where she finds Homer. In an "actual" whisper—as if concerned not to appear mad to those around her—Melinda tells the invisible Homer that she is his "pack leader" and that he needs to . . . "Go!" After repeating this, supplemented with the appropriate hand gestures, Homer exits screen right.

In effect, what this scene establishes is that there is an essential continuity between the two whisperers. Melinda helps ghosts (in this episode Julie's kidnapper/"mother") cross over; and César helps Melinda help Homer to cross over. But the scene also gives new depth to the insistently oblique character of the whisper. First, the plural, the two dogs. César thinks he is helping Bob, but it soon becomes evident that he is also helping a dog that is present only "in a manner of speaking." Within this "manner of speaking" Melinda and César converse about a dog that is not quite a dog, and they do so in a highly coded and thus oblique way. Consider here the notion of "going into the room" that is not a *living* room. To the spectator this coded manner of speaking is metaphorical. She or he knows that the implied "dying room" is "the light." However, given the enunciation of the sequence, where Delia and Bob enter the room of the bookstore precisely as Melinda and César discuss her reluctance to go into "that particular room," *the room* becomes the room of whisperers speaking of death and dogs. It seems crucial that in these rooms the dog whisperer says to the ghost whisperer: "He's not hearing what you are saying." This is not because she is speaking unclearly; it is because—as the final "exchange" with Homer makes clear—she has not been *whispering*.

What foregrounds the allegorical dynamic of the scene is the fact that César uses the session with Melinda to invoke, obliquely, the secret of his "way," his technique. In telling her that until she changes her *own* feelings about "the room," her status as "pack leader" will fail to reach Bob, César is being true to his oft-repeated dictum: "I rehabilitate dogs, and train people." Put differently, to work with dogs, you must not work with *them*. You must work with their owners, as if the world of the dog is split by another scene, the scene of the owner. It is as if the dog, like Bunyan's Christian, is simply acting out a script writ large in the very mesh of its kennel. This finds its direct corollary in Julie's story, where it is clear that her world, and the world of her encounter with her foster parents, Melinda, and Jim, is a "double divide." It is haunted by a "mother" for whom Julie is a failed transitional object, a pure compensation for the loss inflicted on her by the trauma of her miscarriage. The following exchange from Evans's novel confirms that this is indeed about whispering. Responding to an attendee at one of Tom Booker's horse clinics, a woman who has queried the source of his knowledge about horses, Tom says: "'Well Dale, you know a lot of this is nuts and bolts.' She frowned. 'What do you mean?' 'Well, if the rider's nuts, the horse bolts'" (Evans 117). While "Dale" regards this as witty obfuscation, Tom insists that his "wisdom" comes from the horses themselves, as if *they* had softly uttered in his pricked ears secrets about their owners. Moreover, in both novel and film Pilgrim's progress is completely overdetermined by what is going on with Grace, Annie, and Tom. In the film it is only when Grace is able to ride Pilgrim again, when she is able to let go of the guilt she feels about the accident and Judith's death, that Pilgrim is himself "saved." Rehaltered. As in "Children of Ghosts," the encounter with the nonhuman animal is split by the parental scene, the affair between Annie and Tom. Here, too, what Pilgrim has "taught" Annie and Tom about the traumatic wounds that bind them allows them to relinquish, however ambivalently, their adulterous fantasy. At a certain level this simply bears witness to the totemic drive to sacrifice the animal to the labor of fabulation, but what is the source of its appeal? Put simply: whispering speaks *toward* us about the place from which it emanates, a place that is at once too remote and too intimate to be accessible to the speaking animal. This speaking is oblique, allegorical, and traumatic.

But what relation exists between these qualities and the linguistic construal of the whisper as "nonvoiced vocalization"? It is the relation between two absences: the nonvoiced and the unspeakable.

It is useful here to recall the important theoretical link between trauma and voice, or, more precisely, the unspeakable, forged in the writings of Cathy Caruth and Shoshana Felman. In *Trauma: Explorations in Memory* Caruth urges us to recognize that the unspeakability of trauma has everything to do with the inherent "belatedness" of the pathology: "The pathology consists, rather, solely in the *structure of experience* or reception: the event is not assimilated or experienced fully at the time, but only belatedly, in its repeated *possession* of the one who experiences it. To be traumatized is precisely to be possessed by an image or event" (4–5). Here the motif of possession reappears, but now it seems to have less to do with sorcery than with the temporal displacement of the voice. Belatedness means that one does not speak (of) trauma; it speaks you and does so repeatedly.

In *Unclaimed Experiences* Caruth elaborates her appeal to the voice by interpreting Freud's recourse to Torquato Tasso's *Gerusalemme Liberata* in *Beyond the Pleasure Principle*. There, Freud reads this belated epic of the Crusades as an example of what it means to bear a passive relation to repetition. Tasso has Tancredi unknowingly kill Clorinda twice. In Caruth's probing introductory chapter, "Wound and the Voice," Caruth places less emphasis on the motif of repetition, drawing attention instead to Tasso's figure of the wounded tree that "groans" when slashed by Tancredi's sword. Her point, as the chapter title says plainly, is to foreground the literary articulation of the claim that trauma "is always the story of a wound that cries out" (4). Voice is thus marked within the very drive of utterance by a wound, by something that separates it from itself. But one must also note that Tasso frames Clorinda's cry in ways that hark back to Tom and Pilgrim. In Fairfax's early translation her cry is preceded by whistling wind and rustling leaves, a point Caruth's evocation of Freud lets slip. She misses that the voice of the wound traverses the space of whispering. By the same token Caruth invites one to conclude that whispering, as a voice marked by the nonvoiced, by that which separates it from itself, harbors the same belatedness as trauma. As such, the reiterated link between whisperers and trauma emerges as crucial to the linguistic characterization of whispering as a phonemic dead zone, crucial as well to the *sound* of the whisper.

Caruth, her inattention to whispering aside, brings the belatedness of trauma into direct contact with ghosts. She proposes not only that trauma is structured around the absence of what cannot be assimilated but also that this absence lends a ghostly character to every trauma. Indeed, the sense one has of being possessed by a trauma finds expression in the feeling of being haunted by a ghost that *is* the absence of the trauma for its bearer. In this sense *The Ghost Whisperer* is always already about trauma, about wounds that speak. In fact, this is repeatedly displayed in the show's title sequence, where, again in an "actual whisper," one hears, "Can you see us?" Although it seems important here to note that the question concerns seeing, *not* hearing, my point is a different one. In the "Children of Ghosts" episode the trauma affecting Julie's "mother" verges on cliché. Not only has she committed a felony and misrepresented herself to Julie, but she has abandoned Julie. Her guilt is palpable, and when her ghost first speaks, it groans, "Take her back," a line that speaks ambiguously, both to the felony and the abandonment. Indeed, guilt is as fundamental to *The Ghost Whisperer* as it is to Freud's theory of civilization.

And Homer? Nothing in the episode illuminates his trauma, his guilt. César tells us that Bob is behaving territorially toward the dog that isn't there, but this is merely the way in which Homer's haunting of Bob appears. Nor do we know anything of Bob's trauma or guilt such that he might invite such a haunting. As the episode ends, we leave Homer on Melinda and Jim's front porch, where he growls sequel-ishly at something or someone. In this he is a bearer of the absence given voice by Jim when earlier he remarked sadly on Julie's recent departure, and when Melinda teasingly responded by intimating that Julie's absence might be filled by a child of their own. Homer *is* absence; he does not *know* absence unless we are to interpret his status as the ghostly guard dog to be an expressionless expression of his guilt. Did he fail in his duty to protect his human owners? Was he, in Nietzsche's idiom, unable to remember his promise to serve and protect humans? Did he fail, in effect, at being a dog? Such possibilities fall within the realm of plausibility, but what is clearly emphasized in the figure of Homer is that the animal is trauma, is absence, is ghostly. Indeed, it is precisely this that seems to under- lie the "crossover" between the two shows/channels, urging us to consider that what is ghostly about the nonhuman animal, specifically the dog, is its allegorical function, the way it becomes the scene, the body on which what- ever requires rehabilitating in its owners is acted out. The whisperer must address *this* ghost, and what comes up in this exchange of secrets—as Evans stressed—is the fear the animal has of the violence of domesticity. On this score César is certainly correct in insisting that animals must be treated as animals, but the problem is that he does not appreciate the trauma that the nonhuman animal and the human are for each other.

Freud, of course, urged readers to consider that ghosts were, as he says in the well-known footnote to *Totem and Taboo*, "disguises for the patients' parents" (65), an idea with considerable traction in *The Ghost Whisperer* and, if one takes seriously the widespread tendency among pet owners to treat their companion animals as children, then in *The Dog Whisperer* as well. But surely Adorno and Horkheimer are right to pressure the limits of this discourse by insisting on a political dimension to the uncanny fear of ghosts. In the "Notes and Sketches" that follow the five chapters of *Dialectic of Enlightenment*, they write: "Freud's theory that the belief in ghosts comes from the evil thoughts of the living about the dead, from the mem- ory of old death wishes, is too narrow. The hatred of the dead is jealousy as much as a feeling of guilt" (178). What Adorno and Horkheimer are doing here is questioning Freud's question. The issue is not simply why people believe in or fear ghosts but rather why they associate ghosts—even if unconsciously—with those with whom they have experienced the guilt of Oedipal rivalry? The proposal here, condensed around the concept of jealousy, is that ghosts have something essential to do with the conditions of historical life under which families live. If such conditions are hopeless—and recall that *Dialectic* is an exilic text marked profoundly by the war of the worlds—perhaps the living are more frightened of life than death. While this line of argument leads quickly to the stance taken in Adorno's critique of horoscopes ("The Stars Down to Earth") and thus to the conclusion that whisperers are simply avatars of the new irrationalism, a more patient unfolding brings whispering, politics, and the animal into a less dismissive arrangement. After all, the repudiation of irrationalism forgets the fact that jealousy is presented as *supplementing*, not replacing, guilt.

Crucial here, because the sound and sense of whispering remain in the foreground, is the matter of the voice. Recently, both Giorgio Agamben and Mladen Dolar have stressed the continuing relevance of Aristotle's contrast between language and voice in the *Politics*. Agamben in *Homo Sacer* is keen to draw attention to the way this distinction founds what Aristotle understands by the domain of the political as the activity through which beings articulate the means by which to live (and presumably die) in common. In turn, the contrast between language and voice is shown to bear on the human-animal relation. In effect, humans and animals share a voice, but they do not share language. For reasons that may seem obvious, Agamben does not entertain the *langage des oiseaux* thesis, emphasizing instead the way Aristotle links the political ("the association of living beings") to language precisely to exclude nonhuman animals from the political. While humans may be "political animals," it is in the name of the political that they struggle against the animals that they are. Voice then, for the political animal, is marked by what language requires it to take out, by something unvoiced, nonvocalized within it, something that for Agamben and Aristotle designates the animal.

That this line of inquiry leads directly to the animal/trauma link, and does so via the problem of the voice and the excision of the animal in the political animal, is vital to the sound and sense of whispering. Nietzsche, who collapsed while attempting to whisper to a horse, was among the first to recognize that the political animal, the human being, is also—in its very moral fiber—a traumatic animal. In *On the Genealogy of Morality* he not only insisted on the link between punishment and morality, but he confected the term *Selbstierquälerei*, "self animal torture/cruelty," to draw out the foundational role of animal cruelty in the constitution of the human.

The problem is not simply that we experiment with, destroy the habitat of, and consume animals; it is that we do this to ourselves in order to promise *not* to do this to them. We fail. The dog can name Nietzsche's pain not simply because it is faithful, obtrusive, and shameless but because the pain that exposes the human *to* trauma is that of the very domestication that produces "dog" in the first place.

If the whisperer addresses the animal like an animal, then surely whispering engages what produces the animal in the political animal, that is, the *Selbstierquälerei* that founds what stands to the side, not accompanying the animal, namely the human. Evans stressed this even as he failed to spook the human. That said, whispering, as teased out of Redford's film, addresses itself to the nonhuman animal insofar as it appears within language as what haunts language, as it were, obliquely. Regardless of the sorcerer's secrets that it utters softly into pricked ears, whispering is also always about the violence of the animal-human encounter, about the trauma of domestication and specie-ism. This stands always to the side, on the other scene, of the statements uttered by whisperers and is yet cortical to their effects. It is not that whisperers "think like animals" or otherwise establish that they are animals too. It is that they produce a speech haunted by the violent exclusion of the animal from the very medium of communication and for which that communication offers to take responsibility.

This prompts us to consider a distinction between whispering and what I have, from time to time, called "an actual whisper." In Orlando Figes's *The Whisperers,* a history of "private life" within the Soviet Union after the death of Lenin, Figes insists on the importance of the distinction in Russian between *shepchushchii,* and *sheptun,* between those who fear being overheard and those who tattle, inform, on them. While critiques of Stalinism may now strike us as beating a dead horse, Figes's distinction has the advantage of situating whispering squarely on the terrain of a certain construal of the political. As such, it invites one to consider where on this terrain *the sound* of the animal-human encounter belongs. Although the point may seem merely linguistic, the whisperer I have been engaging slips (in) between the two senses of the whisperer in Russian. An "actual whisper" can readily be grasped as either discretion or informing, but what about the whispering of waiting, of the ghostly belatedness of trauma, of a sound that is a problem? It would be a mistake simply to exclude such whispering as nonpolitical, because as we have heard, it is precisely here that the constraints of the political are being pronounced and are thus very much at stake.[3]

If "the politics of the voice" (to use Dolar's formulation) is largely concerned with the issues of possession, expression, efficacy, then concern with the political sense of the voice is obliged to orient itself toward the voice's role in producing the sense of the political. At a crucial level, that of articulation, this manifests as a disciplinary problematic. Which institutionalized forms of knowledge production, and where, are authorized to speak about speech or sound off about sound? In relation to such questions, whispering—precisely because it designates, as did the "murmur," the constraints of the discipline authorized to speak about it to others—becomes crucial to the project of thinking the concept of the political. The fact that it slips between discretion and either tattling or laryngitis prompts us to entertain the notion that it flees altogether. Indeed, the sound of whispering may register precisely as the rush of haunted asides. Political animals will thus only know its likeness, its effect, in the spaces separating disciplines from one another as the sound of whispering spurs us to demand that different and superior ways of organizing the work of being in common remain possible. As Tracy Chapman knew, what is revolutionary about the whisper is its uncertain and split status as similitude—not whispering about the revolution, but revolution as or "*like* a whisper."

4. Gasp

Is it possible to think the concept of the aesthetic, whether organized around the beautiful, imitation, or the distribution of the sensible, in sonic (and not phonic) terms, and, if so, what difference would this, could this, make? Consideration of this possibility, even the tentative elaboration of its attractions, is the aim of this chapter. Although the sound of the gasp—along with the whistle and the whisper a linguistically fraught sound, a nonvocalized vocalization[1]—will serve as a touchstone here, my approach to it will be oblique out of respect for the problems posed by the gasp and the rigors of the method I am trying to bring to its study. Put differently, the place of the gasp in a sonic articulation of the aesthetic requires a certain attention to preliminaries, especially given that, in the era of "visualism," the image, especially the mute image (think here of André Malraux's *The Voices of Silence*), has long dominated this conversation.

While *gasp* might immediately suggest "inspiration" (from the Latin verb *inspirare*, to breathe into), it evokes a sound that mere breathing, inhalation, does not. Although it is routinely rendered pleonastically as "an audible gasp," there is something expostulative, palatal, percussive, moist in the gasp that, among other things, urges one to linger over the entire motif of the role of breath in speech. To approach this, one is compelled to think back through the Greek word and concept of *thymos* and to do so for reasons that no doubt require clarification.

Recently, of course, this term—thought to derive from Plato's discussion of "high spiritedness" (spirit itself derived from *spirare*) in book 2 of the *Republic*—was rehabilitated by Francis Fukuyama in his bestselling *The End of History and the Last Man*. In part 3 of this book Fukuyama deploys *thymos* not so much in the Platonic sense of "spiritedness" as in the rather paradoxical sense of recognition and the desire for it. I say "paradoxical" because

Fukuyama has consistent explanatory recourse to Plato's tidy division of the soul, in which desire is set apart from both "spiritedness" (also sometimes "passion") and reason. Many of his historical insights depend on it—for example, the terms by which he contrasts Hobbes, Locke, and Rousseau. At the same time, the obviously attractive utility of distinguishing between reason and desire is hopelessly muddled by rendering "spiritedness" as a mode of desire—the *desire* for recognition. This does not prevent him from donning the mantle of Alexandre Kojève and reading Hegel as the thinker of the alpha and omega of modernity, and while this deprives Fukuyama of the very originality insistently attributed to his book by reviewers, it does underscore the global theoretical stakes of the motif of "breathing in."

Fukuyama's book was not without its critics. Precisely because the "end of history" was decidedly not communism, he ended up ensnarled with Derrida on the pages of *Specters of Marx*. Derrida's reading, largely conducted in chapter 2, "Conjuring—Marxism," is odd yet suggestive, perhaps even instructive. I say "odd" not because, as a reading, it is uncharacteristically truncated nor because Derrida evinces a certain respect for Fukuyama's project. It is odd because in delineating what he takes to be an unsettling paradox at the heart of Fukuyama's analysis, Derrida risks succumbing to his own version of such a paradox.

Although his name does not appear there, Habermas—and specifically the Habermas of "communicative rationality" and the "public sphere"—palpably haunts the discussion of liberal democracy that unfolds in *The End of History*. If one stresses Habermas's insistence on the sociohistorical force of the *principle* of the public sphere, acknowledging as he does the absence of undistorted communication or public reasoning in any really existing incarnation of the public sphere, then one has the logical template used by Fukuyama to tie liberal democracy and the end of history together. In several careful paragraphs Derrida teases out this tension between the empirical and the transcendental in Fukuyama's argument, showing that only some rather perplexing and self-defeating appeals to Christianity and nature lead him out of what is otherwise an impasse, a vicious circle. In other words, while it may be empirically true that the triumph of liberal democracy has not systematically ended tyranny, in the transcendental moment of the end of history a "democratized" domination will assume the benevolent form of a father who treats all his children as equals. To use Fukuyama's term, a universal *isothymia* will prevail in principle if nowhere else. Derrida's impatient skepticism is palpable.

Isothymia has its binary twin in *megalothymia*. Both are forms of the desire for recognition. *Isothymia* designates a form of recognition in which all subjects are equally recognized/recognized as equals; and *megalothymia*, which Fukuyama aligns with Nietzsche's "will to power," is a demand for recognition through which the many are equal only in being unequal to the one. This is what takes Fukuyama to the figure of the "last man." As forms of the desire for recognition, hence the root, *thymia*, both are rooted in *thymos*, no longer rendered as "spiritedness" but as desire, and—one should add—desire in a decidedly nonpsychoanalytical sense. Fukuyama tries to finesse this philological inconvenience by tying the desire for recognition to the feeling of "indignation" (hence spiritedness) that arises through the denial or frustration of this desire, but here again this seems like a ruse of the very reason Plato insisted on contrasting with desire. Although this philological drift might ordinarily have caught Derrida's attention, he notes the pairing of the thymotic twins only in passing, preferring to dwell on the oddly non-Hegelian form of Fukuyama's enabling paradox and his evangelism.

This would be one way of stating what is odd about Derrida's reading. It thus merits a bit more attention. I would like to suggest that this passing acknowledgment of the *thymos*—and this despite its conspicuous centrality in *The End of History* and not merely in part 2—resembles a symptom. But of what?

A key quasi concept (Derrida's formula for refusing the distinction between concepts and metaphors) in *Specters of Marx* is that of what he calls "the spirit of Marxism." To prevent "spirit" from collapsing back into the Hegelian concept of *Geist*, Derrida teases out its decisive affiliation—especially within Western Marxism—with ghosts, the very specters of his title. Haunting (and, in the end, "hauntology") designates the logic of the border between spirit and matter that is, for Derrida, "properly" undialectical. The relation structuring this border is not yoked to a teleology wherein its development through time is indexed to the logic of negation. That said, throughout *Specters*, and as if anticipating their future collaboration /dialogue (see *Philosophy in a Time of Terror*), Derrida appeals oddly to a version of the Habermasean argument that "haunts" Fukuyama's analysis. He, too, wants to distinguish and separate between the ethical and political compromises of all sociohistorical incarnations of really existing Marxism and not its "idea" (Fukuyama's term) but its spirit. Crucial here, of course, is the different articulation of the distinction between the empirical and the transcendental that is captured in the motif of "haunting," and if Derrida evinces cautious respect for Fukuyama's project, it would seem to be as a result of recognizing this shared, if frayed, thread.

But readers of Derrida will bring to the vexed matter of this difference his long and careful reading of the quasi concept of "spirit" in the work of Heidegger published five years earlier. Now legible as a preemptive strike in the "Heidegger Affair" (the political controversy stirred by Victor Farías's *Heidegger and Nazism*), Derrida's *Of Spirit* derives from a lecture written as the closing remarks for a conference on Heidegger sponsored by the *Collège international de la philosophie* in 1987. It is concerned, among many things, to trace the use and mention of the terms *Geist, geistig,* and *geistlich* in Heidegger's works from the mid-1920s with the publication of *Being and Time* to an essay on Georg Trakl from the 1950s, and to do so as a way to think explicitly about the politics of Heidegger's "destruction" of Western metaphysics. In patiently tracing this material, Derrida shows that Heidegger moves from avoiding the notion of *Geist* ("spirit" but more besides) to avoiding its avoidance through devices as varied as "air" quoting (the late Chris Farley's forte) and adjectivalization. In Heidegger's late work *spirit* has become flame, a philological twist that gives his precise and unequivocal embrace of *spirit* in the infamous Rectoral Address from the 1930s an unmistakably menacing ring.

Aware that his own thought owes an enormous debt to Heidegger, Derrida is scrupulous in underscoring where the deployment of *spirit* leads to conclusions with which he disagrees, while never pretending to disagree from some "remote location," some sheltered, uncompromised site of blameless opposition. What invites our attention to the material—even if one is not a reader of Derrida—is that it not only clearly engages the term deployed against Fukuyama (*spirit* of Marxism, as opposed to the *idea* of liberal democracy), but it does so through recourse to the rhetoric of haunting and ghosts. Indeed, Derrida even proposes that Heidegger's texts are haunted by the ghostly return of spirit, thereby gesturing toward something thoughtless, even unthought, in the latter's use of the term. In light of this one is prompted to speculate on the comparatively uncomplicated use and mention of spirit in the dispute with Fukuyama. To be clear: the entirety of *Specters*—as its title implies—is concerned with teasing out precisely what is thoughtless about a concept of spirit prophylactically shielded from the logic of hauntology. That said, on the matter of the exposition of the "spirit of Marxism," Derrida lets spirit not only do some of the same work it does in Heidegger—for example, complicating its relation to the letter, to the body, to the object—but also in Fukuyama. Perhaps because Heidegger himself risked conflating spirit and Germany, thus avoiding the politico-theoretical problem of an empirical realization of spirit, Derrida's use of *spirit* in the dispute with Fukuyama repeats this avoidance, not in the form of an avoidance of avoidance but in the form of a lapse.

Earlier I proposed there was a symptom to be read here, and I now suggest that this has to do with the passing—and I want to emphasize the gesture of passing—reference to *thymos*. In *Of Spirit* Derrida draws attention to Heidegger's refusal to render *Geist* as a German translation either of the Latin *spiritus* or the Greek *pneuma*, agreeing that such translations operate to subjectivize spirit. Derrida's motivation is to signal his concord with this form of the critique of the subject and to gesture ahead to the network of paths along which one might exit from the flames of spirit that consume Heidegger's "fundamental ontology." Again, readers of Derrida will recognize the distinctive role of *pneuma* in this matrix. Rendered as "breath," *pneuma* belongs to the pneumatological phonocentrism that figured in Derrida's earliest articulations of grammatology. As such, avoiding the translation of *Geist* as *pneuma* appeals to Derrida almost as a matter of principle. But what happens if one accents the "pulmonary" dimension of *pneuma*? What if instead of stressing the "breathing out" of *inspirare*, the breathing or blowing into something, one stresses the breathing or sucking in, what I am calling the gasp?

The tie between breathing in, the gasp, and the *thymos* was twisted well before Derrida read Fukuyama. It was worked out by the classicist Richard Onians in his *On the Origins of European Thought*. Although we have since come to doubt where the Europe is whose origins Onians has located (consider here the thesis of Bernal's *Black Athena* or even David Wallace's edited volume *Europe: A Literary History, 1343–1418*), the philological and philosophical insights he provides can, in certain respects, be detached from the geopolitical assumptions organizing his text. Indeed, some of his sources derive from Asian materials. But, more to the point, his discussion of *thymos* is usefully framed in terms that resonate immediately within the context of the dispute among Fukuyama, Derrida, and Heidegger. There is here what in an earlier chapter I referred to as an echo. Doubtless more than one.

The sentence "What was the *thymos*?" is the first in chapter 3 of Onians's text, a chapter whose title, "The Stuff of Consciousness," tells us directly that Onians approaches the *thymos* as belonging in a decisive way to the Greek (and here, too, precisions are in order) theory of the subject. This becomes crucial both because it points immediately to a flawed assumption of Fukuyama's—that the desire for recognition that drives history is not itself historical—and because it brings the *thymos* into a connotative field that includes decisive sonic elements. As with Foucault, who differentiated between "the history of ideas" and "the history of systems of thought," by insisting on the need to situate philosophic utterances in a multigeneric and transdiscursive network, Onians proceeds by tracing *thymos* and kindred terms through both Plato and Homer, where the notion that it might simply be captured in either "spiritedness" or "the desire for recognition" seems fanciful at best. Above all, this tracing establishes that the *thymos* relates to "spiritedness" insofar as breathing, inhaling, can be related to body heat. Such a relation becomes plausible when we realize that the Greeks thought that heat was imparted to the body through the blood and that air was brought into contact with blood in the lungs. Citing numerous textual sources, Onians shows that the *thymos* was understood to be something that resulted from this contact and that *thymos* was released or lost when this contact was broken, that is, in death:

> Diores, when his leg was crushed by a stone, "fell on his back in the dust and stretched out both his hands to his dear comrades, breathing forth . . . his *thymos*." An arrow pierced Harpalion and "breathing forth . . . his *thymos* he lay stretched upon the ground like a worm." Achilles wounded Hippodamas with his spear and he gasped [*aisthe*] for his *thymos* and roared as when a bull etc." Sarpedon wounded the horse of Pedasos "and he bellowed gasping [*aisthon*] for his *thymos* and fell in the dust moaning and his *thymos* floated away. . . ." Agamemnon sacrificing "cut the lambs'" throats with the pitiless bronze and laid them upon the ground gasping, in want of *thymos*. . . ." (Onians 45)

The list of citations, all but one from the *Iliad*, continues at length, and it is Onians's objective not only to bring out the tie between *thymos* and breath but to deploy this tie to establish that death for the Greeks had little if anything to do with brain function. This is in keeping with his aim to identify the Greek theory of consciousness, its "stuff," as presented in classical materials. I will return to the repeated reference throughout to the gasp, but suffice it to say that it is very hard to hear "desire for recognition" as a suitable translation for *thymos* as the noun appears in these lines.

Plato's dispute with Homer is well-known (see Eric Havelock's *The Preface to Plato*), and while one might thus be tempted to justify Fukuyama's reading of *thymos* by situating it later in the classical period, Onians is not so easily shaken. Indeed, he draws attention to Plato's dialogue the *Cratylus*, in which the word *thymos* is "defined" (Socrates is struggling not to get at the sense of words through other words but through their relation to the origin of language). In Jowett's translation *thymos* is rendered as "passion" (closer obviously to Fukuyama's rendering), but passion is then immediately linked to rushing, boiling, and flowing, associations that Onians ties not to the "blood soul" but to "breath related to blood, not mere air but something vaporous within, blending and interacting with the air without, something which diminishes if the body is ill-nourished, but increases when the body is well-nourished" (Onians 48). Again, the Platonic perspective is shunted back through the pneumatic material. Onians also refers to passages in the *Timaeus* and the *Phaedrus*, indirectly suggesting that Fukuyama's reading of Plato is confined to the *Republic*. The problem here is not whether Plato contrasts *thymos* and intellect/reason but rather what precisely is being contrasted. If what Socrates says in the *Phaedrus* matters, namely that his chest is filled with thoughts from some alien stream (235c), then it is not clear that passion and intellect are to be distinguished in the customary way and certainly not in the way Fukuyama's schema both requires and betrays.

Extending the impulse given expression here, Onians not only draws out the status of the word *thymos*, but he underscores the thymotic dimension of language as such. Citing first Hesiod, who, in *Works and Days*, writes that words are put into the lungs of hearers; then Homer, who develops this thought by observing that the sound of Hermes's lyre once breathed into Apollo was listened to by his *thymos* (Onians 70), Onians motivates his interest in such passages by providing us with the early Greek account of spoken language: "They [the speeches of man] come forth with the breath that is intelligence in them, they are parts of it, and the listener puts them, takes them, into his *thymos*, thus adding to his store, his knowledge. They pass from lung to lung, mind to mind" (Onians 67). Or, more concisely, "The sound, the breath, of which words consist passes through the ears not to the brain but to the lungs" (Onians 69). Here, I would emphasize, it gets harder and harder to render *thymos* simply as the desire for recognition. Instead, it emerges as the cortical layer of a subject whose consciousness is not yet understood to be localized in the head. One puts utterances *in* the *thymos*; one listens *with* the *thymos*. We are a long way from the much-discussed passages in Aristotle's *On Interpretation*, where thoughts are located in the mind and words represent them in the different languages spoken by humans.

A clarification followed by an elaboration: my purpose in turning to Onians's work is not to establish that his account of the *thymos* is the true one. It may certainly be an earlier one, but what matters here is the fact that what his account discloses is the clash between two regimes of subjectivity and, moreover, the persistent relevance of breath, sound, and listening to sorting out what might be at stake in this clash. Perhaps because the "desire for recognition" presumes a subject that is synonymous with the human, as such, Fukuyama resists attending to any discussion of the thymotic that betrays the dubiousness of such a presumption. Nor, it should be said, is he particularly interested in sound as something relevant to the end of history, and this despite his interest in a figure like Nietzsche, for whom ears, listening, sound, voices, music, and so on insistently matter.

Of course, to the extent that this points to something pertinent in the testy exchange between Fukuyama and Derrida, it must be acknowledged that Derrida—much like Nietzsche, Freud, and Heidegger before him—attends assiduously to sound. In fact, one might reasonably suggest that Onians's entire discussion of the *thymos* might be said to confirm Derrida's well-known, even signature, quasi concept of phonocentrism. Even the notion that words travel from lung to lung, that is, as breath exchanged between interlocutors, would appear to conflate language with speech. If, however, it makes sense to distinguish, as I have, between the sonic and the phonic, this is not simply to draw attention to a difference in scale (the sonic being more capacious than the phonic). Instead, this distinction is meant to help identify precisely what is not phonocentric in the classical account of the *thymos*, namely the *sound* of the breath, and especially of the breath as articulated with lungs thought to be the storehouse of language in the human subject. It is useful here to return to Saussure's much-combed *Course in General Linguistics* and emphasize in his wavy diagram of the articulation between sounds and senses (see page 157 in the French edition) the simple fact that if language brings order to this articulation by lining up resultant signifiers and signifieds, then what is not so lined up is left, in effect, un- and thus in-articulated. Derrida is surely right to stress how Saussure's account of this articulation presupposes a certain reduction of language to speech, but this leaves unattended the significance of the sound left in the wake of the phonic reduction of the signifier. To be sure, what I am here referring to as breath is only a part of the resultant field of the sonic, but it is a decisive one, and it points to a dimension of the *thymos* that in eluding the critique of phonocentrism also slips through the dispute between Derrida and Fukuyama.

Herein lies the import of the gasp. Consider again how Onians brought the gasp into contact with the *thymos*. Citing Homer, he writes: "Sarpedon wounded the horse Pedasos, and he bellowed gasping for his *thymos* and fell in the dust moaning and his *thymos* floated away." The line suggests the English expression, "gasping for breath," but precisely because it is pleonastic (breathing for breath), what seems stressed is the sonic quality of what we might also call labored, or even noisy, breathing. Moreover, when the *thymos* is said to float away (retrieving the aqueous or vaporous connotation of the thymotic noted earlier), life rather than breath would seem to be the proper rendering of the *thymos*. If it is also important here to separate gasping from bellowing and moaning, it is not primarily to set up a pain gradient but to stress the biophysical, as well as semantic, tie between life and the sound of the gasp. The absence of a theory of brain death would, of course, enable this particular series of associations, but the point is not whether this account of life and its loss is true but whether life and gasping are indeed associated in the poem. They are.

Having earlier in this study drawn attention to Barthes and Havas's notion of "the alert" (a mode of listening shared between humans and other animals), it seems pertinent to note—and this despite Onians's lack of interest—that the subject whose *thymos* floats away is a horse. Yes, another horse. This citation derives, as do many others, from the *Iliad,* and the pattern of associations that emerges there invites one to conclude that the *thymos* is something not so much shared between humans and other animals (as for example the whisper) but is something shared *by* humans and other animals, and while this breathes life into the cliché about Life (with a capital *L*), it also draws attention to the Homeric inclination to insist that humans and other animals have a life in common. One is not inferior to the other as in the distinction made in Aristotle, Arendt, Agamben, and others between *bios* and *zoe,* and given the role this distinction plays in Arendt's differentiation between the voice and language, one might even consider the pneumatic theory of speech present in Homer as the semantic ground out of which this problematic arose. Here, the animal already exhibits the stuff of consciousness that Western science and philosophy will spend centuries disputing. That said, we are still not yet dealing with a "desire for recognition." In fact, what is truly challenging here is that the nonhuman animal has a relation to our life that cannot simply be set opposite the desire emphasized by Fukuyama, and this inflects what might be meant by the *thymos* in a similar way. It is not the desire for recognition without therefore being its opposite. A desire for misrecognition *(méconnaissance)*?

But Onians also develops the theme of the gasp in an even more intriguing direction. Consider the following discussion from chapter 4, on the five senses:

> Sound was obviously breathed out in the voice and odor must have been observed in the breath. . . . This correlation [among air, breath, and lungs/consciousness] of the earliest Greek evidence perhaps enables us to realize that the Homeric and later Greek word, *aio,* "I perceive," usually of hearing but also of seeing and more generally of "taking in" something, is really identical with the Homeric *aio,* "I breath in," as it appears to be, but as it is currently assumed not to be in the absence of these other considerations. Similarly, we may now see that *aisthomai,* "I perceive" (with the resultant *aisthesis* and the lengthened form *aisthanomai,* our "aesthetics," etc.), is the middle of the Homeric *aistho,* "I gasp, breath in," and we can relate to these and explain the curious fact preserved for us by Alcaeus and Hesychius that in Aeolic *epipnein,*

"to breath at," means "to look at" *(epiblepein)*, the eyes being in fact not only passive and recipient like the ears, but also active outwardly. (Onians 74–75)

As if in anticipation of Bernal's critique of Eurocentrism in classical studies, Onians then develops this fascinating and solicitous line of discussion by adducing a similar example, that of the Sanskrit *prana* (breaths), from the *Chandogya Upanishad*. But to tease out what might lie buried in the common ground between Hinduism and Greek classical thought, details of the preceding passage deserve comment.

Given the express aim of this chapter, namely, to speculate on the tie between aesthetics and sound, the passage is indispensable. It shows Onians following his philological nose to scents deemed malodorous to the classics of his day. But more important is his stress placed on sound in relation to breath and the explicit way, through the motif of "taking in," Onians draws out the intriguing parallel between breathing at and looking at or, to use the terminology whose value I have been mulling throughout: the audit and the gaze. He stresses the activity of both (while oddly insisting on the recipient character of the ear), and this must be kept in mind when thinking about the event of "taking in," which might otherwise seem passive, merely receptive.

On the matter of sound: vital, in the pneumatic realm, is the difference between expiration and inspiration. Both involve breathing, and if thought about tonally, expiration might be said to have a slightly lower pitch than inspiration. To revisit the contrast that perplexed Mallarme: expiration is like *jour* as opposed to *nuit*, that is, semantics be damned, the "darker" sound. But what Onians is driving at in the passage is not this sound but the sound he heard when reporting on the bellowing of Sarpedon's expiring horse: the gasping for its *thymos*. As the reader will recall, that gasp was rendered as *aisthon*, and it is clear that in following the philological Braille that leads from *aio* to *aesthesis*, Onians is hearing the *aisthon*, the gasping, that heralds the event of inspiration, the taking in of breath. One might even propose that the morphological and phonemic units *ai(o)* and *ais(thon)* are onomatopoeic; that is, they are names that assume the contour of the sound of sucking in air suddenly and urgently: inspiration, but in the form of what in another argot might be called a "hit." That said, and here the tie to aesthetics is difficult to ignore, inspiration is more than simply breathing in; it is also receiving something like a message, and if received from one's muse, that message might take the form of an artwork, or at the very least the unsettling passion or urge not simply to perceive but to be moved to move the message. The gasp, then, might be understood as the sound of inspiration or the giving of life to the bearer of the message. Crucially, I will propose, this gasp of inspiration conditions the expiration—the breathing-out or breathing-into—that phonocentrism has long associated with speech. The gasp, like the trace, is prephonic.

Toward the end of the previously cited passage Onians proposes a suggestive parallel between ear and eye, one that appears to shift the discussion away from inspiration and toward expiration or, as his text has it, "breathing *at*." As I have noted, his aim is to grasp both seeing and hearing as activities, but from our perspective his remarks also ask us to recognize in this parallel a certain superimposition of the senses of seeing and hearing, a superimposition that in bringing audit and gaze (here, "looking at") into alignment invites one to wonder about the historical triumph of the gaze, of vision, of the image in the history of aesthetics. Put differently, Onians's discussion gives us a way to think about what might be designated as the "before" of what I have been calling "visualism"—or, if not the before, perhaps something like a constitutive exclusion that both belongs to and beleaguers "visualism"—something an audit might help us think.

To elaborate the point, it is helpful to recall the oddity of the formulation "breathing at" *(epipnein)*. One might more typically think here "breathing out" or even "breathing on," both realizations of what feels like expiration, but here the Greek *epi* seems, as Onians suggests, to find its equal in "at." Perhaps it makes sense here to remember the insistent association made between the gasp and the *thymos*. Recall that when Achilles wounds Hippodamas and he gasps for his *thymos*, he is not simply breathing out or breathing in. He is breathing for or at something, and that something is the *thymos*. This suggests a relationship between the sound of the gasp, the urgent and abrupt sucking in of air, and a "breathing at" that has as its object the *thymos*. And, if via the motif of action this has its parallel in a "looking at," then gasp and gaze may have more to say to one another than we have known to attend to. This is not because "looking at" is the same as gaze (I cautioned against this earlier when distinguishing between eye and vision) but because gaze, indeed *the* gaze, has, despite all its theoretical complications, fallen in step with the tenets of what I have been calling "visualism," especially when tracked through the aesthetic realm. Undoubtedly, this has much to do with the role of vision in the epistemological assumption brought to bear on aesthetic objects, but I will chime in with those who argue that the mode of perception that matters in Western aesthetics has long been that of sight. Consider in support of such an assertion that in Jacques Rancière's recent *Aisthesis: Scenes from the Aesthetic Regime of Art*, a text that proposes to illuminate "the category designating the sensible fabric and intelli-

gible form of what we call 'Art'" (ix), of the fourteen "scenes" covered, only
one of them, "The Immobile Theater" (on Wagner), deals in any sustained
way with sound, despite the fact that he discusses film (Chaplin and Vertov,
so "silent" cinema), theater, poetry, and dance. One is, of course, entitled to
one's limitations, but if one feels thus authorized to presume them, this
might be said to echo, in Rancière's case, precisely the distribution of the
sensible that he is purporting to analyze.[2]

Ultimately, the issue is not Rancière but the relation between the aesthetic and sound that Onians's discussion puts before us. To elaborate this
and bring the chapter back around to the problem of the thymotic character
of the "last man," I turn now to another text I intend to put my ear to,
Terrence McNally's short play, "Last Gasps." As is often the case, one text
leads to another, and McNally's play is no different. It takes us to Salman
Rushdie's *The Moor's Last Sigh*, especially its evocation of Alfred
Dehodencq's pictorial rendering of *"el último suspiro del Moro."* I will say
how and why.[3]

McNally's play, written in 1970, both is and is not a one-act play. It is so
in the sense that in the written text there are no divisions designated as acts.
Everything that takes place happens in a succession that unfolds in one time
and place. The performance is its own spatiotemporal unity. By the same
token it is not a one-act play in that what happens onstage is punctuated by
lighting, a recurrent clock strike, and a siren that suggest that there are as
many acts as there are characters, and there are eleven, although a Boy and
a Girl appear together, complicating, however deftly, any effort to tie acts to
the comings and goings of characters. While this might seem merely formal,
everything that transpires in the play converges on the problem of temporal
stasis, on, in effect, the Benjaminian *Jetzzeit* figured in "On the Concept of
History" as an alarm clock perpetually sounding its alarm. This stasis is
measured off in a repetition structured around the following six elements: a
character, a clock striking 12:00, a siren sounding, a deep breath being taken
(in one case its duration, forty-five seconds, is specified), lines being delivered while holding the breath, and an expiration punctuated by light. The
dramatic arc, such as it is, moves characterologically, from a Man seated to a
black soldier in Vietnam (McNally was not the least bit shy about engaging
in political commentary). This is coupled with two other toggles, namely,
between English and Italian and, through the device of projected subtitles,
between theater and cinema. Indeed, the projection of subtitles virtually
cuts or folds the play in half. The opening and close of the play are marked
by the introduction of the name, Charlie/Charley, first as the name for a
lab mouse and later as the slang designation of Vietcong partisans, a

gesture that beads together on the necklace of the signifier a cartoon and a slur, and animals and enemies (beings who must be exterminated to "save" us). Here is the introduction to the play.

> A large clock, the kind whose minute hand visibly "jumps" every sixty seconds. It is 11:59. We hold there in silence until the minute hand jumps and it is 12:00. And at once the sound of a siren explodes: deafening, urgent, terrifying. Lights up on a Man in a straight back chair bending over to tie his shoelaces. His head and body snap up at the sound of the siren. He sits rigidly in the chair, not moving at all, his eyes staring straight ahead. He fills his lungs with as much air as he possibly can. This is all he does. He does not move. His face shows no emotion. We watch him in silence until his lungs explode for air. About 45 seconds. . . . The moment he gasps for air he falls out of his chair. Light holds a beat on the empty chair. The clock. It is 11:59. (McNally 47)

What distinguishes the Man from the remaining characters is that he says nothing, but in all other respects this is the template that repeats, complete with the resetting of the clock, almost as if time is running backward and everything just cited occurs in exactly one minute. In effect, everything transpires (from the Latin for "breathing out") as transpiration.

Nothing tells us whether the clock is striking midnight or noon, but as the earlier invocation of Benjamin might suggest, it is the hour, or more literally the minute, of emergency. This minute arrives for a Man, a Scientist, a Teacher, a Writer, a Nervous Woman, an Italian Girl, a Boy and a Girl, a Nun, a Middle-Aged Lady, and a Black. Each of them responds to the siren in the same way implying that the emergency is shared. It belongs to, or otherwise bears on, these "types." It has been suggested that the emergency at the core of "Last Gasps" is the then current anxiety about air pollution (not yet "climate change") and the widely shared Western belief that time is running out for humanity. From this perspective the title is at once literal and allegorical: the gasps we hear are but moments in the "last gasp of humanity," at the end of times.

But here's the problem: how precisely does this play reach beyond the environmental to the aesthetic? How is it "about" itself as a piece of aesthetic practice, and how does gasping fit here? If one stresses the presence of the character called the Writer, certain aspects of a response, not an answer, a response, emerge.

The Writer appears seated at his typewriter, literally at the scene of writing. His first spoken lines are presented as representations: he is reading what he has written. What he has written involves a man and a woman, and it is set in the land of Homer; indeed, Homer's "epic simile" of the "wine dark sea" is invoked and commented on from the environmental angle noted before. When the siren sounds, the Writer sucks in a deep breath and begins typing and reading aloud what he is typing. He says: "Since no one will find what I next write, there is no point in writing it. (He pauses.) I loved. (Another pause.) Now is the time for all good men to come to the aid of their country. Now is the time" (49). He then falls dead. Last gasp. End of the world.

If one considers the "dying words" (to use an expression developed powerfully by Kevin Riordan in an as yet unpublished dissertation) as part of the text that began with the scene presenting "John" and "Sarah" gazing out at the Aegean Sea, then it is clearly reflexive. The text is "about" the becoming-conscious of the work of art, couched in a familiar modernist lament about obscurity and the futility of expression. Beckett: "I can't go on, I must go on." The point is not that reflexivity is necessarily art (although this relation is an important one), but here reflexivity is explicitly staged as part of the aesthetic process deflected by the siren(s). If pollution captures this, it does so through the corollary of dilution. Something or someone loved has become inaccessible.

The invocation of Homer here is a rich one. Given the matrix of sea (whether wine dark or not), siren, and falling silent, one senses here issues to be explored in the following chapter around Kafka's parable "The Silence of the Sirens." Here, however, the silence that isn't one assumes the sonic profile of spoken words responding to the audible taps of the writing machine, words conspicuously marked by the strained urgency of their delivery. Moreover, like Kafka, the Writer is concerned to underscore what separates his work from Homer. In "Last Gasps" this separation is measured in terms similar to those that one finds in Georg Lukács's *Theory of the Novel*, where Greece is idealized as a lost "integrated civilization" whose forms of artistic expression, notably the epic, have been rendered difficult if not impossible by modernization. The novel—written/printed prose—is the symptom of this loss. At one level this is captured in the environmental thematics adduced by McNally: Homer's sea is being polluted with raw sewage. But at another level, and Lukács himself is comparatively silent on the matter, there is the whole question of the loss of oral culture, or what Walter Ong called "orality." The Writer is, precisely, writing. In fact, he is typing and thus telescoping the advance of print capitalism as it moved from the sacred/public to the secular/private. As if to underscore this particular aspect of what separates the Writer from Homer, the words that enter into the Writer's text—"Now is the time," etc.—might just as well have been written by the typewriter itself because these are words, typically dictated by instructors, used to train people on how to use the typewriter. McNally might also have used, "the quick brown fox jumped over the lazy dog." It serves the same pedagogical purpose even as it lacks the (in)decisive deictic "now." Here the loss of orality is coupled with the inversion whereby writing, indeed a writing machine, dictates speech. A break (in this case, a historico-epistemological one) is rebroken for emphasis.

Thus, "Last Gasps" engages aesthetics not merely by staging the figure of the work, or worker, of art but by thematizing the hoary theme of the emergence and displacement of the very concept of art in the West. And it does more. It probes directly the contours of the perceptual experience thought to be named through, to reinvoke Rancière's term, *aisthesis*. We now have an inkling of why the gasp leads us here.[4] These issues manifest in the "act" that centers around the Middle-Aged Lady, a farcical bourgeois figure who embodies a familiar form of modernist misogyny. Among other things, in a play concerned at some level with environmental degradation and public health, she is smoking. Her lines, uttered after a siren-induced deep inhalation, read: "I was having my hair done. I was doing my nails and having my hair done. I was reading about a diet and smoking L&Ms and drinking coke and eating chocolate covered cherries . . . *ciliegge,* cherries are *ciliegge* in Italian . . . and doing my nails and having my hair done. My mind won't move. I can't think" (51). Struggling to think, the Middle-Aged Lady says that she can't think of anything other than that she can't think of anything other than nails, cherries, cigarettes, and hairdressing (here presented as the same as not thinking). Her breath gives out, and she expires.

While it might be interesting here to mull the matter of the reintroduction of Italian in the dialogue (earlier we are treated to a phone call by an Italian Girl, in Italian, in which she speaks first to her father and then to her lover), what strikes me as more intriguing is the way this character turns reflexivity not only into a thinking about thinking but into a meditation on wonder.

Wonder is the English word used to translate *admiratio* when it appears in the works of Descartes and Spinoza (among other places, to be sure). It arises in these sources as part of a discourse on affect. Given the fraught, even anxious, relation between these two thinkers, readers will not be surprised to learn that wonder plays quite different roles in their thinking of affect. For Descartes, at least as presented in *The Passions of the Soul*, wonder is the ground of all affect. It is affect in its primordial state. Spinoza disagrees, but it is the terms of his disagreement that are pertinent to McNally's Middle-Aged Lady. In part 3 of *The Ethics*, under the Definition of the Emotions, he says the following:

> *Wonder* is the conception *(imaginatio)* of anything wherein the mind comes to a stand, because the particular concept in question has no connection with other concepts (cf. III. lii. and note).
>
> *Explanation.*—In the note to II. xviii. we showed the reason, why the mind, from the contemplation of one thing, straightway falls to the contemplation of another thing, namely, because the images of the two things are so associated and arranged, that one follows the other. This state of association is impossible, if the image of the thing be new; the mind will then be at a stand in the contemplation thereof, until it is determined by other causes to think of something else. (Spinoza 174)

This line of reasoning is continued until Spinoza, characterizing this form of fixated contemplation as a "distraction of the mind" caused by the absence of a cause (oddly not unlike his immanent god), decides that wonder is not an emotion at all. But apart from this, it seems important to note that wonder is tied directly to the advent of the new and the figure of thought at a standstill, a form of thinking stunned by the intake of a perception that stubbornly refuses to associate with other perceptions. True to the "visualism" that constitutes the very air that Western thought breathes, Spinoza thinks of the object of such a perception as an image, but why not shift the emphasis in accord with McNally's Middle-Aged Lady? Why not treat the siren and the gasp, the sucking in, the *ais*, as a cacophony of sounds that stun a subject who in pulling itself together around the imaginary, the *imago*, has a chance encounter with wonder that precisely calls up or motivates the image as what, in grounding recognition, belies a logically prior event in the becoming-subject of the bearer of perceptions? Put differently, what the concept of the nonconcept *admiratio* invites is acknowledgment of the precisely reactive character of the image insofar as it designates what holds the subject of Western philosophy together.

To be sure, McNally does not put the matter in these terms. His play does, however, stage as part of its reflexive encounter with the work of art a gasp, a last gasp, that conduces directly and without delay to wonder. The point is not that McNally anticipates the "affective turn" but that "Last Gasps" stages a meditation on aesthetics that plunges it in sound and, in so plunging it, submits Eurocentric aesthetics to a violent shaking—its death rattle.

Echoing this treatment of sound and affect, Salman Rushdie in *The Moor's Last Sigh* adds another defining rupture to the Lukácsian mourning of Greece. Specifically, in the novel's opening chapter, and intermittently throughout, Rushdie draws attention to the expulsion of the Moors from Europe that occurred under the reign of Columbus's Catholic sponsors,

Ferdinand and Isabella. Indeed, in chapter 6 he recounts the official story. Although his saga of the Zogoiby family is largely a meditation on the history of India (which, of course, had its own encounter with Islamic expansionism), it makes persistent reference to the episode of Abu Abdallah Muhammad's flight from Grenada, an episode referred to as "*el último suspiro del Moro*" (the last breath/sigh of the Moor) and famously depicted by Alfred Dehodencq in his painting "*Les Adieux du Roi Baobdil à Grenade.*"[5] The mother of the narrator, Aurora, is a painter who has painted not only the "Moorish series" but specifically a canvas titled "The Moor's Last Sigh," thereby casting Aurora in the role of Borges's Menard. This thematic snarl is introduced thus by Rushdie:

> (Here I sit, is more like it. In this dark wood—that is, upon this mount of olives, within this clump of trees, observed by the quizzically tilting stone crosses of a small, overgrown graveyard and a little down the track from the Último Suspiro gas station—without benefit or need of Virgils, in what ought to be the middle pathway of my life, but has become for complicated reasons, the end of the road, I bloody well collapse with exhaustion.) . . . When you're running out of steam, when the puff that blows you onward is almost gone, it's time to make confession. Call it a testament or (what you) will; life's Last Gasp Saloon. Hence this here-I-stand-or-sit with my life's sentences nailed to the landscape and the keys to a red fort in my pocket, these moments of waiting before a final surrender. (Rushdie 3–4)

Prior to this the narrator has been presented as a man in flight, and the allusive suggestion that he is Abu Abdallah Muhammad ("the Moor") is quite clear, despite the numerous intertextual evocations of *The Divine Comedy*, the Bible, and the *Aeneid* (as if thematically compelled by the gasp, Homer's *Iliad* will also later figure in the intertextual matrix).

Like McNally, who brings Homer's sea into contact with sewage, Rushdie brings the last gasp of the last Moor in Spain into contact with gasoline, in fact, with the whole petrochemical drama of a road trip thwarted by an ill-considered refusal to heed signage that reads "last gas for X miles." Not so much the last sigh, as the last sign. Given the title, and the text repeatedly appears within itself under its English name, it reads like the confession called for by arrival at the Last Gasp Saloon. This locus, so named, makes it clear that gasp, sigh, and *suspiro* share semantic turf, turf mapped explicitly in chapter 4, and in so doing, these terms envelop the work of art, in Rushdie's case, the telling of the tale named "the Moor's last sigh." By the same token, what the comparison between Rushdie and McNally amplifies is the vital sense that the world on the wane in "Last Gasps" is less the planet of ecological concern and more "the world" brought into being through the emergence of Judeo-Christian Europe. This invites us to add the Moor to the characters that appear on McNally's playbill, that is, someone whose last gasp not only extends for four hundred–plus pages of utterance but whose end recontextualizes the other last gaspers around him. Another writer has slipped into the theater.

While this may seem merely fanciful, it is important to note that the moment of the conquest and the expulsion of the Moors (with Jews soon to follow) figures prominently in McNally's play. This material is introduced via the Teacher, a figure whose last gasp might just as well be my own. This character's first line is, "Now let's see if one of you [her unseen students, but her audience and readers as well] can tell me the *name* of the queen who gave Columbus the Nina, the Pinta and the Santa Maria" (48). This is followed by the now familiar siren. As "Karen" answers correctly, the Teacher abruptly changes the lesson plan. What ensues is a macabre fusion of Jonestown and a Cold War "duck-and-cover" drill where the students are instructed to collectively inhale their last gasps in a contest to see whose last lasts longest. As the "act" concludes, the Teacher gasps for air and falls, revealing "Columbus and the date 1492" written on the chalkboard. At one level this might be said to enter the paradigm of environmental catastrophe simply by reminding us how "the Conquest" is typically transmitted to students striving for cultural literacy in the West as a bold form of evangelism sustained by scientific curiosity and (ad)venture capital. But the otherwise fortuitous meeting of *this* historical event and the motif of the last gasp urges us to hear in their join the material foregrounded in Rushdie. That is the rush of air that passes between celestial bodies, two worlds, one that is ending and one that is not.

One might insist that the reference to Columbus is just another strand in the play's weave of allusions to Italy and Italians, but that proposition hermeneutically oversteers in the opposite direction. Besides, what stands out in the text is the emphasis—and yes, this emphasis is borne by italics, a typeface developed less than a decade after Columbus's first voyage—the emphasis on the word *name*. Specifically, the Teacher asks for the *name* of the queen who gave Columbus his three ships. As "Karen" correctly responds that the name is "Isabella," a feminine given name that, while it drifts between Spanish and Italian, belongs here to a Hispanophone monarch. Isabella. Why stress that name? Perhaps because when tracked back through Elizabeth to the Hebrew Elisheva, one hears in it "my god is an oath," that is, my god—and Isabella of Castille is renowned for her piety—is as an utterance, an imprecation or vow. The point, I take it, is not that one is making an oath *to* or *before* god but that one's god *is* one's oath, that she/

he/it is the oath by which, in the case of Isabella, one is named. Thus, as much as this material might belong to the code of "Italianicity," it also certainly belongs to the sonic register of the play. For "Karen," Isabella is her last gasp. Her gasp is the oath that is someone's god.[6] In effect, "Isabella" is the *ur*-onomatopoeia.

Again, the sonic character of the gasp, especially as it calls up the *ais* of aesthetic perception, figures prominently in both McNally and Rushdie. But let me now gesture toward a new problem: why all this emphasis on "the last"? To some degree this emphasis derives from the association with death I have already noted in the classical sources. From the *Iliad* Onians teased out many instances of how one's *thymos* is gasped at the moment of expiration. In this sense the gasp has an essential tie to the lastness of one's last breath. But the gasp, precisely to the extent that it has an equally essential relation to aesthetic perception, cannot be reduced to the pneumatic event of expiration, for it is also ensnarled in and with the onset of perception, the sucking in of wonder, the effecting of affect. How does the "last" come into play here?

If we are to believe Spinoza, wonder takes hold precisely in bringing thought to an end. As a radical rationalist Spinoza sees wonder as the conceptual name for the bid to deny the concatenation of all thoughts and things. He is thus deeply skeptical of its philosophical value. Wonder is the *punctum* in the *studium* of immanence (to form a masala of Barthes and Deleuze). One is, of course, tempted to wonder whether Spinoza's own thinking of and about the unthought of *admiratio* rescinds his own argument, with or without an appeal to the "third type of knowledge," but regardless, what is clear is that the sucking in, the inspiration of wonder, touches the last by touching the end of a process mediated, if not by thought as such, then by what Foucault insisted on calling *savoir*. Here, I would argue, we stumble upon the sonic channel into Rancière's "distribution *(partage)* of the sensible" but with a twist. The issue is not primarily that of how "a distribution of the sensible therefore establishes at one and the same time something common that is shared and exclusive parts" (Rancière 12), where aesthetics and politics converge in effecting and legislating this distribution. Instead, the gasp speaks to or even from within the rushing passage between the world in which *this* thinking of aesthetics became possible and a world metaleptically cast back before the sound generated by or through this passage as what had to be last in order for "our" distribution of the sensible to become first. Here is the sucking in of wonder, the last gasp— strictly speaking a pleonasm—of what an emergent knowledge renders unrecognizable. It figures in the *ais* of what deserves to be called aesthetics and, if I may be indulged a provocation, this is where Nietzsche was heading when he grasped tragic theater as emerging out of the *spirit (Geist)* of music (see section 16 of *The Birth of Tragedy*), and this despite his later, self-critical, misgivings. But let me be clear: as a sonic event, the gasp might be considered a name for a shift or rupture of enormous scale (geographic, historical, philosophical) that echoes in aesthetic figures of transpiration.

Returning now to the quarrel between Fukuyama and Derrida—and let us recall that in dispute is the disavowed Christological guarantee that the "last man" will, indeed must, be an adherent of neoliberalism—let me briefly draw out how the atmospheric pressure here applied to the concept of the *thymos* might be made to matter there. As noted, Fukuyama's analysis depends on a construal of *thymos* as the desire for recognition, a desire batted between the excesses of either *isothymia* (where recognition is made irrelevant by its immediate ubiquity) and *megalothymia* (where recognition is made impossibly relevant by its perpetual rarity). Acknowledgment of this impasse constitutes the end of history because it clarifies the need to situate the power of recognition outside history in a monotheistic transcendental instance or, as Adam Smith put it in his essay on astronomy, "an invisible hand." Derrida, for his part, is keen to establish the essential convergence between monotheistic neoliberalism and *megalothymia* and yet to do so, as noted, without sustained recourse to the problem of the *thymos* and the puzzles wound up inside it. The spirit of his Marxism blows in the direction of thinking the end of recognition that radical *isothymia* makes possible. Doubtless a, if not *the*, subtext of this dispute has precisely to do with the figure of the subject presumed by Fukuyama's pre-Hegelian account of the *thymos*, and certainly one of the complicating factors introduced into this debate by Onians is the historical problem of the recognition of recognition, that is, of the emergence of a subject of history organized around recognition, in effect, the first man. And, yes, why "man"?

Now, if I have been at pains not to posit Onians's lung-centered subject as an origin, it is because what is more important is simply the point, to invoke the early Foucault, of insisting on a certain discontinuity in the history of the human mind. Although the term has been largely deployed within the field of geology, it strikes me that Derrida and Fukuyama are worrying over how to conceive of the Anthropocene in the history of the subject. What Onians underscores is the fact that within the Anthropocene, different ways of thinking the subject have come and gone. Thus, when Fukuyama starts brandishing the notion of the "last man" (a term he expressly derives from Nietzsche), he is at once attempting to think the endgame of the Anthropocene, its closure, and trying to formulate what, to use McNally's terms, might constitute its "last gasp." But two additional problems arise here. On the one hand his last is merely the latest (in certain languages, German for example, this semantic relation is obvious). He assumes a certain absolute continuity in the constitution of the subject from one end of the Anthropocene to the other. On the other hand he misses in the concept of the desire for recognition not only its locality but the significance of the gasp, of the *thymos*, as a struggle for breath/life/consciousness as an encounter with wonder, as an encounter with and passion for the unrecognizable. I do not mean an unrecognizable that is absolutely new, without precedent, but an unrecognizable that assumes the form of subjectivity that, by virtue of the sucking in of wonder, finds its earlier form unrecognizable. The work of art, the *ais* of aesthetics, is precisely what bespeaks and thus registers this encounter. In certain respects this is what Lyotard was trying to do when answering the question "What is postmodernism?" and invoking the notion of the *post modo* to do it. He was not, all protestations to the contrary notwithstanding, defining the postmodern condition but thinking the concept and experience of aesthetic perception in terms that fell outside the regime of "visualism," in which the image, and especially its philosophical fetishization, covered over the gap left in the wake of wonder.

What this implies is that what Derrida and Fukuyama are quarreling over is not simply the "end of history" but the role or place of the work of art in thinking, indeed in realizing, this end, an end that would encompass, in principle, the end of thinking the work of art in aesthetic terms. If I have impishly displaced the "last man" with the last gasp, it is because sound, the *ais*, figures here more than either Derrida and Fukuyama recognize. And, if this is not evidence of what a more critically humanistic sound studies might give us to think, I haven't the faintest idea of what is. The gasp is not just another sound; it is the sound of a postphonocentric way of grasping the work of wonder. It is certainly a unique possibility for thinking.

5. Silence

> Silence is all of the sound we don't intend. There is no such thing as absolute silence. Therefore silence may very well include loud sounds and more and more in the twentieth century does. The sound of jet planes, of sirens, et etcetera. For instance now, if we heard sounds coming from the house next door, and we weren't saying anything for the moment, we would say that was part of the silence, wouldn't we? . . . But I think electronics now are essential and I think this is what makes rock and roll so interesting.
>
> —JOHN CAGE, quoted in Kostelanetz, *John Cage*

> Still, to talk about language is even worse than to write about silence.
>
> —HEIDEGGER, *Poetry, Language, Thought*

Splicing these two epigraphs together, we pick up the problem that agitates this chapter, namely, how is sound studies, whether endlessly emerging or booming, to write about that faintest of sounds, silence? Although it is clear that Heidegger is keen to distribute the distinction between language and silence across the now familiar distinction between speech and writing, if Cage is right that silence is as ubiquitous as the expanse of the unintended, then can one intend to take up the unintended? All "writing about" (including "automatic" writing) would appear to run directly into this problem. Room for maneuver is produced if one stresses that intent never absolutely governs writing, but do we then assume that silence is written where writing eludes the writer? While plausible, this is both too easy (merely reactive) and too inscrutable (what does *elude* mean). Here, I will urge that entertaining the concept of the audit may be useful. Perhaps the problem of silence uniquely traces the discursive barrier between the potential and the actual in what can be written about sound. As this might suggest, "the sound of silence" (to echo an early Paul Simon lyric), because it reverberates off the constraints of our knowing, leads us back to the problem of contextualization but along a different channel. We come to the unintended through the intentions of others.

Thus, my approach to the sense of silence will pass before (a locution I will later justify) John Cage and Franz Kafka. Although previously linked to Kafka by Deleuze and Guattari (see chapter 1 of their *Kafka: Toward a Minor Literature*), this surprising pairing calls for more than the passing attention they direct to it despite the fact that the problem of how to enter the burrow *(der Bau)* of Kafka's work explicitly concerns them.[1] What justifies this attention is the way the silence that defines the relation between these two monsters of the twentieth century (to my knowledge despite Cage's interest in Kierkegaard, he had nothing to say about Kafka, who was an attentive reader of Kierkegaard), can be heard to address heated questions that bear on the logic of contextualization, especially as it engages the status of music within critical or "new" musicology. At issue is less the matter of "expression" (dear to Deleuze and Guattari) and more what here I will refer to as "inscription," that is, the process through which music— both as a musicological construct and as a performance practice—can be said to "echo" or otherwise belong to its moment, its time and place. Because much of what passes for "new" under the new musicological sun bears precisely on this process—the contention, variously stated, that the extramusical influences the properly musical (and vice versa)—the amplification of the Cage/Kafka encounter promises to agitate these turbulent waters. Moreover, because the legacy of Adorno looms large over these distinctly disciplinary depths, due in part to the way his "negative dialectics" reconceived inscription so as to include the cultural negation of society within this process, his construal of music as both concept and practice deserves to be put in play. And this despite the fact that he appears to have been silent about what will serve as the textual matrix of these thoughts, Kafka's parable "The Silence of the Sirens" ("Das Schweigen der Sirenen").

What is here referred to as amplifying the Cage/Kafka encounter runs directly into numerous obstacles, some of which demand preliminary comment. I will restrict myself to three: influence, music, and method.

With regard to the first, how precisely are we to understand the influence that Kafka had on Cage, given that the latter appears to have been unaware—except in the most general, "culturally literate" sense—of the former? Or, to make things interesting, how might we make sense of the way in which Cage may have influenced Kafka, a writer who died when Cage was twelve years old? Such questions beg one to recognize that influence and inscription share a family resemblance. Specifically, the former might be said to derive from, or otherwise depend upon, the latter in that if one holds that cultural artifacts are decisively inscribed in a temporal sequence, a historical chronology, then the matter of influence becomes a question of knowledge: given that x preceded y, is there evidence that x was known to and thus mattered to y? Sooner or later the question of knowledge comes to be dominated by the authority of priority, what in an earlier theoretical vocabulary was summarily dispatched in the word "origin."

Missed in this temporal reduction of inscription is precisely the conflicted intricacies of space, the various locations—both subjective and geographic—from within which chronology is not simply lived but contested. Revolutions generate new calendars seeking to unfold in their own time, and, as I have argued, this dynamic is better stated in the term *echo*.

Here it seems crucial to invoke the epistemological scandal of what Freud called *Nachträglichkeit* (afterwardness). Perhaps influence occurs unconsciously, not simply in the sense of happening involuntarily but in the sense of happening "belatedly," that is, after the fact, where *fact* refers to a temporal prior that only assumes its priority in the remote wake of its passing—in effect, from another scene. While one might exemplify what happens to influence under such circumstances by appealing to Foucault's concept of discourse, where a "frame of intelligibility" can be said to condition any number of otherwise unrelated enunciative possibilities, more fecund is the recognition of what Althusser called "structural causality" behind Lacan's oft-repeated contention that Freud *anticipated* Saussurean linguistics. Key here is not simply the way "structural causality," as an elaboration and refinement of the Freudian concept of "overdetermination," obviously derives from the contact, at once personal and professional, between Lacan and Althusser; rather, of primary importance is the way Althusser's concept urges one to stay focused on the problem of inscription, a focus perhaps first urged on us by Fredric Jameson in the methodological introduction to *The Political Unconscious*. What "structural causality" definitively complicates is the concept of reflection, that is, the model of spatial inscription that grasps it as an extension of *mimesis*, wherein the molecular structure of realism—the thing and its representation—becomes *mutatis mutandis* the means by which to think the relation between society and culture. Under such constraints even modernism, often set opposite realism (especially by Jameson), becomes a realism, in effect the theoretical centerpiece of Georg Lukács's still resonant reading of Kafka in "Franz Kafka or Thomas Mann" from 1956. Against this, "structural causality" does not simply invert the priority of the thing and its representation, society and culture; rather, it underscores the spatiotemporal intricacy of cause and its many avatars, notably, of course, determination, when used to describe the relation between society and culture, especially when projected onto the orthodox architecture of the *Bau* and the *Uberbau*, base and superstructure. What Althusser understood is that the intricacy of cause at the level of consciousness, that is, at the level of the subjects of history, is what Lacan had properly formulated through the concept of the unconscious-structured-like-a-language. This is precisely why Lacan could write to Althusser while reading "On the

Materialist Dialectic" from the summer of 1963: "Your article—I'm reading it. It fascinates me, and I discover my questions in it" (Althusser, "Correspondence with Jacques Lacan" 151). Not only might this be thought to confirm a fragment of intellectual history, but it bears testimony to the very question of "influence" as it arose within the event of their friendship. "I discover my questions in it."

Again, what stands out here is the complication of causality, not just what in certain circles goes by the term *presentism*, that is, the somewhat muted, even baffled, critique of historicism that insists that we, in the present, can never know the past on its own terms. Rather, at the core of this complication stands something of a "black box," that is, the site of what is at bottom a relation by which, put in historical terms, the first and the last lose their ordinal simplicity. Indeed, relation is the not-so-secret passageway that allows influence and inscription to communicate. In that spirit, *influence* will be deployed here as the means by which to entertain the notion that Kafka thought Cage's silence for him but only once Cage had, in effect, returned the gesture. By referring to the silence that defines the relation between these two men, I hope both to say something within and about silence while rendering immediately pertinent the procedure, undertaken here, of their pairing.

Music. Perhaps the most obvious place to turn for Kafka's final word about music is "Josephine the Singer, or the Mouse Folk" ("Josephine die Sängerin oder das Volk der Mäuse"), a tale recently bent by Mladen Dolar to the task of salvaging the postdeconstructive voice. As its title signals immediately, through the ambiguously conjunctive *or*, the tale relentlessly complicates what is to be understood by singing. Is it really piping (Pfeifen)? Whistling? A relation between a performer and her audience? In what is certainly the most sustained consideration of the strictly musical implications of this tale, the chapter "Kafka and Silence" from *Music in the Works of Broch, Mann, and Kafka*, John Hargraves is quick to point precisely to this difficulty as it is contained in the term *Pfeifen* (piping/whistling), which is strictly antithetical in the Freudian sense; that is, it can mean both performing and booing. Under these circumstances the question of what precisely counts as music is likewise thrown into radical doubt, not in the sense of whether it can be made the object of a judgment of taste but in the sense of whether we can formulate the frame of intelligibility within which its ontological character can be specified. Kafka's tale seems preoccupied with achieving precisely this effect. Responding to a biographical impulse, Hargraves explores this difficulty in the wake of the well-known diary entries in which Kafka proclaims, at one and the same time, his "unmusicality" and his belief that music can only be understood by the "unmusical," proposing that music for Kafka thus becomes a metaphor for a "latent metaphysical force at work behind the foreground of human existence" (Hargraves 162). This claim is what motivates Hargraves's titular appeal to silence, an appeal that, in the end, he does very little with except to provide musical expression with a rather familiar depth, one whose precise contours are defined by no fewer than four disciplines: philosophy (metaphysical force), linguistics (metaphor), art history (foreground), and psychoanalysis (latency). All the same, Hargraves succeeds in attuning our ears to the problem of the "unmusical" in Kafka, urging us to recognize that music is precisely at stake when it does not otherwise appear to be in question. Thus, instead of bemoaning the fact that, compared to Broch and Mann, Kafka offers "infrequent instances of examples of music" (Hargraves 162), one needs to craft a reading of Kafka that responds to the call of the unmusical, to the resonant deficiency of music.

Method. In his much-read review of Max Brod's study of Kafka, Walter Benjamin detailed, with a cruel precision honed by desperation, the costly paradoxes of Brod's reading, perhaps most memorably accusing him of displaying in his text "a fundamental contradiction between the author's thesis and his attitude" (Benjamin, "Review" 317). Here, as Réda Bensmaïa has argued, Benjamin berates Brod for an error we also risk, namely that of, as Benjamin had earlier put it, "missing the point of Kafka's works" (Benjamin, "Franz Kafka" 806). This error is not simply a misreading but a betrayal. After establishing that Brod's misinterpretation is animated by a variant of Pietism, Benjamin insists that the pious misinterpretation is one that either systematically avoids the irksome distractions of psychoanalysis and dialectical theology or succumbs to them without resistance. Alas, the promise held out by such an observation—that of properly engaging psychoanalysis and dialectical theology and thus getting Kafka right—is not fulfilled in Benjamin's own commemorative essay on Kafka, an outcome summarized and distilled in Adorno's bitter methodological precaution: "Each sentence says, 'interpret me,' and none will permit it" (Adorno, *Prisms* 246). And although Adorno in his "Notes on Kafka" goes to some length to establish the startling solidarity between Kafka and Freud (both recognize the ego as a "mere organizational principle" [251]), his doubts regarding the hermeneutics of dialectical theology are unequivocally stated. Through such a method, and here Adorno offers his assessment of the failure of his friend's essay, Benjamin succumbs to myth, even if knowingly. While this might suggest that Adorno's reading lands comfortably on the side of psychoanalysis, it does not. Aware that it is precisely

Kafka's "literalness" that pushes him out ahead of Freud, Adorno urges that Kafka be read as an allegorist (here reviving one of Benjamin's signature constructs), not of the sort to be found in Goethe but rather as one who recognizes that the literal and the figural are, as it were, worlds apart. In this Adorno prepares to align himself with the very "textualism" now widely held to have superseded him.

Does this bring one to a true *aporia* in methodological reflection on the challenges posed by Kafka's texts? Can we truly navigate the channel between the Scylla (who strikes from above) of theology (whether dialectical or not) and the Charybdis (who sucks from below) of psychoanalysis, especially without benefit of Circe's fateful counsel? Adorno's recasting of this channel as the space of secular allegory contains a suggestive codicil. For him, Kafka's relation to Freud is realized not only in his radicalization, his literalization of the critique of the ego, but also, and more importantly, in their shared struggle to snatch "psychoanalysis from the grasp of psychology" (*Prisms* 251). Precisely because Adorno associates this gesture with the Kafkaesque impulse to push beyond metaphor to flesh, in effect, to reaffirm the so-called seduction theory, it would appear that the space of secular allegory, that of letter and spirit, is understood to be active within and along the disciplinary "zone" (as Adorno names it) between psychoanalysis and psychology. Decisive here is the rather unsettling notion that Kafka's texts operate to scramble disciplinary frontiers, that they deploy what Derrida once called the "law of genre," not merely within the field of the literary—are his texts "novels," "stories," or even "meditations"?—but on or against all that the literary fronts upon—including, of course, music. As if buffeted by Poseidon's *ressentiment*, all of this bounces us back to the problem of how to read for the musical or, to up the ante, the musicological in Kafka's texts? The preceding discussion of Hargraves's analysis has already indicated the heading of such a reading but without yet clarifying the matter to which we have returned, that of inscription.

If "The Silence of the Sirens" is the appropriate text on which to focus such a reading, this is in no small part due to the decisive role played by book 12 of the *Odyssey* in Adorno's thinking about Enlightenment culture in general and music in particular. The reading of the Sirens episode occurs in the first chapter of *Dialectic of Enlightenment*, setting the stage for the more extended treatment of Homer's poem in chapter 2, a treatment wherein "enchantment" (Verzauberung) emerges as the term shared by and thus (con)fusing myth and enlightenment. Forgive me if I do not rehash this well-known discussion, choosing instead to foreground two elements: the motifs of inscription and music. With regard to the first, recall that Adorno and Horkheimer concentrate our attention on the dialectical interplay between Ulysses and the crew. Each follows one of two escape routes: Ulysses fetters himself in order to open his ears; the crew seals its ears shut in order to work. Taken together, the two escapes map the contradictions of class society wherein domination becomes, both within and between subjects, the precondition for aesthetic experience, the lived encounter with the sonic beauty of the Sirens' song. As Adorno and Horkheimer are keen to stress, the point is not that one class has access to the beautiful while the other does not but that both classes engage aesthetic enjoyment as a compensation for the constraints imposed on them by the social order they inhabit. The nature and scale of these constraints are certainly different—although Adorno and Horkheimer have been charged with abandoning "class analysis" (see the "Afterword" to the Jephcott translation)—but key is the proposition that the dialectical tension between art and society arises from yet transcends the social division of class. Thus, art bears the inscription of the social order in its essentially compromised isolation from it, an account of inscription that takes reflection theory to its very limit in proposing that art reflects society in refusing to reflect it. How one thinks "cause" here is obviously a vexed issue and stands at the heart of what Adorno sought to articulate as a "negative" dialectic.

The Homeric episode centers on song and in that sense would appear to sound the motif of music blatantly. Clearly though, the ease with which Adorno and Horkheimer pass from a discussion of singing to art in general suggests that music is the means by which to think the modern incarnation of the contradiction between art and society in general. Richard Leppert, across the pages of *Essays on Music,* has made it difficult, if not impossible, to ignore such a claim. Be that as it may, the specifically musical character of the episode, when conceived in the broad framework of aesthetics, effectively leaps out in Adorno's words, written half a decade before the exilic collaboration with Horkheimer: "Complaints about the decline of musical taste begin only a little later than mankind's twofold discovery, on the threshold of historical time, that music represents at once the immediate manifestation of impulse and the locus of its taming" (Leppert 288). This, the opening sentence of Adorno's blistering reply to Benjamin's "The Work of Art in the Age of Its Technological Reproducibility," segues within the space of a few pages to book 3 of the *Republic,* where Socrates recommends banning soft and excessively sorrowful musical modes from his state, a gesture suggesting that "the threshold of historical time" is precisely the abyss thought by Adorno and Horkheimer to conjoin the mythic past and the enlightened future. Moreover, the dialectical interplay between the manifestation and taming of impulse is what the two men find, in effect, allegorized in the Sirens episode. In this sense the episode is centrally about music and its fate. But this should make us all the more attentive to the locus of silence in the episode. It resides in the experience of the crew, an experience found at the opposite end of the apian chain from the "honey sweet" voice of the Sirens, that is, in the "sweet wax of honey" shutting the holes in their heads to this voice. Although the point escapes the authors of *Dialectic*, it would appear that Homer seeks here, at the very core of a telling on/off binary (open/close, hear/not hear, succumb/survive, etc.), to locate the dialectical interplay of beauty and domination but now staged as the relation between humans and nonhuman animals. No wonder the bees have abandoned us. Silence then, to use a term put in play by Adorno and Horkheimer, is "entwined" with music, not sound, but music as the locus of the manifestation and taming, the domesticating, of impulse, a taming here understood in the Nietzschean sense of the "breeding" fundamental to the very production of the human animal itself. But how precisely is one to think the "entwinement" of music and silence? Is this a matter of appreciating, at the level of musical notation, the function of the rest or, at the level of jazz performance, the function of "sitting out?" Is silence simply a matter of not playing?

The disciplinary reflections with which my preliminary remarks concluded open onto other problems. Is entwinement, perhaps, another avatar of the "zone" between psychoanalysis and psychology, or between philosophy and nonphilosophy, say musicology? Is silence a name for and thus a means by which to think what acts within this zone without succumbing to its topographic protocols? By linking silence and the unintentional, Cage points us precisely in this direction, for intention might well be read as the "instinct for knowledge" (as Freud would put it) of a discipline. And it is surely not by accident that the thinker of disciplinary reason, Michel Foucault, comments in *The Hermeneutics of the Subject* lectures on the Sirens episode in the *Odyssey*, zeroing in on the acutely pedagogical significance of outmaneuvering the passivity of listening (335). In any case, a version of this disciplinary puzzle is one of the many disturbing challenges put before us by Kafka's parable "The Silence of the Sirens." Pending whatever transformation of the Brod-organized Kafka canon results from combing the remains found in the late Esther Hoffe's apartment, "Silence" is preceded in volume 5 of *Gesammelte Schriften* by what would qualify as an "allegory of reading." Literally two entries before appears "Von den Gleichnissen" (On parables), in which Kafka, certainly in Brod's mind, provides something like a key for the sketches, aphorisms, and parables that surround it. Adorno cites, in support of his appeal to the enabling concept of allegory, Benjamin's discussion of parable in "Franz Kafka," reminding us that, like Scylla and Charybdis, this metacritical mouthful stands like an ordeal, a test, on the way into one's reading of Kafka.[2] Although the closing line, quoting the first of two interlocutors, "Nein, in Wirklichkeit; im Gleichnis hast du verloren" (no in reality, in parable you have lost) (Kafka 95), would appear to support Adorno's championing of "literalness" (parsing *Wirklichkeit* as actuality or reality), the more striking feature of the parable is the way it revisits the philosopheme, deployed repeatedly within the West from Plato to Heidegger, of "uselessness." Consider, for example, the way the parable on parables takes up the theme of "use": "Viele beklagen sich, dass die Worte der Weisen immer wieder nur Gleichnisse seien aber unverwendbar im täglichen Leben, und nur dieses allein haben wir" (Many complain that the words of the wise are always merely parables and of no use in daily life, and this is the only life we have) (Kafka 95). Kafka's insistence that daily life is the only one we have later effects a collapse between the unusable—the transcendental hallmark of philosophy—and parables as such. Not only do philosophy and parables share the quality of lacking use, but Kafka's repudiation of an actuality outside or above daily life suggests that philosophy uses its expository recourse to parable to blur the ordinary, lived distinction between uselessness and the rule of the wise. The parable stands thus revealed as the alibi of philosophic domination. Kafka, as the consummate gadfly, asserts that if we really wanted to go where philosophers are pointing, to the "sagenhaftes Drüben" (fabulous beyond), we would have already left. Clearly we don't. But what kind of "key" is one that stresses—in a paradoxically philosophical register—its lack of utility? Strictly speaking, it is an inadequate key, as we will see.

Surviving the ordeal of "On Parables," then, one passes to the Sirens, counseled to read the parable—qua parable—not simply as an alibi but as a site wherein a certain disciplinary friction produces the available light, that is, as a site within which the questions "Is there (not what is, but is there) philosophy?" and "Is it about domination?" are insistently posed. As I intimated above, the fact that silence arises here will prove instructive, and the task of figuring out how to "read" the already read will prove essential to receiving these instructions.

"Beweis dessen, das auch unzulängliche, ja kindische Mittel zur Rettung dienen können" (proof that inadequate, even childish methods, can save us) (Kafka 97). Thus begins the parable. It reads oddly as something of a *quod erat demonstrandum*, a conclusion, as if the whole parable is an example of philosophy in reverse, perhaps even capsized. What is demonstrated? That inadequate, even childish methods (kindische Mittel) can save us (Kafka uses here *Rettung*, which has the strong theological resonance of salvation, not simply rescue). His stress on the "unzulängliche" (inadequate) would suggest that here, too, he wishes to agitate the matter of the uselessness of philosophy by pressuring the relation between Ulysses and what Plato in book 6 of the *Republic* called the "true pilot."[3] What brings this into contact with the figure of the child, or the quality of childishness, appears to be the Schillerean notion of *die Naïve* (the naïve, as opposed to the sentimental)— that is, the fact that in heading out to confront the Sirens, Ulysses deploys a variant of the infantile fantasy: if I close my eyes, and I can't see the other, the other can't see me, or, restated in the proper sensory register, if I plug the ears of my crew, then I will be able to hear what I am not to hear, giving no sign—in the extreme case, shipwreck—that I am indeed hearing what I am not to hear. To clarify in what sense this method is "inadequate" requires that the arc of the parable be sketched in.

It comprises six paragraphs followed by an "appendix" (ein Anhang). In the first Kafka reconstructs Ulysses's preparation for the encounter with the Sirens. Taking extreme, even ridiculous (naive?), precaution, he both plugs his ears *and* binds himself to the mast. As if to draw out the vital symmetry between Circe (who is never mentioned) and the Sirens, the paragraph introduces a preemptive aural complication in the encounter through the figure of hearsay. Which is more risky, hearsay or singing? In stressing Ulysses's "unschuldiger Freude über seine Mittelchen" (innocent joy over his little stratagem) (Kafka 97), Kafka places the child of the founding premise/conclusion at the helm. The first paragraph concludes with what will turn out to be an avatar of the lexical and conceptual driver of the parable, the slippery preposition *entgegen* (towards, out to).

The second paragraph, in justifying the title assigned to the parable, opens with perhaps the most brilliant "oh shit" line in the European canon: "Nun haben aber die Sirenen eine noch schrecklichere Waffe als den Gesang, nämlich ihr Schweigen" (Now the Sirens have still a more terrifying weapon than their singing, namely, their silence) (Kafka 97). Immediately, we sense that Ulysses is ill prepared, that, in effect, he has been betrayed by everyone—by Circe, who thus becomes a femme fatale; by all those who might have counseled him; and, of course, by his own naive self-confidence. We also vividly see, and this is an issue agitated to great effect in Blanchot's reading of the episode (about which more later), that this is not Homer's Ulysses.[4] As if to stress this, the paragraph contrasts the respective dangers of singing and silence from the vantage point of a future wherein reports of Ulysses's exploits have become legend. Some may have survived the

Sirens' song, but no one or nothing "irdisches" (earthly) can endure their silence. Crucial here is the insistence throughout on "ihr Schweigen" (their silence), not silence in general (whatever that might be) but the silence of the Sirens, that is, the silence that takes the place of a singing too beautiful to endure.

The third paragraph presents the scenario of the failed encounter. It unfolds as if the Sirens intended to sing but don't. Their silence comes not as the decisive well-aimed blow but mysteriously. Do they recognize and respond to his tactic of sensory deprivation (with ears plugged he could hear neither their silence nor their song), or does his "Anblick der Glückseligkeit" (look of bliss) so stun them that they forget to sing? Either way, the third paragraph casts silence as reactive, stripped of unambiguous tactical intentions.

The fourth paragraph extends the "preemptive complication" of the first down into the sonic enigma of silence itself. "Odysseus aber, um es so auszudrücken, hörte ihr Schweigen nicht, er glaubte, sie sängen, und nur er sei behütet, es zu hören" (But Ulysses, if it can be so expressed, did not hear their silence, he believed they were singing and only he did not hear them) (Kafka 97–98). Crucial here is the entwining of the perception of a singing that *is* silence, an event so singular as to cast doubt on its communicability, and the metalinguistic gesture of "if it can be so expressed," where the "use" (or "uselessness") of parabolic expression arises as the means by which to point at the limits not simply of a certain code (in this case German) but of a frame of intelligibility within which hearing falls unthinkably *between* "das Schweigen" and "den Arien," the arias echoing in the mere gestures of singing. As if to sear this predicament into an image, the paragraph concludes with Ulysses sailing out of range of the Sirens, his eyes fixed on a distance set opposite their singing faces (the implication being that the Sirens were lip-synching to a tape that malfunctioned), a distance nearer to the danger they represented than he could grasp.

The fifth paragraph exploits the structure of what Lacan would call extimacy to effect a pivot, a conceptual whirlpool. Now it is Ulysses who plays the siren. He does not, of course, sing. Instead he looks resolutely ahead. The Sirens, who have already forgotten to sing, now forget everything and seek only to fall within his gaze, Ulysses's Gaze (*pace* Theo Angelopoulos). They seek what Kafka calls his "Abglanz," the light reflecting from his two great eyes. Crucial here is the sensory *agon* of the eyes and the ears, especially as it might herald an encounter between two frames of intelligibility.

The sixth paragraph is only two sentences. In it Kafka propounds a theory of consciousness, suggesting that had the Sirens possessed consciousness, the pivot wherein they fell within the gaze of the other would have destroyed them. The temptation of a psychoanalytic reading, indeed a Lacanian one at that, is nearly irresistible. To succumb to it, however, is not only to restore the seductive (the *verführerisch,* the misleading) invulnerability of the Sirens in hermeneutic guise, but it is to fill in the very figure of the channel between dialectical theology and psychoanalysis that I am struggling to chart. As if to remind us of this, the second sentence is utterly perfunctory, Adorno would say, "literal": "So aber blieben sie, nur Odysseus ist ihnen entgangen" (So they remained as they had been, all that happened is that Ulysses escaped them) (Kafka 98). Thus, read philologically, the paragraphs prior to the appendix tack from *entgegen* to *entgangen* (escaped), from set out to meet to elude, toward and away.

The appendix moves, as if to gut everything, to restore the *metis* of Ulysses by suggesting that even his blissful face was nothing but a knowing way, a bluff. He thus reduces the gods to poker players with weak hands. At the same time, Kafka here restates the "uselessness" of the parable, noting, in the tone of an afterthought, that "Es wird übrigens noch ein Anhang hierzu überliefert" (An appendix to the foregoing has also been handed down) (Kafka 98). In effect, he is saying "Oh, and by the way, we also already know that it might have been otherwise." This, too, is part of the myth. As if to underscore the way this laces and relaces back through all that has preceded, the last word of the paragraph and of the parable is *entgegengehalten,* a term used to characterize the cunning use of Ulysses's shield to counter or oppose the Sirens and the gods but one that in the context of the parable (functioning if not as a rhyme-word then certainly as a thought-word) appears almost anagrammatic, as a collection of letters in which *entgegen* and *entgangen* are, as it were, *gehalten* or contained, caged.

If we right the parable, the Q.E.D. would follow here. Thus, in the foregoing sequence of major and minor premises we learn that inadequate or childish techniques can save us; that Ulysses saved himself; therefore, Ulysses probably used childish techniques. But what precisely were they? In the course of the six paragraphs and appendix these techniques flicker by as if repeating the enigmatic exchange that concludes, "Von den Gleichnissen": parables can make parables of those who use them; isn't that a parable? you're right; yes, but only in parable; no, in reality you are right, in parable you are wrong. A version of the Cretan's paradox. The Kafkan/ Homeric paradox might be phrased: a child would prepare for battle only to misjudge the adversary; realizing this, the adversary would assume this to be a bluff and avoid drawing attention to the misjudgment, hoping to exploit it later; baffled, the child would ignore and thereby eliminate the tactical difference between judgment and misjudgment (the weapons of song and silence) and simply proceed with belligerent confidence; likewise baffled, the adversary would misjudge the sign of confidence as a presentiment of victory and capitulate to the invincible child; after coming to terms, the child reveals itself to be the master of bluffing, capable, in effect, of making total adequacy look and sound exactly like utter inadequacy. Stated thus, the parable scuttles itself, showing that if inadequacy and adequacy are indistinguishable, then inadequate means can indeed save us; in fact, we are always already saved. No sweat.[5]

Crucial here is the motor of the paradox, that is, the circumstance under which the inadequate and the adequate become the same without thereby being identical. Given the subject matter of the parable, perhaps the decisive presentation of this structure occurs when Ulysses "hears" (his ears are plugged) the silence *as* song. This situation conforms literally to what earlier I referred to as the "entwinement" of silence and music; indeed, I would suggest that the entire parable is designed to pose this problem and to invite speculation about it. This is why Kafka rewords Homer in precisely the way he does, displacing the Homeric locus of silence—namely the crew (there is no mention of them in "The Silence")—thereby resituating the conflict between freedom and necessity *within* the child and therefore between the child and the adversary. Moreover, if I have insisted on the anagrammatic status of the last word, *entgegengehalten*, this is because the language of the parable is bound up in the problem it poses. The going toward, *entgegen*, and the going past, *entgangen*, are subsumed within the going nowhere, the counter or parry of the shield, *entgegengehalten*. This is not an evocation of fixity but of a disquieting negativity, of a constitutive instability, as if the appendix, in metabolizing the coming and the going, hopes to draw attention to the nonrelation at the heart of relation, at the core of encounter. This would appear to be a radicalization of the Lacanian dictum—there is no sexual relation—one that in emphasizing the several and repeated ways that Ulysses and the Sirens, the child and the adversary, anticipate and misread one another critiques relation in general. Indeed, this critique of relation finds expression in the language of the parable, a circumstance perhaps predicted in the very name, *Sirens*, which derives from the Greek *seira*, or cord, binding, at once evoking the grip of their song, the physics of enthrallment, but at the same time evoking the strategy deployed by Ulysses to resist their power. Whether speaking of binding or entwinement, the parable frets beatifically over the relation that holds through release.

Marcel Detienne and Jean-Pierre Vernant, in *Cunning Intelligence*, add an important wrinkle here by reminding us that precisely to the extent that *metis,* the virtue or skill Ulysses was thought to embody, involved being able to slip through the fingers, the grasp, of one's adversary by turning its strength against it (Detienne and Vernant 21), not only does *metis* speak directly to the relation, the grasp that cannot hold, but it places a contest over types of knowledge at the core of Ulysses's encounter with the Sirens. Of course, this is what Adorno and Horkheimer seek to emphasize in trying to situate the origin of philosophy in the abysmal shift from myth to enlightenment. But what Detienne and Vernant stress is that the contest over knowledge is itself subject to the wiles of *metis* and that this must be kept in mind when thinking about Kafka's attention to the silent song. Again, what is accented in the parable is the silence of the Sirens, that is, *their* silence, as if what is crucial is precisely the contest of knowledges, the expectations simultaneously solicited and refused. Precisely because the Sirens' song is "known" to be fatal, Ulysses prepares for it. In attempting to outfox the fox, or, as Kafka posits, in being stunned by the inadequate preparation of the foxiest fox, the Sirens counter with an even more lethal weapon, one thought to fall outside the frame of intelligibility within which Ulysses's opening gambit was planned. And so on. The point is that the entwinement of silence and song puts in play divisions of knowledge that can be grasped (indeed?) as predisciplinary articulations of disciplinary reason, as if the parable, through its fraught relation to philosophy, insists that such issues demand the reader's attention.

Might one then consider that the parable, with all that we have come now to associate with it, answers to the question: how can/should we write about silence or even sound? Especially promising, it would seem, is the fact that true to the humanistic spirit of finding problems, the parable enables us to engage the problem of sound without factoring out the problematic character of the problem. As its name might suggest, the parable traces an arc around the problem it thereby continuously refinds. In other words the "uselessness" of parable, instead of being understood as its complicity with the transcendental remoteness of philosophy, might be read as evidence of its ability to discover without dispelling provocations for thought. The parable does not "solve" the paradox of a sound that is a silence. It writes so as to preserve the problem that attracts us to silence, even as it obliges us to approach it differently, to know it otherwise. As Barthes once said about writing about myths: one proceeds neither cynically nor in the mode of demystification, but dynamically (Barthes, *Mythologies* 128). Matters only become more interesting when, in heeding such counsel, one attempts to write in accord with what imposes itself on our attention in listening to the relation between a literary and a musical silence.

The problem—what is silence, and how would we know?—is one John Cage stumbled on in the early 1950s. This is how he tells it:

> There is always something to see, something to hear. In fact, try as we
> may to make a silence, we cannot. For certain engineering purposes, it is
> desirable to have as silent a situation as possible. Such a room is called
> an anechoic chamber, its six walls made of special material, a room
> without echoes. I entered one at Harvard University several years ago
> and heard two sounds, one high and one low. When I described them to
> the engineer in charge, he informed me that the high one was my
> nervous system in operation, the low one my blood in circulation. Until
> I die there will be sounds. And they will continue following my death.
> One need not fear about the future of music. (Cage 8)

There is some doubt about whether the reported event—regarded by many as the founding articulation of Cage's aesthetic theory—ever took place. According to Cage's biographer, David Revill, there were two anechoic chambers at Harvard, neither of which clearly matches Cage's description. If one counts the hyperechoic chamber that Douglas Kahn notes was also at Harvard, then precisely where this encounter between Cage and silence took place is itself concealed in a black box. But this is as it should be. Cage sets out on a quest for silence, seeking reassurance that experimental music has a future. Instead of encountering silence, he encounters two sounds, one of which, given the implausibility of hearing one's nervous system, may have been the ringing in his own ears. Regardless, in those two pitches what he encounters, what he hears, is the limit of his assumptions (his musicological or even acoustical knowledge) about the nature of silence, an encounter that obliges him to rethink both those assumptions and the entwinement of silence and sound. The issue here is less about the impossibility of silence faced with the embodiment of human listening than it is about the way this missed encounter poses questions about the categories—including, lest it pass unremarked, the category of the human subject—within which its possibility makes sense. Strikingly, Cage segues abruptly from the sounds happening on either side of his death to the "future of music." While this is typically understood to have provided listeners, even if metaleptically, with the music for *4′33″* (which Deleuze and Guattari find staged in Kafka's story "Descriptions of a Struggle"), that is, whatever ambient sounds happened while the keyboard of the piano was exposed during the four "movements" of the piece (including the stopwatch), more important is the motif of "intention" sounded in the epigraph of this chapter. When Cage says, as reported by Revill, "Silence is not acoustic. It is a change of mind. A turning around" (Revill 164), he is gesturing directly at the way acoustics, a particular interdisciplinary field of knowledge, gives form to our intentions such that one might go about "making" silence precisely by defeating echoes. "Turning around" here does not presumably mean changing direction or rotating one's head. It means troping; it means changing the way knowledge informs our intentions. It means catching hold of the deafening work of the audit in the field of sonic attention. That Cage was motivated by Robert Rauschenberg's blank canvases, his "mirrors of the air," would strongly suggest that both men understood clearly the challenge they were posing to the frame of intelligibility within which either painting or music had been understood.

It is especially telling that in light of this, as the first of my epigraphs has it, Cage heard sirens in the silent field of the unintended. What this underscores, aside from an intriguing etymological genealogy, is that what Kafka grasped, and Cage takes from him—a relay that took place, as I have noted, in silence—is that silence is less "entwined" with song, or music, than it names, however inadequately, what escapes in or as the nonrelation, the channel, *between* sound and what no longer is even its opposite. This is what Derrida appears to have been driving at when he titled a decisive chapter of *Voice and Phenomenon* "The Voice That Keeps Silent," a text that was always more about philosophical ideology than it was about the faculty of speaking.

Let me then approach the musicological aspect of *Dialectic of Enlightenment* from a different angle. Signposting this approach are two essays of Jean-François Lyotard from the early 1970s—"Adorno as the Devil" (*diavolo* in the original, as if to underscore the Italian cover for his Jewish, Wiesengrund, identity) and "Several Silences"—both pieces that, as the second title suggests plainly, engage the work of John Cage. Both were written during the period of Lyotard's career when he, like so many others, was concerned to weigh in on the encounter between Marx and Freud. *Libidinal Economy*, where, in his chapter on "the tensor" he provides his own reading of Ulysses, dates from this period. Unlike many of his compatriots concerned with this encounter, however, Lyotard was distinctive in paying keen attention to its German articulation. It thus comes as no surprise that as he moved to articulate its aesthetic implications, he found himself face-to-face with Adorno. In "Adorno as the Devil" and "Several Silences" this face-off occurs in and around the musicological inflection of Adorno's aesthetic theory. The argument unfolds a bit differently in each case, and since the evaluation of Cage's significance changes accordingly, my comments will proceed *in seriatum*.

"Adorno as the Devil" asks to be read as a theoretical and political challenge to the evaluative distinction drawn by Adorno between Stravinsky and Schönberg in *Philosophy of New Music*. Lyotard's point is not to reverse this evaluation—to delineate what might be either salvaged or championed in Stravinsky's "poetics of music"—but to challenge the musicological implications of the terms deployed to advance it. At issue, simply put, is the critical force of *Kritische Theorie* (the project, not the genre), a matter, given the enormous import Adorno now has for the "new musicology," of considerable note. As the title implies, Lyotard seeks to establish the ultimately theological character of Adorno's position, showing that his investment in the redemptive power of the negative obliges Adorno not to ally himself with the devil (Lyotard regards this as the failure of Mann's presentation of the matter in *Doktor Faustus*) but to fulfill the satanic function in a struggle over meaning that is fundamentally Judeo-Christian in character. Sounding a theme then making its rounds on the Parisian scene, Lyotard worries over the capacity of philosophy to think negativity outside the box of the sociodiscursive conditions of philosophy, including—perhaps especially including—a philosophy impatient with merely interpreting the world as opposed to changing it. Crucial here is *Kritische Theorie*'s account of the subject, an account hampered by an all-too-reasoned assessment of the significance of Freud. Stated within the concerns of *Philosophy of New Music*, this now somewhat dated line of criticism takes the form of showing that Schönberg's dodecaphonic serialism is, at best, the sonic articulation of the satanic function and thus precisely the spectral lure for Adorno's musicology—Schönberg as Siren.

Cage becomes urgently relevant because through him Lyotard shows what Adorno misses by posing the problem in terms of an opposition between Stravinsky and Schönberg and the social tendencies their compositions are said to "represent." The issue is not whose music is more or less progressive but what is understood by *music* and who controls this? Lyotard is aware that Adorno recognizes that progressivism cannot be adjudicated without *some* account of musical substance, but for Lyotard Cage represents a more fecund probing of the theoretical and political matters at stake. Because of its obvious connection with the unintentional, and therefore a distinctly post-Freudian subject, Lyotard places strong emphasis on Cage's embrace of the aleatory, even going so far as to organize the form of his own exposition as if dictated by procedures derived from the *I Ching*—not a parable but something like it. This gesture underscores what Lyotard perceives as the practical continuities between composing the new music and theorizing within audible range of music so composed. While this heightens attention to the musicological problematic, Lyotard seems content to do little more with Cage than to posit his work as nondiabolical, as post-Judeo-Christian. Unequivocally he sides with

Cage, who famously—to cite the title of his interviews with French musicologist Daniel Charles—declared himself to be "for the birds" and against himself, that is, their cages.

Doubtless this terseness is due to the fact that the year before, in "Several Silences," Lyotard had developed more thoroughly, but also more critically, what Cage brought to musicological and philosophical reflection on the nature of music. In turning explicitly to the question of silence, Lyotard wrote:

> When Cage says: there is no silence, he says: no Other holds dominion over sound, there is no God, no Signifier as principle of unification of composition. There is no filtering, no set blank spaces, no exclusions: neither is there a work anymore, no more limits #1 [the element or quality deemed to be musical] to determine musicality as a region. We make music all the time, "no sooner finish one than begin making another just as people keep on washing dishes, brushing their teeth, getting sleepy and so on: noise, noise, noise. The wisest thing to do is to open one's ears immediately and hear a sound before one's thinking has a chance to turn [it] into something logical, abstract, or symbolical." (Lyotard, *Driftworks* 108)

Here Lyotard's impatience with the Frankfurt School's concept of the subject complicates his own embrace of psychoanalysis by pointedly challenging the work of *L'École freudienne* and Lacan's concepts of the Other and the Signifier in particular. Striking, though, is his alignment of Cage's concept of the silence that isn't one, with the absence of the Other, here conceived under the broad heading of the undisclosed location of the signifier, followed by a citation in which Cage stresses the urgency of listening for sounds *before* they are recognized, that is, before they come to belong to a frame of intelligibility in which they signify. As he says elsewhere in the essay, "A sound *(son)* is a noise *(bruit)* that is bound *(lié)*" (92).[6] While one might wish to insist on a distinction between the symbolical and the symbolic, what leaps out in Lyotard's formulation is the relation between the Other and the discourse within which sounds assume their musical character. Silence points deliberately at the before or the between of discourses charged with monitoring what Cage here calls "noise, noise, noise," and thus also at the limits of the psychoanalytical Other. In drawing attention to this aspect of Cage's thought, Lyotard spares us from the "new age" Cage, that is, the riddling sage content simply to still the mind through Zen-like paradoxes.

Nor, however, is Cage spared from criticism. Specifically, Lyotard picks up on Cage's concept of the body in the latter's account of the anechoic chamber, arguing that what he and Adorno share is a phenomenological notion of the body, "a body that composes." He goes on to argue that this body filters and binds, drawing attention, if only terminologically, to the fact that the body matters not in and of itself but from within a field of practices that includes a set of lived assumptions about who or what makes sounds. In this sense music generates, as a horizon of sense, the body that enjoys sending and receiving it. Against this, Lyotard appears to invoke something like "true" silence, that is, what Cage filtered out of his anechoic experience, namely, the death drive. Invoking the authority of Freud, he declares that "the death drive is never heard, it is silent" (91). But as if to parry immediately a misreading, Lyotard links the silence of the death drive with both the Paris Commune of 1871 and the student uprising of May 1968, making it obvious that two exceedingly noisy events—events, as he says, "we did not hear coming" (91; translation modified)—took place in, or perhaps as, the silence of the death drive. Again, this field of associations shifts death away from mortality toward limit, or closure; away, in effect, from death to drive although not as modeled on the compulsion to repeat but on something like the compulsion to repeat differently, to break down.

Running with the point, Lyotard moves to justify his title, "Several Silences," by proliferating silences. In this he reinforces the import attached by Kafka to "their [the Sirens'] silence." Two of the most resonant are the silence of analysis (which he subdivides into the silence of the imaginary, the silence of the symbolic, and the silence of the analyst) and the silence of *Kapital* (a term left in German presumably to conflate Marx's text and its object). Ostensibly developed to radicalize Cage—wouldn't there be as many silences as there are frames of intelligibility, and in not seeing this, aren't you, all protestations to the contrary notwithstanding, just being a musician?—this series of silences blatantly underscores the question of limit, of break, of closure, drawing direct attention to the deployment of silence as a way to think, a way to conceptualize what passes through the channel between, say, dialectical theology and psychoanalysis, or between philosophy and musicology, or, for that matter, between the singing the Sirens withheld and the silence Ulysses took for the singing to which he did not succumb.

Blanchot in "Ars Nova," from *The Infinite Conversation*, pursues a similar line, although his touchstone is not that of silence but of the work and the space of its absence (a motif, as has been noted, put to work differently in Foucault's later treatment of madness as "the absence of work"). Despite this, what emerges unmistakably in the alignment of Blanchot and Lyotard is the question posed to Adorno as to whether he has risen to the actual challenge posed to musicology by the new music. Although Blanchot does not link "Ars Nova" to "The Song of the Sirens" section of his *The Book to Come,* a not so hidden, or hidden in plain sight, passageway allows the essays to correspond. In both texts Blanchot places the accent on the absence of the work, although in his reading of the episode from Homer he insists "that enigmatic song is powerful because of its defect" (*Book to Come* 5). As if extending his hand through this passageway toward us, Blanchot invites us to see that it is precisely the concept of music generated in Adorno and Horkheimer's reading of Homer that supports his philosophy of the new music, in short, the championing of Schönberg, with whom, in the interest of full disclosure, Cage briefly studied. Perhaps because Blanchot's accents fall where they do, Cage does not come up. But the defect in the Sirens' song, a defect he formulates with a knowing glance at Kafka's parable—"The Sirens, it seems, they did indeed sing, but in an unfulfilling way" (*Book to Come* 3)—touches on their silence in a manner that Lyotard helps us to hear as "Cagey," that is, as a deft and cunning move against a certain musicological construal of the musical work. Is this not what Blanchot is gesturing toward in the opening of "Encountering the Imaginary," when he characterizes the island of the Sirens as the place where music "had itself disappeared more completely than in any other place in the world" (*Book to Come* 3)?

In silence, then, something has been passed between Kafka and Cage. If music is indeed best grasped (a decisively polyvalent verb in this context) by the unmusical, by one approaching music from the outside, and if this slippery grasp, this seizure of the nonrelation at the heart of relation, is what is expressed in the elusive silence taken for song in "The Silence," then what has been thought there, precisely to the extent that it rhymes conceptually with what Cage understands by the domain of the unintended, anticipates the deployment of silence in Cage's aesthetic theory. "The Silence" is Kafka's Cage, its bottled message of musicological critique, unfolding (think here of Benjamin's contrast between the flower bud and the paper boat in "Franz Kafka") on the deserted shore of a different discourse, one set adrift in the recesses of an anechoic chamber some twenty years later. Perhaps it is in this sense, if not specifically with regard to this example, that Benjamin, in his radio lecture "Beim Bau der Chinesischen Mauer," not only characterizes Kafka as "prophetic" but later reads "The Silence" as prophesy, as an utterance possessed by what it cannot yet imagine, a "token of escape" (Benjamin, "Franz Kafka" 799).

But what, then, of inscription? At issue here is how one contextualizes music, and it is plain that Adorno's extraordinary contribution to this intellectual task is his ability to think the specificity of music—what Lyotard calls the apparatus, "le dispositif," that is music (*Driftworks* 94)—while not simply connecting it to social history but grounding its new incarnation in capitalist modernity. Crucial here is the logic of negative dialectics, wherein, through the motif of negativity—and expressly the residue that survives the negation of negation—an irreducible structural instability is placed at the contact point between the apparatus of music and the social process. In his own pass over these troubled waters Lyotard is content to make the following observation:

> To produce a surface as appearance is to produce surface as a site of inscription. But imagine that the Renaissance had not invented or re-invented appearance in painting, music, architecture, politics: that there would be no general theatricalization. Then there would have been no surface as a site of inscription, even the category of inscription would be impossible. . . . One has to think the primary processes on this side of generalized theatricalization and inscription, as connections and transformation of either influx or flux, without ever being able to decide what is active or passive in the connection. Thus, without inscriptibility and without surface. (*Driftworks* 98; translation modified)

Aside from reminding us that perhaps we are asking the wrong question, that is, a question that in its very language has conceded the matter prematurely, what does this really tell us about the problem of situating art in its social or historical context? It tells us that the effort to do so has a history. It tells us that the category of inscription belongs to this history. And it tells us that appearance construed as the surface of a depth, in effect, "theatricalization," is the template put in circulation by this history. That the alternative—modeled on Freud's account of the primary processes, where the agency of connectivity is undecidable—hardly clarifies things only underscores the paradoxical and ultimately feckless character of Lyotard's formulation. Doesn't the claim that the category of inscription belongs to history beg the question: what does "belong" mean in such a sentence? Or, formulated even less charitably, given that Lyotard is writing in the wake of the Renaissance, in what sense doesn't the category of the "primary processes" belong to this same history? It merely locates reality in a depth that is pure surface. Put differently, while Lyotard's quarrel with Adorno over the political meaning of Schönberg is compelling on its own terms, the implications of this quarrel for the question of inscription are at best unclear.

But perhaps here the silence that falls between Cage and Kafka is instructive. If it makes sense to deploy the notion of the "black box" as a way to approach this silence, this is because the "black box," in framing the point of contact at the core of inscription, simultaneously raises the problem of causation. What happens to the influx such that a certain flux results? For

Adorno, and here his Marxism trumps his Hegelianism, society must cause art to repudiate it. Schönberg embodies a progressive politics because his music is determined to hate tradition properly, not just thematically but down to the most fundamental musical parameters. But it is socially determined to do this. As Lucien Goldmann might say—and he and Adorno famously quarreled (see the former's "To Describe, Understand, Explain")—Schönberg's consciousness was formed within the "worldview" organized by the situation of a nonorganic intellectual caught up within the forward stumbling of late modernity. In fact, however, rare is Adorno's recourse to a formulation like, "In the eyes of the Viennese composer, coming from a parochial background, the norms of a closed, semi-feudal society seemed the will of God" (Adorno, *Prisms* 151) from his late essay on Schönberg. More typical is his recourse to precisely what Engels, in his remarkable 1893 letter to Franz Mehring, concedes as having been neglected in his and Marx's account of ideology, namely, "the formal side, the ways and means" (Baxandall and Morawski 99) by which ideological contents come about. In Schönberg's case, where, as Adorno insists, content consistently risked succumbing to procedure, such an emphasis might seem so immanently derived as to have been foretold. Moreover, one might legitimately argue that Max Weber, in "The Rational and Social Foundations of Music," specifically through the concept of "rationalization," had already secured a rich sociological, and to that extent "causal," account of musical form, its ways and its means. So is Adorno's centrality within critical musicology due simply to the fact that he composed string quartets and that he wrote prolifically and beautifully on music? This, though necessary, is hardly sufficient.

Even if we concede the legitimacy of critiques such as those of Lyotard or Blanchot, we do run up against, perhaps even aground upon, the remainders, the as yet unassimilated aspects of Adorno's struggle with inscription. Once one folds reason, and by extension rationalization, into the dialectic of enlightenment, that is, once one situates the terms of one's own analysis within the troubled process they seek to analyze, then the explanatory force of a concept like "determination" (the hold, the grip, of the *Bau* on the *Uberbau*, society on music) is checked, not neutralized but profoundly and intractably challenged. Is Adorno not drawing attention to the theoretical and political opportunity generated here when in the methodological section of the introduction to *Philosophy of New Music* he inveighs against both reducing music to the status of an "exponent of society" and the error of "applying" philosophical concepts to either music or society? While it is clear that neither tendency thinks adequately the inscription of an unsettling negativity, it should also be noted that here Adorno is repeating the motif of wresting psychoanalysis from psychology; that is, he is drawing attention to the fact that the disquiet of negativity is bound up with a conflict within disciplinary reason between, in this case, sociology and philosophy. This points less at the problem of what can be said about music once we recognize it as inscribed within the social process, and more at the fact that coiled up within this problem is the problem of the "knowledges" that stand to be authenticated by prevailing in the struggle to produce the concepts by which one account of social determination versus another might be thought to hold sway. Put differently, what Adorno has come to represent is a properly "nonvulgar" sociology of music, as opposed to a philosopher of Marxism who urges those of us concerned with the latter to recognize that the very nature of Marxism is at stake in making sense of music. Adorno himself had trouble recognizing, much less sustaining, this, failing to see in his dismissal of the "crafty naiveté" of mass culture precisely what Kafka "heard" in the silent song of the Sirens. For in the end what slips through the *mano a mano* of philosophy and sociology is the silence *of the Sirens*, that is, the naming of a held release where a different way of knowing—not the irrational, not unreason, and emphatically not Hegel's "cunning of reason"—works, however absently, its charms. This silence, the one that forms along the disciplinary frontiers that establish yet limit both our intentions and our expectations, is where *metis* is called for. Answering this call means wondering aloud, and with frequency, whether we have the right concepts for thinking everything from influence to determination, whether, in the end, we have missed what Benjamin had the temerity to call "the point." One might say that Bataille was certainly onto something when he observed that Kafka, as if anticipating the tendentious query published by *Action* (a postwar French Communist weekly), "Should Kafka Be Burned?"—weighed in, as it were, in advance by instructing Brod to do precisely that. Doubtless, although no reference is made to "The Silence," this is what leads Bataille to characterize Kafka not simply as childlike but of all writers "the most cunning" (Bataille 85). It is from within Cage's echoless chamber, his "black box" I propose, that we hear how faintly yet forcefully this observation bespeaks Cage's and Kafka's "unmusical" challenge to musicology.[7] For if music sets the high-water mark of the *Uberbau*, then critical musicology must commit itself to the task of reworking if not Marxism per se then the critical practice that engages the social order over which music contemptuously yet vainly soars. This also means that musicology, whether critical or simply new (or perhaps even what Reggie Watts calls "social musicology"), must also engage sound studies on the matter of whether either theoretical initiative knows how to write about its objects—objects, as the silence attended to here, that withdraw into their own strangeness.

6. *Tercer Sonido*

In film, the living fresco of image and sound.
—SOLANAS AND GETINO, "Hacia un tercer cine"

Music has meant a lot to me, both as a distraction and as part of my culture. Everyone in my family is a musician. . . . It is strange that I have not spoken of music in my books.
—SARTRE, *Life/Situations*

I

Having to this point concentrated largely on sounds of which we are "hard of hearing," I turn now to a different dimension of the same problem, namely, the status of sound in sound cinema—not as an "unheard melody," as music was famously characterized first by Keats and then Claudia Gorbman, but sound as a "missed moment" or undertheorized element in a cinematic practice otherwise world-renowned for its principled reflexivity. Sound here vibrates between its adjectival and nominal forms, radiating beyond or through silence and confronting us with an alarming ordinal resonance. In this chapter I will restrict myself to making three points about this practice. First, *tercer cine* ("third cinema," as it is known in the Anglophone world) consistently risked compromising with both imperial and auteurist cinemas by repeating, however differently, their theoretical and political commitments to "visualism." Second, although *tercer cine* was clearly a cinema of the left, it was also always a cinema where Marxist theory was in question. It was, in effect, a theorization of Marxism. And third, the relation between points 1 and 2 is one of contingent necessity. Put differently, sound, and specifically what I am calling "third sound," is a matrix through or around which a certain set of propositions about Marxism can be, indeed should be, posited and examined. These propositions bear on the status of immanence within Marxism, a matter long considered under the heading "Spinoza or Hegel," to invoke the title of Pierre Macherey's 1979 study. For reasons to be adduced, the terms *mediation* and *impersonality* will serve here as my points of entry into the problem of immanence, Marxism, and sound. Again, the problem at issue is not chiefly the sound either of or in *tercer cine* but sound as the thirdness of third cinema.

Thus, before turning directly to the elaboration of these points, an essential set of remarks about "thirdness."[1]

In 1986 the Edinburgh Film Festival convened its activities under the banner "third cinema"; indeed, a well-known anthology edited by Jim Pines and Paul Willemen was formed from a selection of the proceedings. When this volume was later reviewed by Robert Stam (a leading US cinema scholar and vigorous proponent of multiculturalism), it was contrasted favorably with Roy Armes's contemporaneous *Third World Filmmaking and the West*.[2] At issue was not simply the greater attunement of the former to matters of aesthetics but the tendency in the latter to, in effect, nationalize culture by understanding "third" as a strictly geopolitical locator. For Armes, thirdness was articulated with cinema through the world system, an approach that rendered the specificities of the medium if not irrelevant then certainly inessential. Whether one agrees with Stam or not, what floats to the top of his review is the question of what happens to the term *third* as it politically inflects cinema and world. My formulation of *tercer sonido* will not be able to evade this question.

In point of fact, even if I were in a position to rationalize such an evasion, it would be immediately complicated by the fact that "thirdness" has figured insistently in thinking about sound. I am, again, thinking here both of Barthes and Havas's "Listening" from 1976 and Michel Chion's chapter from *Audio-Vision*, "Modes of Listening," two statements that have surfaced repeatedly in this study. Although Chion, whose discussion follows Barthes and Havas by more than a dozen years, makes no reference to the earlier text, it is clear that he has borrowed their expository template, even as he more directly links listening to the cinema. Striking here is how the third mode or type of listening brings otherwise disparate concepts and problems into proximity. For Barthes and Havas, who index listening to particular objects, the third mode of listening is distinctive in taking Lacan's concept (or, strictly speaking, the process it designates) of *significance* (as noted earlier, "signifierness") as its object. This is a listening that attends to one's being heard by another or, as Lacan would insist, from the place of *the* other. Audited. Because they offer no explicit name for it, I am tempted to call it transferential listening. This is not an allusion to Reik's "third ear" per se, because it surpasses the notion of "hovering" attention, but key in both formulations is precisely the status of the third. Chion, however, names the third mode of listening "reduced," by which he means an aural attending to the *event* of listening. Reduced listening does not seek the source or cause of a sound; it listens to how the sound takes place within our listening. If taken together, these analyses situate thirdness in sound at the point where sonic substance folds, as if deploying a spatula, the subjective field into itself. It is not the agent of listening but the agency of sound as it orients its listener, a formulation meant to call up the theoretical vocabulary of "positioning," while accenting the motif of "permeation." Clearly, the construct of a *tercer sonido* must confront the implications of these inflections of thirdness, especially as they bear on the cinema as a medium of sound and image.

Famously, of course, Barthes developed his own reading of the cinematic apparatus under the heading of what he called "the third meaning." But before assessing the relevance of this discussion for my own, it behooves us to entertain some sort of explanation for the remarkable tenacity of thirdness across the topoi of cinema, world, and sound. I will propose that such an explanation is to be found in the Western philosophical tradition, the very one in which Spinoza and Hegel figure as vexed precursors to the Marxism that mattered to the partisans of *tercer cine*.[3] Under the rubric of "thirdness" one might immediately think here of the triadic structure of dialectical reasoning (although Hegel himself generally avoided the thesis, antithesis, synthesis formula) or of Spinoza's three forms of knowledge, the third being intuition or the intellectual love of God. And while this would not be a mistake, it overlooks the decisive "thirdness" of mediation itself, that is, the process by which, to use the language common to both Spinoza and Hegel, substance and subject pass in and out of one another. I will return to the distinctly sonic aspect of this matter, but here I stress only that mediation is precisely what is at stake in thinking about cinema and world as "modified" by thirdness (as in "third world cinema" or, to take the more humble case of Uruguay, the *Cinemateca del tercer mundo*), where, as I have suggested, the subjective field is decisively in play. Although digressive (but what is exposition without digression?), it is not without relevance that in Foucault's gloss on the concept of *le dispositif* (the apparatus), he expressly thinks it as the machine of mediation that submits both substance and subject to its operation.[4]

II

In Barthes's 1970 essay "The Third Meaning" Barthes develops "thirdness" in relation to something he contrasts with the "obvious," namely, the "obtuse." As such, this piece registers his commitment to the critique of semiology announced in the contemporaneous Collection Points reprint of *Mythologies* (see "Change the Object Itself") and thus his broad alignment with colleagues in various fields concerned to pressure the sign with notions such as signifierness, textuality, or even the figural. Thus, the obtuse does not mean "dull" or "slow"; it means excessive, that which slips through or slops over a sign system however finely or capaciously reticulated. Famously, Barthes teases out "the third meaning" from a series of stills from Eisenstein's corpus, a move—however counterintuitive—designed to frustrate any attempt to link excess and the mere furtive motility of the cinematic image.

What interests me about this analysis—and it is not without its critics— becomes manifest when we translate the title back into French, "*Le troisième sens*," where what comes into play is the relation between meaning and direction or way. Such emphasis draws attention to the didactic role played in Barthes's essay by the contrast between the signs of communism and fascism. Although it is easy to miss, "The Third Meaning" actually discusses two Soviet filmmakers: Eisenstein and the less well-known Mikhail Romm. Only a single still from the latter's *Ordinary Fascism* (1965) appears in the piece, but it is set up in precarious opposition to the Eisenstein stills, in which Barthes ferrets out not signs of excess but that which in traversing the sign system of the stills, literally the syntagma of their placement in the essay, makes way for an alternative. Stated in political terms, this alternative, this "third way," is not the typical one, that is, fascism as the position pitched against the familiar dyad of capitalism and socialism. Rather it is a differ- ence, indeed a sloppy and thus excessive difference, passing *within* commu- nism (in the Soviet context, on one side [Romm] or the other [Eisenstein] of Stalinism) and *between* communism and fascism as these ideologies articu- late themselves in cinematic, but more broadly aesthetic, terms. As such, the third meaning/way draws attention to the structural parallel—Barthes calls it a "fold"—between political and aesthetic difference when that difference names both a relation between modes of production (capitalism and com- munism) and one between modes of production and the practices of repro- duction both parties call "art" (political modernism and realism).

Anyone familiar with Solanas and Getino's 1969 manifesto "Hacia un tercer cine" ("Toward a Third Cinema") remembers that "third cinema" is a cinema of struggle, of emancipation, of, broadly speaking, the left. Would this not then imply that it cannot therefore be a "third way," between capi- talism and socialism, that it is *simply* an alignment with the socialist left in the region? I want to argue that *tercer cine* is not, that it is more than this, but to clarify how, I return to the three points with which I opened.

Let us start with the problem of Marxist theory, not only in "Toward a Third Cinema" but in the film referred to throughout their essay, *La hora de los hornos* (The hour of the ovens). This practice of self-reiteration, regarded as merely indulgent by some, is actually crucial to the political posturing of the essay, both because it textualizes the principle of mediating theory through practice and practice through theory and, even more importantly, because self-reiteration "performs" a version of the decisive political argument of the entire essay. Stated bluntly, that argument concerns the problem of whether a revolutionary cinema is possible outside of, or before, a revolutionized social order. While this may seem like a tactical question resonant only within the context of sectarian debate, it in fact sounds the very depths of an international Marxism struggling with the famous eleventh thesis on Feuerbach: until now philosophers have only interpreted the world; the point is to change it. Put differently, Solanas and Getino pitch their essay against those who conclude, on the basis of the correct ideas contained with the eleventh thesis, that interpreting the world cinematically must yield or otherwise defer to the "real" work of changing it, thus aligning (or nonaligning)[5] with those who argue that transformations of the superstructure can produce transformations of the base, a move that when pursued up until the "last instance" reverses the causal arrow of a certain Marxist orthodoxy. In some cases this is the very repudiation of Marxism. Although one finds no such explicit repudiation in Walter Benjamin's "Work of Art" essay, one might reasonably argue that in it he, however desperately, entertains the notion that the destruction of aura is a decisive, enabling achievement in the real political struggle for communism. And, it is a sure if surprising sign of Adorno's commitment to orthodoxy that he so abreacted to this essay.

Crucial here is the matter of transformation: what threshold must be crossed in order for a particular transformation to matter; what ontological substance must be engaged and so on. I will observe, if only in passing, that Jacques Rancière's concept of the distribution of the sensible implicitly answers the question of what kind of ontological transformation is called for by Solanas and Getino, by foregrounding what the base and superstructure presuppose, namely its "bearers." On Rancière's account a causal reversal of the sort they entertain (film leading the fight) is possible because the sensible—our unevenly distributed experience/perception of the common—exists at the same level of reality as the mode of production. Real social classes consist of and are animated by no less real subjects. Although their discussion stubbornly worries over the division of labor within film production and the problems of exhibition and distribution of state-censored films—matters that underscore the risks of prematurity, that is, filming before the fight is won—Solanas and Getino concentrate on producing the necessity both of their concept, *tercer cine*, and their gesture of thinking/making it. Put differently, their elaboration of the motif of transformation focuses on differentiating the three cinemas: the cinema of Northern Imperialism—Hollywood, the cinema of auteurism; the various European countercurrents exemplified for them by Godard; and the cinema of liberation, that is, the cinema to come and that in coming promises to overcome the unimpressive if tenacious dichotomy between number one and number two.

Their task, urgent as it is for their own practice, is not made easier by their reluctance to attach "third cinema" to the "Third World." They do this, from time to time (for example, in the subtitle of their manifesto), but they also insist on tendencies they locate within the United States and Western Europe—that is, the First World—tendencies that are not merely doctrinal but, more importantly, aesthetic. In this they signal that the concept of "thirdness" is rooted primarily in the cinematic practices they are advocating rather than in geopolitical locations. This makes it hard to read such practices as "national" in any simple way, a gesture that puts their thinking in dialogue with later currents in postcolonial theory,[6] if not Fanon himself in *The Wretched of the Earth* when he warns against the traps of national consciousness when dominated by the middle class, *les évolués* (*los asimilados* in the Latin American context). But how are we to grasp and thereby appreciate the political aesthetics of this articulation of "thirdness?"

One section of "Toward a Third Cinema" is titled "A Perfect Cinema? Practice and Error," a title that resonates closely with Julio García Espinosa's "For an Imperfect Cinema" of the following year, where "imperfection" is elaborated as a distinctly aesthetic category that attempts to square the political circle of modernism and realism. That is, for Espinosa films that appear both technically and aesthetically "slick" ("perfect" in that sense) are by definition reactionary. The things they depict and the stories they tell may *feel* real, but this is only because they are hiding the signs of the interests animating their construction. By contrast, an imperfect cinema seeks to achieve realism by awakening the slumbering spectator through the careful exposure of such signs. In this Espinosa anticipates the concept of "political modernism" developed by Silvia Harvey in her appropriation of Brecht for film theory later in the decade.[7]

But there is a more fleshed-out discussion of the aesthetics of *tercer cine* in Solanas and Getino's manifesto. Beyond realism they also talk about beauty:

> Imperialism and capitalism, whether in consumer society or in a neocolonialized country, conceal everything behind a veil of images and appearances. The interested image of reality is more important than reality itself. It is a world peopled with fantasies and phantasms in which monstrosity dresses in beauty, while beauty is clothed in

> monstrosity. . . . In a world where the unreal rules *(impera)*, artistic expression is pushed along the channels of fantasy, fiction, language in code, signs and messages whispered between the lines. Art is cut off from the concrete facts . . . to turn back on itself, strutting about in a world of abstractions and phantasms where it becomes a-temporal and a-historical. (Chanan 22; translation modified)

Swathed in a familiar Platonic rhetoric of reality and its mimetic distortion, the aesthetics of third cinema are presented here, albeit *ex negativo*. To use a formulation Solanas and Getino care deeply about, this is an account of "their" beauty, not "ours." Presumably, the latter can be grasped outside the discourse of aesthetic autonomy and be thus definitively separated from the monstrosity with which it is now confused. Be that as it may, it is unfortunate that despite their repeated gesturing to a formal cinematic language cut to the shape of this aesthetic, *nuestra belleza* (echoing, presumably, José Martí's *"nuestra América"*), they never quite specify its terms, leaving one to presume that the proof is in the proverbial pudding, that is, the films themselves. However, before putting this claim to the test in a reading of *La hora,* a summary comment on the cited passage.

Despite the polemical energy of the characterization of "their" beauty, the text insists on a distinct epistemological investment in the image as a way to think—not the subtle tenacity of the aesthetics of imperialism ("their beauty") but the structural logic of distortion figured in the familiar and now politically fraught trope of veiling or masking. Key here is the notion of the "interested image" that has substituted itself for reality. While this leads somewhat predictably to a clumsy, even precritical, embrace of documentary filmmaking, it does not pause to consider that documentary films are themselves partially made of images, many of them "found," or that what I have been calling "visualism" might be ideologically active in one's thinking about images. Worse still, and this is only the most pronounced form of the same symptom, what falls out completely is sound. Despite occasional gestures toward the audiovisual character of the cinema (see the first of my epigraphs, where "fresco" thinks the unity of sound and image), Solanas and Getino never really work out in what way "our" beauty might give expression to an articulation of sound *and* vision not subject to the ideology of "visualism." In failing to do so, not only do they allow their own project to be pushed into the channels of capitalist fantasy, that is, into the circuits of Northern consumerism, where "visualism" runs rampant, but they let go of an important, perhaps even decisive, thesis of a Marxism no longer defined by its unthinking if heroic preference for changing as opposed to interpreting the world.[8]

III

To begin to tease this out, consider how sound functions in the opening sequence of *La hora*.[9]

Assuming that the opening screen announcing the Pesaro Prize was not part of the film as originally screened, there are roughly one hundred shots in the opening six-and-a-half-minute sequence. I say "roughly" because the punctuation between shots is difficult to determine with precision because Solanas and Getino have sustained recourse to the device of the blank, or in this case black, screen throughout. I will return to this shortly. Two minutes into the film, in shot 16, sound enters the film for the first time in the form of a percussion track. We hear beneath or behind the black screen a conga beat in ¾ time, punctuated intermittently with a snare drum whose timbral qualities accentuate the "poignant" contact between the two instruments. In shot 17 the first moving image appears. It is a torch (or match, the scale is difficult to determine), at night, and its appearance is synchronized with a fill on the snare drum, as if the sound and the image were calling to each other. Put differently, the torch appears as the image of the sound, and the sound appears as the cue for the torch. The snare drum, in effect, "strikes" (up) the torch. This chiasmus is intensified through the punctuation device of the black screen because the device cements the form and content of the film by using a formal technique specific to the cinema as the sign of the very night illuminated by the torch "struck" by the snare drum. That this also casts light on the medium itself, the cinema, is not in doubt. Why else have the first "moving" image arise precisely here? To be sure, there is movement within the graphics that have preceded this shot— Solanas and Getino are fond of geometric irises in and out—but these shots, driven by the twin principles of literacy and legibility, achieve a certain immobility or stasis that finds its echo in the death mask of Che with which the first section of the two-part film concludes—from flame ignited to flame extinguished. In effect, the first part of the film resolves the matter of the place within Marxism of armed struggle and in doing so makes the film into the place where the struggle continues.

The percussion music (other drums and voices are steadily layered on) builds to an impressive din during the unwinding of the six-minute opening sequence. It culminates in a diegetic gesture when, in shot 98, Che is quoted as saying: "Toda nuestra acción es un grito de guerra contra el imperialismo y un clamor (outcry or demand) por la unidad de los pueblos contra el gran enemigo del género humano: los EE. UU" (All of our action is a war cry against imperialism and an outcry for, or on behalf of, the unity of the people against the great enemy of the human race: the US). Against a black screen music subsides, as if withdrawing behind the screen, and a human voice, the first, is heard to say: "América Latina es un continente en guerra" (Latin America is a continent at war). This percussion music repeats in the film, significantly at the beginning of part 2, where, in a truly remarkable sequence, it withdraws and hovers at low volume behind a black screen—one of several used for this effect in the film—over which a voice counsels the audience to enter into a Brechtean state of self-awareness, a gesture repeated, though differently, at the end of part 3, where the black screen accompanies a narrator's voice-over inviting the audience to enter into conversation and debate about what they have just witnessed visually and aurally. Doubtless, for the readers of "Toward a Third Cinema," one of the first topics of discussion might well be the question of whether the film is an instance of monstrosity dressed as beauty or beauty clothed as monstrosity—screen, black frame, cloth/dress, cinema, aesthetics, all imperfectly folded on top of each other.

As I have noted, *La hora* is "cited" several times in the manifesto, and one such citation draws attention to the deplorable status of the neocolonialized intellectual as a mere copyist or spectator (18), precisely the position being thematized and presumably countered in the closing black-screen sequence of the film. Although this invites various forms of critical attention, I will focus on the way this articulation of the aesthetics of *tercer cine* draws attention to the problem of limits or, stated in temporal terms, starts and stops. Yes, the relation between the manifesto and the film certainly exemplifies a certain dialectical sensibility, but it also rhymes with precisely those features in the film that link the sonic manipulation of its form and content to the very problem—as given through the formal device of the black screen—of when and where the film moves from one shot to the next, but—even more consequently—of where the film begins? Or, and the point is perhaps clearer in this version, where does *it* end? Is the film over once the narrator's solicitation of debate concludes, or does it continue in the debate itself? Does it continue in the actions that follow from the debate? Is it projecting in the essay that repeatedly gestures to its insights and achievements? To come back to an earlier formulation that puts the problem of Marxism within the film: is the film changing the world or just interpreting it?

But what justifies the emphasis I have placed here on sound, and how does this engage my second and third points as stated at the beginning of the chapter? I will take up the problem without resolving it. And deliberately so.

If one agrees with Adorno and Eisler that music was added to the silent cinema to, as they put it in *Composing for the Films* (citing Kurt London), "drown out the noise of the projector" (Adorno and Eisler 75), then beyond simply recognizing here an important distinction between music and noise—both sounds—there is the important acknowledgment not only that the image arises against the blackness into which it is projected but that films always begin (and, for that matter, end) within a material process that exceeds them. The auditorium sounds that drowned out the silent film are now inscribed in the soundtrack that cancels them. In effect, they have always already begun and thus cannot end. They "echo," as I have argued elsewhere in this study. "Sound" might be a fitting term by which to think this condition if we concede that Aden Evens is on to something when he writes in *Sound Ideas:* "Thus, every sound interacts with all the vibrations already present in the surrounding space; the sound, the total timbre of an instrument is never just that instrument, but that instrument in concert with all the other vibrations in the room, other instruments, the creaking of chairs, even the constant, barely perceptible motion of the air" (Evens 6). Having earlier reminded us that hearing, unlike seeing, cannot conveniently be subjected to the will (for example, the decision to close one's eyes), and that it is all a matter of perceiving differences in air pressure, Evens is urging us to consider that sound, beyond its distinctive sonic and acoustic properties, might also be grasped as a materialization of what lacks either beginning or end. In terms that he borrows from Gilles Deleuze, sound realizes the ontology of immanence; it locates it in the field of human perception while simultaneously pointing to the problem of delimiting such a field. In this sense sound is not so much an event that unfolds in the manifold of sense perception (whether auditory or tactile), as it is a concept/metaphor beamed in the direction of a problem, the problem of delimiting the frame of intelligibility in which sense perception makes sense. Or, to use the formulation that Evens introduces in *Sound Ideas:* "Sound is a problem posing itself while working itself out" (58).

But what precisely does this have to do with Marxist theory? In what way does this engage with the matter I raised earlier regarding the distinction between interpreting and changing the world or, put differently, with the problem of which Marxism (if any) is in a position to embrace the political centrality of the superstructure, of cultural practice, in the struggle for liberation?

Here one profits from a serious and sustained consideration of what is at stake for Marxism in the study mentioned earlier, Pierre Macherey's *Hegel or Spinoza.* This text systematizes with excruciating precision a pairing that had already appeared in Althusser's master's thesis, "On Content in the Thought of G.W.F. Hegel," from 1947, but as its date of publication would suggest (1979), it is deployed by Macherey for the purpose of separating himself from Althusser during the waning of French structuralism. As if following the script written by Perry Anderson in *Western Marxism* (where Marxism becomes occidental through a theoretical sublimation of politics), *Hegel or Spinoza* turns back to the philosophical reassessment of Spinoza begun by Deleuze in the preceding decade in order to rearticulate the political struggles and defeats of the 1960s as theoretical problems. What this adds to Deleuze's project (note that his first book on Spinoza appears at the same time as both *Difference and Repetition* and *The Logic of Sense*) is the explicit political problematic of sorting the matter of "whither Marxism" in the wake of the repudiation (heard as loudly in Heidegger as in Fanon) of humanism. As Warren Montag, Susan Ruddick, and others have noted, Macherey's text approaches this monumental task by thinking symptomatically (thus as a loyal, if conflicted, Althusserian) about the French Hegel, a Hegel, as characterized by Foucault in his inaugural lecture at the Collège de France, from whom we can only escape through an "exact appreciation of what it costs to detach ourselves from him" ("The Order of Discourse" 74). Thus, if one accepts the notion—certainly accepted by Lenin himself—that there is no Marxism without Hegel, then it matters to what extent Hegelianism is, as Macherey then argues, ensnarled in a systematic misreading of Spinoza's corpus. The point is not that Hegel is "wrong" but that much of what is right in his work, and thus pertinent to Marxism, emerges from his—and I think Macherey would accept the term—anxious struggle to master—to assimilate, correct, and forget—Spinoza. While even a partial consideration of Macherey's text would take us very far afield, it seems fitting in the present context to point briefly to his chapter "Hegel Reads Spinoza," especially the section of it titled, "A Philosophy of Beginning."

At issue here is precisely what I have been addressing in relation to *La hora*, that is, the question, at once ontological and political, of where or whether it and the liberation struggle it *is* begins or ends. To summarize abusively, Macherey is concerned to tease out how Hegel and Spinoza resolve differently the contradiction of how they—as historical subjects— can think the absolute. According to Alain Badiou, this is a dilemma also, even foundationally shared with the apostle Paul. Spinoza resolves this by entertaining the theological principle of eternity—the absolute, including one's thought of it, has always already begun—while Hegel resolves this by logically articulating the absolute and thought through a dialectic that grasps their relation as coincident with human history itself. Deftly,

Macherey shows that Hegel's need to think his own superiority to Spinoza prompts him to produce a reading of eternity that can be summarily dismissed so that the vexing question of the *beginning* of the dialectic can be set aside. Yes, it has something irreducible to do with the advent of human consciousness, but how does a consistent materialism think the rupture believed to condition this advent? Rupture in or of what?

As Kojève, Lukács, Sartre, and others have stressed, there is a tenacious anthropological element in Hegel. The long meditation on the distinction between consciousness and self-consciousness in *The Phenomenology* makes this plain enough, even in the early Hegel. This is further accentuated in Marx, who, after all, famously stands the Hegel doll on its feet (see the "Postface to the Second Edition" of *Capital* I), thus endorsing if not even producing *homo erectus* as Engels was later to recognize in "The Part Played by Labor in the Becoming Man of the Ape." Both insist that something absolutely begins with the human; indeed, the absolute itself begins absolutely with the human. It is this "anthropologism" that Spinoza seeks to counter, not by deriving the human from the divine but, according to Macherey, by proposing that the very concept of derivation generates a problem, that of the absolute, originary cause, whose sole necessity derives from the dialectical solution designed to fix it. As Macherey points out repeatedly, Spinoza, as with any rigorous thinker, is often blinded by his own insight, but it is clear that the principle of an eternal, universal mediation, or what in my introduction I invoked through the concept of "thirdness," is what both powers and contradicts Hegel's thinking.[10] Macherey does not, in this study, entertain the implications of this for Marxism—except to say that the status of a *truly* materialist dialectic is raised by Spinoza's understanding of substance—but it seems to me that such implications are indeed put in play, if not precisely explored, in *La hora*.

To more carefully elaborate the problem of mediation as it engages the status of sound in *La hora* specifically, and *tercer cine* more generally, I wish to draw attention to another French statement on "thirdness" that appeared in 1970 (and is thus contemporaneous with Barthes's "The Third Meaning"): Hélène Cixous's *The Third Body [Le troisième corps]*. Certainly one sense of "thirdness" rendered in this difficult text refers to the structural fact that it is woven of three texts or corpuses. Throughout, there is a sustained engagement with the figure of Gradiva, both as she pumps (much is made of the nearly vertical angle of her back foot) her fateful way through the eponymous novel of Wilhelm Jensen and as that novel is taken up by Freud. There is also a somewhat more intermittent, but no less tenacious, engagement with Kleist's novella "The Earthquake in Chile" (and a few sidelong glances at *The Marquise von O*). What motivates this textual encounter is the superimposition of desire and destruction, a mix famously toyed with in Duras's screenplay *Hiroshima mon amour*. The third textual corpus—and they are not sequenced in any usefully numerical way—is the one in which the narrator figures as a body transferred between a certain T. t. and someone designated in the Cohen translation as "my father." Desire and destruction figure here, as well, but less at the level of world historical events and more at the level of subjectivation itself. Because the figure of T. t., after Tristan and Titan, comes to be rendered as Tout [all or everything], his (and the masculine pronoun is consistently used) contrast with the narrator's father urges the reader to hear the narrator's voice as emerging from the position of the not-all or, in the Lacanian vernacular, the place of Woman. Subjectivation here is then very much organized around the drama of feminine desire. As with *Hiroshima*, the text unthreads as if Sabina Spielrein's "Destruction as Cause of Becoming" is being read in a whisper just off (the) page.

As one might expect, Cixous's text contains several perplexing presentations of its title, or, as I prefer, moments of "entitlement." In thereby opening the echo chamber of reflexivity, the text draws attention to something highly pertinent about the concept of "thirdness" it puts in play. Of the seven events of entitlement woven into her exposition, the following one from late in the text is especially suggestive. It appears in an encounter between T. t. and the narrator where the event of writing is at issue. Insisting that a book knows no times/tenses *(temps)* the narrator specifies:

> It (the writing) says "tu" [you] to us, it gives us orders. It suggests to us to walk one in front of the other. But the right belongs to T(ou)t for I am the right, and because T(ou)t is the left, the left belongs to me, and we go across the writing with the same turning, rising motion, by means of the same third body, and I am the left and T. t. is the right; I see him move his right foot over the gap between two pages while his left foot prepares to follow suit; I write, I write till day springs forth from night. (Cixous 156)

Introduced through the figure of the step *(pas, thus "step" but also "not")* as a way to think a text without time, this passage not only motivates the sustained reading of Gradiva, but it also stresses that the third body is shared by and between T(ou)t and the narrator, the one who here says "I." An earlier event of entitlement tells us to think this sharing in terms of a lawless intersection of tongues *(langues)* and thus urges us to attend to the language, especially the language about language in the passage (Cixous 70). I am thinking here of the deixis. In the first sentence alone we have "it," "you," "us." This is soon followed by "one," "I," "him," "we." What is consistently missing, and not only here, is "her/she"—that is, the feminine third person. Despite this, if the shared third body facilitates a writerly encounter between him and (not) her, if it arises at the intersection of tongues, then perhaps what enables what can be shared in the third body is the fact that languages—whether written or not—share the grammatical category of person. This is also true of the three corpuses stitched together in and as this text. While there may not be time, there are persons both grammatical and characterological.

But what, precisely, does this teach us about "thirdness"? This can be clarified by turning to Roberto Esposito's probing study, *Third Person (Terza persona)* from 2007. Esposito's analysis begins with a bang. He zeroes immediately in on the paradox that despite the juridical and philosophical power of the concept of "the person" (and not uniquely in the North or West), at the level of political practice respect for "personhood" is rare. What drives his study is the hunch that the ordinary explanation for this—that "human rights" and their protection of persons have simply not been extended far enough—is absolutely wrong. For him the paradox results from the very concept of person, and the more it is practically extended, the worse things will become. Thus, *Third Person* embarks on a genealogical critique of the concept of "the person," one that shows how its function as "the bridge" between human being and citizen, or "overlap" between law and humanity (Esposito 3), burdens it with conceptual responsibilities it cannot carry. Put differently, the person is a figure of mediation that succumbs to the very pressure of mediation. In this vein Esposito takes up Cixous's concerns by teasing out how personhood is that within the body that is more than the body, referencing Kojève's vision of the end of history (see chapter 4 in this study) in which human beings attain personhood by freeing themselves from the animal within.

Against this backdrop he takes up the titular theme of "the third person." Although it is clear from his discussion that this term is freighted with literary critical baggage (it speaks to Levinas's "other," Foucault's "outside," but most essentially to Blanchot's "neutral"), he derives it from Benveniste's remarkable little essay "The Nature of Pronouns." The key emphasis that attracts Esposito's attention is Benveniste's insistence that in spite of its name, "the third person" is *not* another iteration of first (I/we) or second (you) person. Instead, the third person opposes first and second person by not referring to person at all. It is radically "impersonal" (recall that in French *personne* can mean no one). Given what concerns Esposito about "the person" in law, philosophy, and politics, it is clear why this formulation appeals, even as he is keen at a certain point to stress that *oppose* is probably not the right way to designate the difference between the personal and the impersonal. Aware that such maneuvers have implications for what is then meant by *third* in *third person,* he writes: "This complex—rather than merely oppositional—relation of the impersonal to the person is what explains the 'third' figure that lends its name to this entire inquiry. Rather than destroying the person—as the thanatopolitics of the 20th century claimed to do, although it ended up reinforcing it instead—to do conceptual work on the 'third person' means creating an opening to a set of forces that push it beyond its logical and even grammatical boundaries" (Esposito 14). Thirdness thus becomes "an opening to a set of forces." In the closing pages of his study Esposito elaborates this opening in terms of Deleuze's approach to "haecceity," which "never has an origin or an end—it is not a point: it is a line of slippage and assemblage" (Esposito 149). It marks the flux between the impersonal and the indefinite (Deleuze's "Immanence: A Life") and points even more insistently to what I have been calling mediation, the missing event that marks all elements of a system (a language, a social formation, a life form) with their relation to what does and does not fall within the system.[11] As I have intimated, this rhymes with the "thirdness" of the third body animated by Cixous, but it is a rhyme that draws the philosophical register of her text up closer to its outer, most legible, edge. In doing so, it allows us to sense that the third body—to the extent that it belongs to the "thisness" (its haecceity) of her text—traces a skin or surface that in passing between her fiction and her philosophy articulates and offers this relation to the set of forces called mediation. Correlatively, what this rhyme releases in one's reading of Esposito is the mood or tone of interrogation: what do we make of the impersonality, the singular multiplicity of the she/he/it that, in spite of everything, ties the third (non)person to gender?

What I hope is becoming less faint is the relation between mediation and thirdness, and while I have, through Evens's account of sound as immanent vibration, sketched the articulation of sound and thirdness, what deserves more thorough elaboration is the matter of how this bears on what I have called *tercer sonido.*

Vladimir Jankélévitch, probably best known to Anglophone readers as the author of an insightful if hagiographic study of Ravel and, more recently, as the author of *Music and the Ineffable,* takes an unexpected turn in Esposito's third chapter on thirdness. Specifically, Esposito presents Jankélévitch's *Treatise on the Virtues* as a brilliant, if ultimately mistaken, articulation of the I/thou (you) dyad. Like Levinas, with whom Esposito also has his quarrels ("the wholly other" as impersonality in theological guise), Jankélévitch falls prey to the temptations of *opposing* the third person to the I and the you. As this might suggest, Jankélévitch—despite his sustained impact on Barthes's thinking about music—figures here largely as grist for Esposito's mill. Except for one thing: silence. As if cast as Kafka's Ulysses, Esposito is drawn to the siren of silence that appears in Jankélévitch's writing. Not only does a carefully placed note point us to Lisciani-Petrini's introduction to the Italian translation of *Music and the Ineffable*, but he distills the following formulation from the *Treatise*: "a person may be temporarily absent, but always in relation to its moments of presence, . . . in the same way . . . silence is made 'audible' only by the cessation of the sounds that come before and after it, thereby creating and interrupting it" (Esposito 118).

The "audibility of silence" is a puzzle that figured cortically in my chapter devoted to silence. It speaks not only to Cage's dynamization of silence but also to the epistemological and perceptual challenge of thinking how it is that one encounters what can be known or perhaps audited as silence. In Esposito's invocation of Jankélévitch the audibility of silence is derived from the interplay of presence and absence, where, presumably, it would constitute the third term: the present absence. Or is it the absent presence? This antimetabolic turnstile complicates the charge that Jankélévitch's analysis founders on the logic of opposition, but insofar as his analysis attunes us to the challenge of thinking the third person, it also foregrounds the *sound* problem of silence—silence as the thirdness of the person who is and is not a person, an absent present person or mediation between the human and citizen. Silence as *tercer sonido* is a formulation that challenges us not only to hear silence but to read sound in the putatively nonsonic event of grammatical *(third* modifies *sound* or *cinema)* modification.

If I have deployed the passages from Sartre's "Self Portrait at Seventy" as epigraphic material, it is because I think what is said there about music—it is everywhere in his work, and yet he is/was silent about it—both conforms to the logic of sound as mediation and specifically to what happens to sound in the theory and practice of *tercer cine*. As noted, despite the prominent—and not merely dialogic (whether diegetic or extradiegetic)—role of sound in films like *La hora,* attention to sound as part of what participates distinctively in the thirdness of third cinema is for all intents and purposes absent.[12] This is distinctively complicated in *La hora* as a result of its absent presence/present absence in "Toward a Third Cinema," the essay by Solanas and Getino that, in repeatedly adducing the text of the film (including *extradiegetic* dialogue from the film), brings the silence of the essay on the matter of *tercer sonido* into the zone of mediation between the film and essay. Here a different form of the problem of the limits of the film emerges. Less about beginning and endings, this is about where the film is in the set of forces that mediate between it and its theory: the theory that the film itself is, but also the theory ("Toward a Third Cinema") that thinks the film without thinking its sound. This inevitably places sound in the midst of the political (but not therefore nontheoretical) quandary about interpreting versus changing the world, filming versus fighting. And it thereby enters into conversation with the issues circulating in the matter of the Marxian inheritance of Hegel or Spinoza. Sound, its present absence in the film, and its absent presence in the theory of *tercer cinema*, designates here the problem of a missing mediation, not a mediation mistakenly or incorrectly overlooked but one that in resonating at the level of the impersonal designates the structure of agency that refuses to align with either the human being or the citizen. It is silent only because unthought, inaudited, and in that sense it is third. Even if, as I have proposed, silence is *tercer sonido*, it is undercut rather than foregrounded by an essay that maintains a rather conventional, even predictable, silence about it. This is simply unthinking, not the unthought, the thinking baffled by the audit.

It is not, of course, that Solanas and Getino are or were seeking to participate in the debate over Hegel and Spinoza that was going on around them. But if we accept that philosophy, especially political philosophy (and one may ask whether there is any other kind), struggles to tease out the conditions of intelligibility for, among other things, aesthetic practice, then whether Solanas and Getino are concerned with this debate or not is not, in the end, decisive. What is decisive is that their work was and is concerned to express a critique of neocolonialism whose discursive coordinates, at the very least, *presuppose* Hegelianism. Consider, in this respect, the prominence of Fanon's perspective on violence in the "argument" of the film, a perspective Sartre—no stranger to Fanon—insistently tied to the dialectic of the master and the slave, lord and bondsman, thus to Hegelianism. In this sense they are in the problem of Marxism and its enabling precursors up to their proverbial necks. That *peronismo* answered to the strategic demands of their thinking suggests that left populism in the Southern Cone was itself in dialogue with this legacy. What I want to insist on is that part of this situation—sociohistorical, theoretical, political—required not simply a complication of the Third World but of thirdness as such. *Sonido* may be the Spanish name for it.

A unique possibility for sound thinking indeed.

Notes

1. Pinging, of course, also designates the practice of raising someone on the so-called social network. The fact that this usage converges with a black-box beacon eerily confirms what detractors have long been saying about social networks: they are messages to and from those missing in action.

2. I wish here to draw attention to Walter Benjamin's early and bewildering fragment, "Perception Is Reading." I do so not only to comfort those who have decided that "reading" reduces all signs to linguistic ones (it need not; in fact, it does not) but also to warn those who prefer theory to be merely "consulted" (rather than read), and literature to be glossed (rather than read), that *Sounds* seeks to make other demands of its readers. It does so in the name of humanistic inquiry, which is difficult and slow and has become all the more so in the era of its digitalization, where the field of scholarly perception races ahead and vanishes in all directions. Put methodologically, I am essaying here to read what I read so as to encourage not only a "return to the texts themselves" (Husserl's insistence on "things" notwithstanding) but also to urge more reading in general.

3. This is a fraught and hoary issue. While I, too, have grown impatient with the knee-jerk condemnation of "humanism," it does seem that if one accepts the connection, at once philological and political, connecting the human, humanism, and the humanities, then at the very least the kinds of critiques one finds of sociology or anthropology, critiques delineating their essential complicity with empire, are ones whose implications ought to be brought to bear on the humanities as such. This kind of argument is well-rehearsed in the debates over human rights and humanitarianism; indeed, a version of it is to be found in animal studies, so perhaps instead of mounting yet another feckless defense of the humanities from the predations of capital, perhaps it is time for a more serious consideration of what in the humanities is unredeemable. In short, the problem-finding that heralds the work of the field needs to be turned on itself.

4. "Visualism" is deployed by Ihde (see *Listening and Voice*) to tease out the philosophical privilege given to sight and vision in the tradition of Western epistemology. One might think here of the "allegory of the cave" found in Plato's *Republic,* where the trajectory from obscured vision to illumination simultaneously plots the movement from belief to knowledge. My larger point will be that "reflection aesthetics" (a prominent theory of contextualization) rests on a specular, thus visual, structure wherein the medium of art, say the literary text, is understood to derive its epistemic value as a representation from the world it mirrors. The same, obviously, can be said of the concept of *mimesis.* In "Whistle" I pressure Ihde's concept by bringing out the differences between it and what French theorists working in and around the *Cahiers du cinéma* referred to using the concepts *ocularcentrisme* and *photologie,* concepts that emphasize the cultural politics of privileging the philosopheme of the image. As important as these nuances are, "visualism" has a better ring.

5. Strictly speaking, Lacan comes to the matter of the gaze already in the 1950s. In his early seminar "Freud's Papers on Technique" he takes up the status of the gaze in Sartre's discussion of the intersubjective field, but there he settles for the formula: "It [the gaze] is an x, the object when faced with which the subject becomes an object" (*Freud's Papers on Technique* 220). Following the Ariadnean thread from Seminar I to Seminar XI, from the object to the symbol to the letter to the signifier, though fascinating, would take us too far afield.

6. A quite different, and therefore instructive, rethinking of the gaze is to be found in the work of Kiarina Kordela. See her "The Gaze of Biocinema," in which the gaze is presented in an ontohistorical register as a designation for what film theory comes to recognize about the cinema once the psychologism of a Münsterberg fails as an account of how the subject engages film (Kordela 151–64).

7. A similar pun appears in the introduction to the more recent collaboration between Pinch and Bijsterveld, *The Oxford Handbook of Sound Studies.* There it takes the form of a section title, "Now That Sound Is in the Air," where air refers both to the medium of sound transmission and to the motif of concern. In effect, buzz. As if called forth by the very medium of language, the introduction to the handbook also restates the emphasis on materiality. Pinch and Bijsterveld write: "Sound becomes more materially mediated in a whole host of newfangled ways," and they go on to gloss these newfangled ways by referring to devices deployed in the areas of "science, technology and medicine" (*Oxford Handbook* 6). The implicit reiteration of their reluctance to thinking the "materiality" of sound (think here of Aden Evans's *Sound Ideas*) suggests that little has changed between their two collaborative projects. To be clear: while their approach exhibits a certain technophilia, my point is not that their project fails or is even fatally flawed. All are. The point is to demonstrate how it is that "unique possibilities of thinking" express themselves in the twists and turns of argument with noteworthy, even symptomatic, tenacity.

8. One thinks here of the mellifluous phrase, "*l'homme et l'œuvre,*" where the task of situating seems exhausted in a largely biographical gesture. Once

the work is attached to the life of the author, then it becomes legible, decipher-able, and if it does so, it is because the life constrains or otherwise rei(g)ns in the gregariousness of the signs that constitute the work's texture. They cannot mean just anything, even if we are confident that we cannot anticipate what they *might* mean in some place at some time. Famously, both Barthes and Foucault put the concept of the author (in effect, the embodied principle of leg-ibility) under erasure, but they did so without really resolving the question of how a work might then be situated in relation to anything other than its own excess. This is not good enough.

9. "Sounds" is also the title of a beautiful chapter in Thoreau's *Walden*. Like Nabokov, Thoreau distributes his sources—machines (notably trains and car-riages), animals (notably roosters, owls, and frogs), events—in a soundscape that, although unnarrativized, tends to render them as occasions for what Heidegger might call "worlding." Sounds refer back to the one who says "I" in the text, and, in the course of the chapter, they tend to alert this figure to the ambivalent proc-esses of commerce. One might say that Jacques Attali's *Bruits* ("noise" in the Massumi translation) traces a similar arc but in relation to a genealogy of musical practice. Perhaps for this reason he ends on a less elegiac note.

CHAPTER 1. ECHO

1. This might also cast a different light on Lewis's observation about the merely apparent formlessness of Bolden's music, the fact that it was actually tormented by what was outside it. Animal studies have urged caution when placing the animal strictly outside the human, but this has not always led to an adequate diagnosis of either the animals' alterity or the politics of knowledge in which the animal has been made subject to human/animal attention. *Coming through Slaughter* repeatedly invites an unfree association between animality and madness without broaching a reflection on the latter that, in the spirit of Foucault, would expose its sociopolitical character. By the same token, the notion of "the language of the birds" (colloquial in French), which invokes a prelapsarian pedagogical encounter between animals and humans, in fact, shifts the origin of language into the space of alterity at the heart of this encounter. This Lacan-friendly gesture seems repeated in Ondaatje's suggestion, following John Lilly (his source for the sonographs), that cetaceans taught us music.

2. The oft-cited example occurs when Narcissus, eager to repel Echo's advance, says, "Hands off! Embrace me not! May I die before I give you power o'er me." And the echo repeats as, "I give you power o'er me" (Ovid 151, 153). A treatment of this material that has influenced my own but is passed over by Scott appears in John Sallis's "Echoes: Philosophy and Non-philosophy after Heidegger," esp. 84–86.

3. It is interesting that the text separator that appears throughout "Punctuation Marks" is also used by the designer, Teresa Bonner, to ornament the covers of volumes 1 and 2 of *Notes to Literature*. Specifically, these marks are distributed around the photograph of Adorno that appears at the center bottom

of both covers. Indeed, a slightly embellished version of the text separator appears as the caption of the photograph, as if to acknowledge that it is precisely this relation, that between name and image, that the asterisk could not designate, except to mark that relation, as psychoanalysis might insist, as unattested.

CHAPTER 2. WHISTLE

1. It must also be stressed here that a blaring silence in Benjamin's discussion of Proust—one that, were it filled in, might have preempted, even predicted, Reik's study—is his lack of interest in the fragment from the Vinteuil Sonata. This fragment haunts Proust's text in general and its mediation on the interweaving of reading and writing in particular. It does so in a way that brings the apparatus of the book and the politics of memory together in rather suggestive fashion.

2. This term, no doubt more familiar to us in its prefixed form, *decriminalization*, derives largely from the legal discourse that has grown up around the "war on drugs." It points to a logic—whereby drugs promote criminal activity if and only if their use has been criminalized—that has been carefully delineated in Jacques Derrida's "The Force of Law." In particular, Derrida draws out the relation of supplementation that binds law and force, reminding us that criminalization first proceeds by violently separating crime from law and then authorizing the latter to police both crime and the law/crime relation. Thus, what is criminal is so not "in itself" but only insofar as it helps discriminate the criminal and the lawful, a discrimination that must itself be neither law nor crime. In this sense criminalization is entirely about foreclosure. What makes the law lawful simply goes without saying. When earlier I noted the "criminalization" of terrorism, my point was slightly different. Specifically, I was emphasizing not only that this renders democracy incapable of terror but that terrorism, in falling before or outside the law, is deprived of politics. It has no reasons.

3. Another aspect of this dynamic is organized around the name of Beckert's victim, Elsie Beckmann (note the patronymic articulation of the collapse of law/innocence and crime/guilt). Early in the film we see and hear Elsie's mother, Frau Beckmann, calling out for her daughter, who has not returned from school. Over a series of violently emptied scenes, one obviously the source of Hitchcock's "vertigo-effect," we hear Frau Beckmann call out, "Elsie," each time with more anguish. The internal mark of this anguish is the sonic hyphenation of the girl's name, "El-sie." When, in the final scene, Beckert is obliged to confront his accuser, the blind balloon vendor, this same effect is realized, sonically overdubbing Beckert and Frau Beckmann. Important here is the effect of the hyphenation, whereby another sibilant is released into the acoustic space of M—that is, *Sie*, as in El-*Sie*. This is the formal plural personal pronoun "you," and as it whistles through the film, it links the diegetic victim with all those buried in the extradiegetic space of the film, notably all those bodies huddled together in the film auditorium.

4. It is worth stressing that this scene also brings out in its purest form the pattern whereby when we hear the whistling of Grieg's theme, we do not see Beckert's face. Here, the camera is positioned over his left ear, and while our ears fill with the whistle, the back of Beckert's head conspicuously fills the portion of the screen not given over to the text of his message. As Chion has pointed out, this concretizes the acousmatic character of the whistling, although he does not tease out what might be said about the directorial supplement at work here. Perhaps the most intriguing confirmation of this general pattern is contained in the one episode of failed stalking. Here, we actually do see Beckert puckering as though whistling. Does this not suggest that when the whistle is no longer acousmatic, its menace loses its sting, thereby fusing its threat to its disappearance from the visual field?

5. It must be acknowledged that another potential intertext for these materials is the radio show *The Whistler*, which was broadcast on CBS Radio from 1942 until 1955. It was effectively recycled when Leslie Charteris's *The Saint* was transposed from print to radio. Vincent Price played the title character. In both of these incarnations the shows open with the sounds of whistling and footsteps, sound that comes to be attached to what turns out to be a space of omniscient, but not therefore malevolent, narration. *The Whistler* also later became a film project in the hands of William Castle.

6. The task of sorting out the relation between Wittgenstein's thought and his whistling has at least been initiated in P.M.S. Hacker's "Was He Trying to Whistle It?" This paper was delivered at the Boston Colloquium on the History and Philosophy of Science in the spring of 1998. Hacker proceeds by exploring how whistling might supplement language when subject to the strictures of having to either show or leave in silence what cannot be said. His title, however, suggests that he is unaware of the aphorism attributed to Wittgenstein by his friend Frank Ramsey: "What we can't say, we can't say and we can't whistle it either." More recently, the relation between Wittgenstein and whistling assumed prominence in a 2011 exhibition at the Schwules Museum in Berlin, "Ludwig Wittgenstein: Contextualization of a Genius." An entire evening was devoted to reading passages from "the genius'" writings on whistling, and a professional whistler, Helmuth Drevs, was engaged for demonstrative performances. For my part I wish to draw attention to a moment in the posthumous collection *Vermischte Bemerkungen* (rendered in the Winch translation as "Culture and Value"), where Wittgenstein reports giving expression to a haunting melody. This occurs in a note on the difference between Brahms and Mendelssohn (Wittgenstein characterizes Brahms as "Mendelssohn without the flaws" [21e]). Wittgenstein then inserts two bars of notes in the treble clef with the marking, "With Passion," followed by the comments: "That must be the end of a theme which I cannot place (in the German, *das Ich nicht weiss*, that I do not know). It came into my head today as I was thinking about my philosophical work and saying to myself: I destroy, I destroy, I destroy [in English in the original]" (21e). Whistling these notes would be out of the question because among them there are four chords, but the tie between musical sound, involuntary memory (he does not know/recognize the

music), and violence, a tie linked to his own philosophical project and strung between German and English, invites elaboration. A problem to be revisited another day.

CHAPTER 3. WHISPER

1. For those unfamiliar with either the novel or the film: both tell the story of a family put at risk by trauma. It is set in the present, and the trauma at issue concerns a riding accident that spooks a horse, mangles a daughter, and kills a friend. The mother sets out to heal her daughter and the horse and engages a horse whisperer who, although struggling with issues of his own, manages to do both but not before tempting the mother to leave her husband for him. The horse serves as a metonymy for a nature that operates like an analyst, precisely the kind of material that Redford has been drawn to repeatedly as a director.

2. The character of Grace is played by a very young Scarlett Johansson. As if to suggest that she has an intimate relation to whispering, Johansson stars opposite Bill Murray five years later in Sofia Coppola's *Lost in Translation*, a film that ends famously, perhaps even scandalously, with a whispered bit of dialogue. Although Charlotte's line is now thought to be, "I have to be leaving, but I won't let that come between us," it is presented in the film as the very seal of intimacy, even as it is so conspicuously *for us*, thus sonically gesturing through the fourth wall. I refer to it here to signal that while it plays to the "double divide," it does so in a much more clichéd manner. It operates as the secret that promises to unlock an otherwise untranslatable narrative.

3. Although situated in a very different geopolitical context, the presentation of "actual whispering" one finds in Frieda Ekotto's novel *Chuchote pas trop* resonates provocatively with Figes's discussion. In the novel the young female protagonists, Siliki and Ada, aware that too much whispering only draws unwanted attention to the intensity of their relationship, resort to a mode of written exchange that situates the novel itself within their intercourse, but it also obliges "actual whispering" to range beyond the well-policed fields of aurality and the sonic. See Frieda Ekotto, *Chuchote pas trop*. I am grateful to her for sharing with me this remarkable first novel.

CHAPTER 4. GASP

1. Although I am unaware of any linguistic engagement with it, there is an interesting exception to consider here: the inhaled *oui* in French. It is almost always deployed in the mode of response, so its usage resembles the toggle between *oui* and *si*. Whereas in the case of the adverbial *si* the toggle belongs to the paradigm of reacting to a negative construction, how the inhaled *oui* functions is less clear. But let's put it this way: it is an example of how a sucked-in sound can be given some sort of phonemic and ultimately semantic value.

2. In 2003 Alain Badiou conducted a seminar in Buenos Aires titled "To Think the Cinema." In its published form it contains a section/session called, "A Tribute

to Gilles Deleuze," and it clarifies something about the status of the image in Deleuze that deserves attention here. Specifically, Badiou explains Deleuze's interest in Bergson by arguing that Bergson provided Deleuze with a nonpsychological account of the image. Of what does such an image consist? It is not a reproduction that appears to a consciousness but the equivalent of motion itself. In effect, it is through the image that the cinema participates in the movement of thought. What this foregrounds is the particular ground on which Deleuze's image has little to do with "the gaze" and, thus, would appear to have even less to do with "visualism." As important as it is to concede this complication, it is equally important to demonstrate its limits. In the classification of signs that Deleuze adapts from Peirce, and in his actual analyses of films, he says precious little about the soundtrack. Moreover, the proposition that thought articulates itself distinctly in images is largely consistent with the tenets of "visualism," which, let us not forget, is the designation for a certain philosophical ideology as much as it calls out the faculty of vision per se. Surely, external motion is rendered as vividly in sound, so why the image? There is a fascination here that, to be fair, is not especially well-captured in Badiou's own proposition that the cinema holds our attention because it is "the high point of the visual as semblance" (Badiou 236), a proposition that begs the very question it purports to answer.

3. In light of the preceding discussion of Derrida on "spirit," one might also expect here extended consideration of his engagement with the work of Paul Celan in, for example, *Sovereignties in Question, The Beast and the Sovereign, Volume I,* or even to some extent, *Cinders.* Such a turn would seem invited by the importance in Celan's corpus of the collection of poems titled *Atemwende* (Breath shift or turn), a collection in which mouths and pores as expressive orifices figure prominently. In Derrida's reading, one that famously teases out and lifts up the figure of the circumcised word, the problem of the breath (whether inhaled or exhaled) is downplayed. It is not elaborated in the spirit of the gasp, perhaps in accord with Celan's own attraction to the mouth that smokes where the moistness of the gasp, its suck, is rendered in the phonological trope of that which signals fire, perhaps the very flames that burn in Heidegger's spirit. The intricacies and difficulties of this material are legion. Rather than fall short of them before starting, I'll not start except to note, as I do here, that such matters matter.

4. In an interview with Toby Silverman Zinnan, McNally praised Nathan Lane's acting in the following terms: "He's never added an 'uh' or a comma—he's impeccable, 100% what I wrote, not a breath more" (Zinnan 9). Aside from putting enormous, perhaps even fetishistic, dramatic weight on the written text, this formulation also suggests an overlay among the work of art, the play, and breath that ties the end of one with the end of the other. In this sense, "Last Gasps" puts before us, and puts before us repeatedly, a pneumatic theory of art. Art is or happens where breath lasts.

5. A peculiar feature of this canvas, painted in 1860 during the "heyday" of the Orientalist School, is, despite its title, the strong emphasis on vision. Indeed, the entire center of the picture plane is defined by a twist whereby Boabdil has rotated back over the stifle and tail of his horse to cast a parting look at the

Grenada from which he is being exiled. His eyes are open wide; they even appear to be bulging forward to catch not the last gasp but the last glimpse of his former dominion. Although his lips are parted, no sign of breath, gasp, or sigh is especially visible. In fact, his ears appear fully obscured under his turban. It is a soundless painting about sight. It is thus interesting to note that on the dust jacket of the novel a somewhat different rendition of Boabdil appears. Commissioned from Dennis Leigh (better known as John Foxx, a British musician long associated with the band Ultravox), the painting shows "the Moor" in three-quarter profile riding into (the ear?) or across the face of a woman, perhaps Aurora herself. The look of Boabdil is directly at the spectator, and his lips are closed, distinctly visible under a thick mustache. It is the horse that is given the wild backward glance and a mouth that, while forced by a bit, is clearly wide open. Perhaps gasping. Perhaps not. This is a soundless painting about the echo between it and Dehodencq's canvas.

6. I note in passing that both Derrida and Agamben have had much to say about "the oath." In the second volume of the latter's study of "homo sacer," *The Sacrament of Language*, he develops the concept of the oath *(horkos)* as that which articulates the human as both a linguistic and a political animal. The oath binds together words and worlds such that communication is both possible and trustworthy. In Derrida, oath figures prominently in the text from which we began, namely, *Specters of Marx*, where it belongs to his subtle commentary on "conjuration" as it figures in the opening scenes in *Hamlet*. Perhaps predictably, Derrida stresses both sides of the oath: its role as bond and its role as threat. His interest in the motif of "the name" and what it means to invoke an oath, to swear in one's name or in the name of the other, might usefully be brought to bear on McNally's play—but not by me.

CHAPTER 5. SILENCE

1. The distinctly and significantly sonic character of *der Bau* (the burrow, but also the base) has been recently excavated by Mladen Dolar. See "The Burrow of Sound" (Dolar 112–39). Similarly, in *Radio: Essays in Bad Reception* I suggest some crossovers between Adorno's thinking about radio and Kafka's tale.

2. Benjamin's own fragment "On Proverbs" might also have attracted Adorno's attention but did not. In it Benjamin develops the notion of a constitutive gap between proverbs and experience, picking up nicely on Kafka's rewrite of cunning through the juridical formulation *noli me tangere* conceived as the prosopopoeial self-presentation of the proverb. Or, as M. C. Hammer put it: "Can't touch this."

3. Perusal of this Platonic material might well suggest that it is itself a reading of the Homeric figure of the sirens but as such the template for Adorno and Horkheimer's own discussion. At issue, through the figure of the ship and its rudder, is the question, in fact the *Ur*-question of the *Republic*, of who properly ought to steer/lead the ship of state. In typical Socratic fashion the one most

qualified, the "true pilot" (*kubernetes*, governor or rudder), is not the one trained by the most skilled pilot but one with the least interest in whatever benefits might accrue upon demonstrating one's competence. Sound here is not localized in the Sirens but in the boisterous and distracting quarreling of those vying for control of the rudder. Surely *this* will set the ship of state off course.

4. Lars Ilyer, in philosophy at Newcastle-on-Tyne, has written exhaustively on this material and in ways that invite immediate comparison with what I am arguing with regard to Kafka. See "Blanchot, Narration and the Event," in *Postmodern Culture*.

5. Under the general heading of "Berichtigungen alter Mythen" Brecht has revisited this Homeric episode as well (Brecht 207). He, too, casts doubt on whether the Sirens sang, but he does so by emphasizing the class politics of the episode, asking the reader whether one should believe Ulysses's account of the encounter. Like Adorno and Horkheimer he recognizes that at stake in the myth is precisely the question of the nature of art, but true to the politics of engagement, Brecht calls up the specter of the grumbling crew members, who take some small consolation in knowing that the Sirens would never waste their art on someone eager to enchain himself precisely in order to dominate others. Brecht, as one might expect, draws attention to Kafka's "correction" of the myth but stresses that current events have rendered it less convincing. See, on the entire project of "myth correction" as taken up by Brecht and Kafka, Frank Wagner's recent study *Antike Mythen*.

6. It is worth noting that this distinction between noise and sound, where the former is, as it were, more raw and less cooked, appeals to noise five years before its systematic deployment by Jacques Attali in his political economy of music, *Noise*. For what it is worth, Attali's interest in Cage, although sustained, is less philosophically and politically rich than one finds in Lyotard in that Attali seems content to group Cage among various "representatives" of the era of what Attali calls "composing," and this despite the fact that his concept of "heralding" (in the end not really different from Adorno's invocation of the utopic) is clearly concerned with, as Jameson notes, the problem of inscription.

7. In the concluding chapter of Veit Erlmann's *Reason and Resonance* Erlmann takes up the theme and concept of the "echoless." Through a sustained and provocative reading of the work of Günther Anders (neé Stern), Erlmann develops the anechoic as a sonic inscription of Descartes's *cogito*, where "certainty" is grounded not only solipsistically but outside or before the temporal delay of a sound that returns. Heidegger's concept of *Dasein* is similarly rendered; indeed, Anders is credited with recognizing the fundamental if repressed status of the ear in the Heideggerian corpus. Erlmann treats this as an incarnation of "modern aurality," a period and duration that extends out through Cage (among others), without however really confronting Cage's rather explicit repudiation of the echoless in his anechoic encounter with the silence that is not one. This invites rather predictable recourse to the postmodern, which Erlmann wisely resists, but the dilemma remains. As a symptom of its persistence one might point to Erlmann's unreflective recourse to "echoing" when referring to

both Anders's relation to Heidegger (327), and to the alpha and omega of his own text (341). The echoless echo?

CHAPTER 6. *TERCER SONIDO*

1. Not long ago the Department of Literature at the University of Constance embarked on a graduate research project with the theme *Die Figur des Dritten* (Figures or figuration of the third). In the call for proposals the organizers make explicit that they see "thirdness" as a defining theoretical problem not only in literary studies (Girard on "mimetic desire," or Serres on "the parasite," for example) but for much of the cultural and theoretical work of the twentieth century, including the founding of the discipline of sociology. My own work seeks to weave an additional strand into this unruly project, and I am grateful to Silvia López for bringing it to my attention.

2. See Stam's "Eurocentrism, Afrocentrism, Polycentrism: Theories of Third Cinema," in Naficy and Gabriel, *Otherness and the Media*. Dated though this material is, it speaks eloquently to a moment forged by a set of geopolitical coordinates now routinely, and thus defensively, characterized as forgotten.

3. In the case of Fernando Solanas and Octavio Getino the question of Marxism orbited tightly around the figure of Perón and the status within Argentina of *peronismo*, a "populist" left. While clearly sympathetic to the Leninism of "Che" Guevara, that is, the historical necessity of armed struggle and violence, Solanas and Getino avidly supported the electoral project of Perón, who, in his early postwar campaign, was given to contrasting the workers movement with both communism and socialism. At issue here are two concepts of the state apparatus, both of which belong—albeit not exclusively—to Marxism, concepts that find their philosophical footing in the intellectual traditions I have evoked here. For Hegel, the state is an institutional concretization of reason in human time, whereas for Lenin, the state is an instrument in the world historical struggle of the proletariat.

4. See Foucault's discussion of the "apparatus" in the interview, "Confessions of the Flesh"; and Giorgio Agamben's commentary on this material in *What Is an Apparatus?*

5. This turn of phrase is meant to remind readers that during the 1960s an important countercurrent to communist internationalism, namely, the nonaligned movement, was refiguring the geopolitical framework of the Cold War. With enabling links to both the Cuban Revolution and Indian Independence, the nonaligned movement lends itself to being reduced to an alibi for the projection of Soviet power, but in fact, it represented a modality of "global" thinking that pointed both to and beyond the state system stabilized, however, precariously by the Cold War. Here, too, the question of Marxism was in play in ways ill-captured, if at all, by the rhetoric of revisionism.

6. I am thinking here of Partha Chatterjee's *Nationalist Thought and the Colonial World*, where he sets out to problematize both the concept of the nation and the practice of nationalism while broaching a reading of Gandhi in which the

lineaments of an indigenous, even subaltern, concept of national community can be discerned. However great the distance between Chatterjee and Fanon might be, they converge in attempting to salvage the nation by locating that which within it allows it to travel by meeting its other halfway. In Fanon's case this is defined in terms of class, in Chatterjee in terms of colonialism.

7. See Harvey, "Whose Brecht?"; and Rodowick's influential commentary and elaboration in *The Crisis of Political Modernism*.

8. During the International Congress of Americanists convened in Vienna in July of 2012, Mario Handler brought to the event several films produced by the Third World Cinémathèque. In one, *C3M—La cinemateca del tercer mundo*, he appears and, among other things, comments on the use of music in "Me gustan los estudiantes," a short (six minutes) screened earlier in the week. His comments in the film make it clear that (a) he is aware that the soundtrack of his early films has been neglected, and (b) he is proud of the musical achievement of this particular film. In justifying his pride, he points out that the two key protagonists of the film (the students and the military police) each have their own "song," its own musical theme. In screening the film, this is perfectly obvious, as is, alas, the fact that this is an absolutely standard technique of scoring in the cinemas of the First World (think here of the Darth Vader theme in Williams's *Star Wars* scores). My point is not that Handler's pride is undeserved (the film is superb) but that it is "ill-gotten," as it were. Only a reluctance or failure to attend to sound in first cinema would enable such a feckless form of self-criticism.

9. For those unfamiliar with the film a few general comments may prove helpful. The film is typically characterized as a political documentary. Indeed, some might argue, for example Nicole Brenez, that it is the exemplar of the genre. It runs 208 minutes (although when first released, only part of it was screened), and it is organized into two parts, with three sections and fourteen chapters. Roughly speaking, the first part conducts an exhaustive social, cultural, economic and political analysis not only of Argentina but of Latin America in the late nineteenth and early twentieth centuries. The second part turns to the agenda for action in the wake of the death of Che Guevara. In certain respects its form echoes that of José Carlos Mariátegui's *Seven Interpretive Essays on Peruvian Reality* from the 1920s. Made clandestinely, it is largely composed of what my former student Benedict Stork calls "image documents" with voice-over narration, and insofar as it enunciates a narrative, it unfolds as something of an *apologia:* because this is what has happened, this is what must be done. To the dismay of many, "what must be done" is presented in terms of the electoral struggle to bring Juan Perón to power. As I hope this summary has made clear: there is no substitute for screening the film in its entirety. I discuss only the overture to part 1.

10. In the *Cinema* books Deleuze, long preoccupied with Spinoza's philosophical legacy, also points us toward Charles S. Peirce, whose foundational category of "thirdness" invites consideration in this context. A reference note, however capacious, is not the place to trace the evolution of this category in

Peirce, its early, decisive relation to semiosis on through to its late relation to the cosmological concept of *agape*, but already in "On a New List of Categories" from 1868, "thirdness" designates what allows any "it" whatsoever to be grasped as a "this." Stated in semiotic terms, it operates as the "interpretant" that mediates the relation between an object and its *representamen*. Although the matter is disputed, this view reconciles the "conflict" between thought and matter in a way (Peirce insisted that he was a "realist") that invites comparison with Spinoza's thought. I'll not accept this invitation here but reserve the right to at some other time.

11. Reference to Deleuze's thought in the context of a discussion of third cinema, especially given the crucial status of Italian neorealism to the latter, invites further comment on his *Cinema* books (see note 2 in chapter 4 herein). To be sure, Deleuze's insistence on the capacity of the cinema to think, to invent theoretical concepts ("friends"), gives expression to the principle of an immanentist ontology, but this does not then develop into an examination of the impersonality of the cinema. It was Christian Metz, in his last work, *Enunciation: Or the Impersonal Site of Film*, who pursued this possibility most passionately. Likewise drawing on Benveniste, and his concept of enunciation in particular, Metz set out to pin instances of cinematic reflexivity to an agency operating beneath and before the deictic surface of the narration—whence its *impersonality*. Given what film scholars have since come to learn about the complexities of what Chion called "points of audition," one might have expected Metz to articulate a distinctly sonic aspect of the impersonal site of film, but he did not. Deleuze, eager to set Metz aside, lets the opportunity slip as well. Both, I would argue, would have profited from thinking more deliberately about third cinema.

12. As a further intriguing "fictional" example, one might think of the intricate work of sound in Tomás Gutiérrez Alea's *Memorias del subdesarrollo* (Memories of underdevelopment). Derived from a novel and film treatment written by Edmundo Desnoes, whose voice at a certain point is heard in the film, the plot of the film winds around and through an apartment in central Havana on the eve of the Events of October (missile crisis) and the botched Bay of Pigs invasion. In this apartment, at a certain point "nationalized" by the revolution, we hear voices, music, and radio broadcasts. It is the scene of an adulterous seduction that goes bad, an outcome predicted by the clash of musical tastes between Sergio and Elena, the principal characters. An important moment of dialogue contains a brilliant moment of sonic intertextuality. After showing up at Sergio's apartment unannounced, Elena at a certain point turns to flip through his record collection, pulling out an album by "Elena" Burke. The matter at hand is likes and dislikes:

ELENA. Don't make fun of me.

SERGIO. I am not making fun of you.

ELENA. You just don't have any feelings. Besides (then singing), you don't have to criticize/the way I live/If all I have now—

She is silenced by a kiss planted on her lips by Sergio. What makes the moment sonically resonant is the pronunciation of "feelings." Specifically, Elena not only says the word in English, but she pronounces it so that it sounds like *"filín"* the name of a form of Cuban pop music that in style and name (it is a Hispanicized pronunciation of "feeling") reflected the encounter between US and Cuban music from the 1940s to the 1960s. As such, it would both evoke the sort of music to be heard on Radio Reloj Nacional (Sergio's station) and stand in sharp contrast to Elena Burke, revered as a passionate singer of boleros. Like the private apartment in which the word resounds, *filín* would not survive the revolution. Regardless, and this is part of the brilliance of its evocation, it does accurately name the affect of Sergio as concerns the very sociopolitical transformation he, unlike his family, has insisted on being part of, if only as a witness.

Works Cited

Adorno, Theodor W. *Current of Music.* Ed. Robert Hullot-Kentor. Cambridge: Polity, 2009.

———. *Notes to Literature.* Vol. 1. Trans. Shierry Weber Nicholsen. New York: Columbia UP, 1991.

———. "On the Fetish Character of Music and the Regression of Listening." *Essays on Music."* Ed. Richard Leppert. Trans. Susan Gillespie. Berkeley: U of California P, 2002. 288–317.

———. *Prisms.* Trans. Samuel Weber and Shierry Weber. Cambridge: Massachusetts Institute of Technology UP, 1981.

———, and Hanns Eisler. *Composing for the Films.* Cambridge: Athlone, 1994.

———, and Max Horkheimer. *Dialectic of Enlightenment.* Ed. Gunzelin Schmid Noerr. Trans. Edmund Jephcott. Stanford: Stanford UP, 2002.

Agamben, Giorgio. *Homo Sacer: Sovereign Power and Bare Life.* Trans. Daniel Heller-Roazen. Stanford: Stanford UP, 1998.

———*The Sacrament of Language: An Archaeology of the Oath (Homo Sacer II).* Trans. Adam Kotsko. Stanford: Stanford UP, 2011.

———. *What Is an Apparatus?* Trans. David Kishick and Stefan Padatella. Stanford: Stanford UP, 2009.

Alea, Tomás Gutiérrez. *Memorias del subdesarrollo.* Havana: Cuban Institute of Cinematographic Art and Industry, 1984.

Althusser, Louis. "Ideology and Ideological State Apparatuses." *Lenin and Philosophy and Other Essays.* Trans. Ben Brewster. London: Monthly Review P, 1971.

———. "On Content in the Thought of G. W. F. Hegel." *The Spectre of Hegel: Early Writings.* Trans. G. M. Goshgarian. London: Verso, 1997. 36–169.

———. *Writings on Psychoanalysis: Freud and Lacan.* Ed. Olivier Corpet and François Matheron. Trans. Jeffrey Mehlman. New York: Columbia UP, 1996.

Aristotle. *The Basic Works of Aristotle.* Ed. Richard McKeon. New York: Modern Library, 1941.

Badiou, Alain. *Cinema*. Ed. Antoine de Baecque. Trans. Susan Spitzer. Cambridge: Polity, 2013.

Barthes, Roland. "From Work to Text." *The Rustle of Language*, 56–68.

———. "Les deux sociologies de roman." *Œuvres complètes*. Vol. 2. Ed. Eric Marty. Paris: Seuil, 2002. 248–50.

———. *Mythologies*. Trans. Annette Lavers. New York: Hill and Wang, 1972.

———. *The Responsibility of Forms: Critical Essays on Music, Art, and Representation*. Trans. Richard Howard. New York: Hill and Wang, 1985.

———. "Rhetorical Analysis." *The Rustle of Language*, 83–89.

———. *Roland Barthes*. Trans. Richard Howard. New York: Hill and Wang, 1977.

———. *The Rustle of Language*. Trans. Richard Howard. New York: Hill and Wang, 1989.

———. "Sociology and Socio-logic: Apropos of Two Recent Works by Lévi-Strauss." *The Semiotic Challenge*. Trans. Richard Howard. Berkeley: U of California P, 1994. 160–72.

———. "The Third Meaning" (1970). *The Responsibility of Forms*, 41–62.

Barthes, Roland, with Roland Havas. "Listening" (1976). *The Responsibility of Forms*, 245–60.

Bataille, George. *Literature and Evil*. Trans. Alistair Hamilton. New York: Urizen, 1973.

Baxandall, Lee, and Stefan Morawski, eds. *Marx and Engels on Literature and Art*. Trans. Lee Baxandall and Stefan Morawski. St. Louis, MO: Telos, 1973.

Bellour, Raymond. *The Analysis of Film*. Ed. Constance Penley. Bloomington: Indiana UP, 2000.

Benjamin, Walter. "The Formula in Which the Dialectical Structure of Film Finds Expression." *Selected Writings*, 3: 94–95.

———. "Franz Kafka." *Selected Writings*, 2: 794–818.

———. "On Some Motifs in Baudelaire." *Selected Writings*, 4: 313–55.

———. "On the Concept of History." *Selected Writings*, 4: 389–400.

———. "On the Image of Proust." *Selected Writings*, 2: 237–47.

———. "Perception and Reading." *Selected Writings*, 1: 92.

———. "Review of Brod's *Franz Kafka*." *Selected Writings*, 3: 317–21.

———. "The Work of Art in the Age of Its Technological Reproducibility." *Selected Writings*, 4: 251–83.

———. *Selected Writings*. Ed. Marcus Bullock, Michael W. Jennings, Howard Eiland, and Gary Smith. 4 vols. Cambridge, MA: Harvard UP, 1996–2003.

Blanchot, Maurice. *The Book to Come*. Trans. Charlotte Mandell. Palo Alto: Stanford UP, 2003.

———. *The Infinite Conversation*. Trans. Susan Hanson. Minneapolis: U of Minnesota P, 1993.

Boulting, Roy, dir. *Twisted Nerve*. Charter Film Productions, 1968.

Brecht, Bertolt. *Bertolt Brecht: Gesammelte Werke in acht Bänden*. Berlin: Suhrkamp, 1967.

Cage, John. *Silence*. Middleton: Wesleyan UP, 1961.

Caruth, Cathy, ed. *Trauma: Explorations in Memory*. Baltimore: Johns Hopkins UP, 1995.

———. *Unclaimed Experiences: Trauma, Narrative, and History*. Baltimore: Johns Hopkins UP, 1996.

Chanan, Michael. *Twenty-Five Years of the New Latin American Cinema*. London: British Film Institute, 1983.

Chatterjee, Partha. *Nationalist Thought and the Colonial World: A Derivative Discourse*. London: Zed, 1986.

"Children of Ghosts." *The Ghost Whisperer*. Writ. John Gray and Teddy Tenenbaum. Dir. Frederick E. O. Toye. CBS. March 30, 2007.

Chion, Michel. *Audio-Vision: Sound on Screen*. Trans. Claudia Gorbman. New York: Columbia UP, 1994.

———. *The Voice in Cinema*. Trans. Claudia Gorbman. New York: Columbia UP, 1999.

Cixous, Hélène. *The Third Body*. Trans. Keith Cohen. Evanston, IL: Northwestern UP, 1999.

Debord, Guy. *Comments on the Society of the Spectacle*. Trans. Malcom Imrie. London: Verso, 1998.

Deleuze, Gilles. *Difference and Repetition*. Trans. Paul Patton. New York: Columbia UP, 1994.

de Man, Paul. "The Rhetoric of Temporality." *Blindness and Insight: Essays in the Rhetoric of Contemporary Criticism*. Minneapolis: U of Minnesota P, 1983. 187–228.

Derrida, Jacques. *Of Spirit: Heidegger and the Question*. Trans. Geoffrey Bennington and Rachel Bowlby. Chicago: U of Chicago P, 1989.

———. *Specters of Marx: The State of the Debt, the Work of Mourning and the New International*. Trans. Peggy Kamuf. New York: Routledge, 1994.

Detienne, Marcel, and Jean-Pierre Vernant. *Cunning Intelligence in Greek Culture and Society*. Trans. Janet Lloyd. Sussex: Harvester, 1978.

Dolar, Mladen. "The Burrow of Sound." *differences* 22.2–3 (2011): 112–39.

Ekotto, Frieda. *Chuchote pas trop*. Paris: L' Harmattan, 2005.

Erlmann, Veit. *Reason and Resonance: A History of Modern Aurality*. New York: Zone, 2010.

Esposito, Roberto. *Third Person: Politics of Life and Philosophy of the Impersonal*. Trans. Zakiya Hanafi. Cambridge: Polity, 2012.

Evans, Nicholas. *The Horse Whisperer*. New York: Delacorte, 1995.

Evens, Aden. *Sound Ideas: Music, Machines, and Experience*. Minneapolis: U of Minnesota P, 2005.

Fink, Bruce. *Lacan to the Letter*. Minneapolis: U of Minnesota P, 2004.

Foster, Hal, ed. *Vision and Visuality*. Seattle: Bay P, 1988.

Foucault, Michel. *The Birth of the Clinic: An Archaeology of Medical Perception*. Trans. Alan Sheridan-Smith. New York: Vintage, 1975.

———. "The Confession of the Flesh." *Power/Knowledge: Selected Interviews and Writings, 1972–1977*. Ed. Colin Gordon. New York: Pantheon, 1980. 194–228.

————. *The Hermeneutics of the Subject: Lectures at the Collège de France, 1981–82.* Ed. Frédéric Gros. Trans. Graham Burchell. New York: Palgrave Macmillan, 2005.

————. "History, Discourse and Discontinuity." *Foucault Live: Collected Interviews, 1961–1984.* Ed. Sylvère Lotringer. New York: Semiotext(e), 1989. 33–50.

————. *History of Madness.* Trans. Jonathan Murphy and Jean Khalfa. London: Routledge, 2006.

————. "The Order of Discourse." *Untying the Text: A Post-structuralist Reader.* Ed. Robert Young. London: RKP, 1981. 48–78.

Freud, Sigmund. *The Standard Edition of the Complete Psychological Works of Sigmund Freud.* Trans. James Strachey et al. Vol. 13. London: Hogarth, 2001.

Fukuyama, Francis. *The End of History and the Last Man.* New York: Avon, 1992.

Hacker, P.M.S. "Was He Trying to Whistle It?" *The New Wittgenstein.* Ed. Alice Crary and Rupert Read. New York: Routledge, 2000. 353–88.

Hargraves, John A. *Music in the Works of Broch, Mann, and Kafka.* Rochester, NY: Camden House, 2002.

Harvey, Sylvia. "Whose Brecht? Memories for the Eighties." *Screen* 23.1 (1982): 45–59.

Havelock, Eric. *The Preface to Plato.* New York: Grosset and Dunlap, 1967.

Heidegger, Martin. *Poetry, Language, Thought.* Trans. Albert Hofstadter. New York: Harper and Row, 1975.

Heller-Roazen, Daniel. *Echolalias: On the Forgetting of Language.* New York: Zone, 2005.

Hilmes, Michelle. "Is There a Field Called Sound Cultural Studies? And Does It Matter? *American Quarterly* 57.1 (March 2005): 249–59.

Hoeller, Keith, ed. *Merleau-Ponty and Psychology.* New Jersey: Humanities, 1994.

Homer. *The Odyssey of Homer.* Trans. Richard Lattimore. New York: Harper Colophon, 1967.

Ihde, Don. *Listening and Voice: A Phenomenology of Sound.* Athens: Ohio UP, 1976.

Ilyer, Lars. "Blanchot, Narration, and the Event." *Postmodern Culture* 12.3 (May 2002): 25–48.

Jay, Martin. *Downcast Eyes: The Denigration of Vision in Twentieth-Century French Thought.* Berkeley: U of California P, 1993.

Kafka, Franz. *Franz Kafka: Gesammelte Schriften.* Vol. 5. Ed. Max Brod. New York: Schocken, 1946.

Kordela, Kiarina. "The Gaze of Biocinema." *European Film Theory.* Ed. Temenuga Trifonova. New York: Routledge, 2008. 151–64.

Kostelanetz, Richard, ed. *John Cage.* New York: Penguin, 1970.

Kristeva, Julia. *Time and Sense: Proust and the Experience of Literature.* Trans. Ross Guberman. New York: Columbia UP, 1996.

Lacan, Jacques. *The Four Fundamental Concepts of Psychoanalysis. The Seminar of Jacques Lacan, Book 11*. Ed. Jacques-Alain Miller. Trans. Alan Sheridan. New York: Norton, 1978.

———. *Freud's Papers on Technique, 1953–1954. The Seminar of Jacques Lacan, Book 1*. Ed. Jacques-Alain Miller. Trans. John Forrester.

Lacoue-Labarthe, Philippe. "The Echo of the Subject." *Typography: Mimesis, Philosophy, Politics*. Ed. Christopher Fynsk. Cambridge, MA: Harvard UP, 1989. 139–207.

Lang, Fritz, dir. *M*. Ufa, 1931.

Laver, John. *The Gift of Speech: Papers in the Analysis of Speech and Voice*. Edinburgh: Edinburgh UP, 1991.

Leppert, Richard, ed. *Essays on Music: Theodor Adorno*. Trans. Susan Gillespie. Berkeley: U of California P, 2002.

Levinas, Emmanuel. *Difficult Freedom: Essays on Judaism*. Trans. Seán Hand. Baltimore: Johns Hopkins UP, 1990.

Lyotard, Jean-François. "Adorno as the Devil." Trans. Robert Hurley. *Telos*, no. 19 (Spring 1974): 127–37.

———. *Driftworks*. Ed. Roger McKeon. New York: Semiotext(e), 1984.

Macherey, Pierre. *Hegel or Spinoza*. Trans. Susan Ruddick. Minneapolis: U of Minnesota P, 2011.

———. "The Problem of Reflection." *Substance* 15 (1976): 6–20.

McNally, Terrence. *Cuba Si! Bringing It All Back Home, Last Gasps: Three Plays by Terrence McNally*. New York: Dramatists Play Service, 1970.

Merleau-Ponty, Maurice. *The Visible and the Invisible*. Ed. Claude Lefort. Trans. Alphonso Lingus. Evanston, IL: Northwestern UP, 1968.

Mowitt, John. *Radio: Essays in Bad Reception*. Berkeley: U of California P, 2011.

———. "Spins." *Postmodern Culture* 18.3 (2008): 1–21.

Nabokov, Vladimir. "Sounds." *The Stories of Vladimir Nabokov*. Ed. Dimitri Nabokov. New York: Vintage, 1997. 14–24.

Naficy, Hamid, and Teshome Gabriel, eds. *Otherness and the Media: The Ethnography of the Imagined and the Imaged*. Chur, Switzerland: Harwood Academic Publishers, 1993.

Nancy, Jean-Luc. "Ascoltando." Trans. Charlotte Mandell. Foreword to Szendy, *Listen*, ix–xiii.

Nietzsche, Friedrich. *Beyond Good and Evil/On the Genealogy of Morality*. Stanford: Stanford UP, 2014.

Ondaatje, Michael. *Coming through Slaughter*. New York: Vintage, 1996.

Onians, Richard Broxton. *The Origins of European Thought: About the Body, the Mind, the Soul, the World, Time and Fate*. Cambridge: Cambridge UP, 1951.

Ovid. *Metamorphoses, I–VIII*. Loeb Classical Library. Trans. G.P. Goold and Frank Justus Miller. London: St. Edmundsbury, 1964.

Peirce, Charles Sanders. "On a New List of Categories." *The Essential Peirce: Selected Philosophical Writings*. Vol. 1. Ed. Nathan Houser and Christian Kloesel. Bloomington: Indiana UP, 1992. 1–10.

Pinch, Trevor, and Karin Bijsterveld. "New Keys to the World of Sound." *Oxford Handbook of Sound Studies.* Oxford: Oxford UP, 2011. 3–35.

———. "Sound Studies: New Technologies and Music." *Social Studies of Science* 34.5 (2004): 635–48.

Plato. *The Collected Dialogues of Plato.* Ed. Edith Hamilton and Huntington Cairns. New York: Pantheon, 1961.

Rancière, Jacques. *Aisthesis: Scenes from the Aesthetic Regime of Art.* Trans. Zakir Paul. London: Verso, 2013.

———. *The Politics of Aesthetics: The Distribution of the Sensible.* Trans. Gabriel Rockhill. London: Continuum, 2004.

Redford, Robert, dir. *The Horse Whisperer.* Touchstone Pictures, 1998.

Reik, Theodor. *The Haunting Melody: Psychoanalytic Experiences in Life and Art.* New York: Grove, 1960.

———. *Surprise and the Psychoanalyst: On the Conjuncture and Comprehension of Unconscious Processes.* 1929. New York: Routledge, 1999.

Revill, David. *The Roaring Silence: John Cage: A Life.* New York: Arcade, 1992.

Rodowick, David. *The Crisis of Political Modernism: Criticism and Ideology on Contemporary Film.* Urbana: U of Illinois P, 1988.

Rushdie, Salman. *The Moor's Last Sigh.* New York: Vintage, 1995.

Sallis, John. "Echoes: Philosophy and Non-philosophy in Heidegger." *Philosophy and Non-philosophy since Maurice Merleau-Ponty.* Ed. Hugh Silverman. Evanston, IL: Northwestern UP, 1988. 84–105.

Sartre, Jean-Paul. *Life/Situations: Essays Written and Spoken.* Trans. Paul Auster and Lydia Davis. New York: Vintage, 1977.

Saussure, Ferdinand de. *Course in General Linguistics.* Trans. Wade Baskin. New York: Columbia UP, 2011.

Scott, Joan Wallach. "Fantasy Echo: History and the Construction of Identity." *Critical Inquiry* 27 (Winter 2001): 284–304.

Scott, Peter Dale. *American War Machine: Deep Politics, the CIA Global Drug Connection, and the Road to Afghanistan.* Lanham, MD: Rowman and Littlefield, 2010.

Sennett, Richard. *The Craftsman.* New Haven, CT: Yale UP, 2008.

Solanas, Fernando E., and Octavio Getino. "Hacia un tercer cine: Notas y experiencias para el desarrollo de un cine de liberación en el tercer mundo." *Cine, Cultura y Descolonización.* México: Siglo Veintiuno, 1979. 55–91.

———, dirs. *La hora de los hornos.* Cinema Club, 2006. DVD.

Spinoza, Baruch. *The Chief Works of Spinoza.* Trans. R. H. M. Elwes. New York: Dover, 1951.

Spivak, Gayatri Chakravorty. *A Critique of Postcolonial Reason: Toward a History of the Vanishing Present.* Cambridge, MA: Harvard UP, 1999.

———. *Death of a Discipline.* New York: Columbia UP, 2003.

———. "Echo." *New Literary History* 24.1 (1993): 17–43.

Stadler, Gustavus. "Introduction: Breaking Sound Barriers." *Social Text* 102 (Spring 2010): 1–12.

Suisman, David, and Susan Strasser, eds. *Sound in the Age of Mechanical Reproduction.* Philadelphia: U of Pennsylvania P, 2009.

Szendy, Peter. *Listen: A History of Our Ears.* New York: Fordham UP, 2008.

Wagner, Frank. *Antike Mythen: Kafka und Brecht.* Würzburg: Königshausen und Neumann, 2009.

Wittgenstein, Ludwig. *Culture and Value.* Ed. G. H. von Wright. Trans. Peter Winch. Chicago: U of Chicago P, 1980.

Zinnan, Toby Silverman. "Conversation with Nathan Lane." *Terrence McNally: A Casebook.* New York: Garland, 1997. 89–94.

Index